DEAD MAN IN PARADISE

J.B. MACKINNON

DEAD MAN

in PARADISE

UNRAVELING A MURDER
FROM A TIME OF REVOLUTION

THE NEW PRESS

NEW YORK
LONDON

Requests for permission to reproduce selections from this book should be mailed to:
Permissions Department, The New Press, 38 Greene Street, New York, NY 10013.

Originally published in Canada by Douglas & McIntyre Ltd., 2005
Published in the United States by The New Press, New York, 2007
Distributed by W. W. Norton & Company, Inc., New York

Library of Congress Cataloging-in-Publication Data
MacKinnon, J. B. (James Bernard), 1970–
Dead man in paradise : unraveling a murder from a time of revolution / J.B. MacKinnon.
p. cm.
ISBN 978-1-59558-181-5 (hc.)
1. MacKinnon, J. B. (James Bernard), 1970–   2. MacKinnon, Art, 1932–1965.
3. Murder—Dominican Republic—Case studies.   4. Homicide investigation—
Dominican Republic—Case studies.   I. Title.
HV6535.D65M335 2007   364.15'3092—dc22
2007001369

The New Press was established in 1990 as a not-for-profit alternative to the large,
commercial publishing houses currently dominating the book publishing industry.
The New Press operates in the public interest rather than for private gain, and is committed to
publishing, in innovative ways, works of educational, cultural,
and community value that are often deemed insufficiently profitable.

www.thenewpress.com

This book was set in Fournier

Printed in the United States of America

2 4 6 8 10 9 7 5 3 1

for Padre Arturo MacKinnon,
my companion on the journey

DEAD MAN IN PARADISE

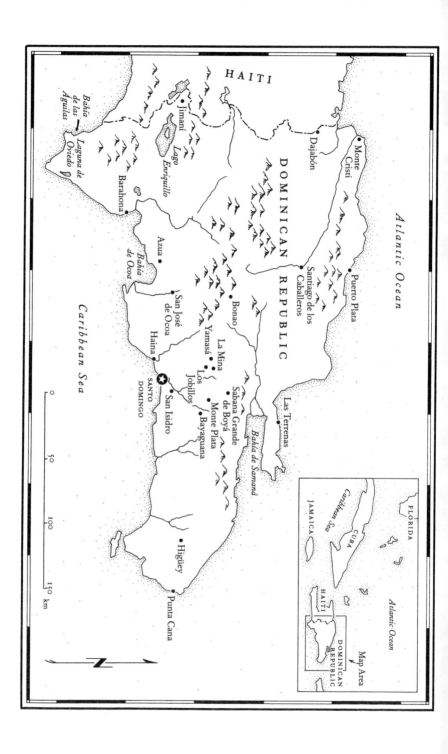

Part

ONE

.

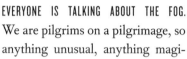

I

EVERYONE IS TALKING ABOUT THE FOG.
We are pilgrims on a pilgrimage, so
anything unusual, anything magi-
cal, also seems fated, propitious, ordained. It is rare here, in the searing
eastern basin of the Dominican Republic, to see the world obliterated by
mist and the night like a pale shroud. Men and women climb the stairs of
the *guagua*, the bus, and it fills quickly, even urgently. One of the last to
come aboard is a campesino with the oil-black skin that speaks of Haitian blood. He wears dark slacks, a painter's cap, a threadbare *guayabera*
that once was bright white. "I love our King, Jesus Christ, above all," he
declares, standing at the head of the aisle. "These are the end times."
Then he walks down to sit in one of the few remaining seats, beside me,
the gringo.

Tomorrow is the Day of Our Lady of Highest Grace, and the pilgrims are thronging toward Higüey. Some are devout, but most are simply miracle-seekers, not fussy about where those miracles might come
from, and Higüey is the city of miracles. They pour in from every corner of the country and beyond, from Haiti, that restless nation that lies
across the border dividing the island of Hispaniola. They sail from
Puerto Rico to the east, or fly in from Cuba, which rises to the west like
a doubting eyebrow. Some come from other worlds, diaspora Dominicans from New York, Miami, Montreal, Madrid, each wearing the uncomfortable expression of the exile. All come first to the guaguas that
hurtle across the island through the sugar-cane fields that surround the
sacred city. The cane is beginning to flower, and because sugar cane was
once the lifeblood of this nation, the flower has its own name, *el pendón,*

which people speak of in the way they might a friend who comes to visit only once or twice a year. The blossoms hang in silvery wisps above the stalks, sweetening the mist.

As the bus pulls out for the last leg of the journey, video screens light the darkness: Arnold Schwarzenegger as an everyday American in a struggle against Colombian terrorists. The man who believes in the end times moves forward in the bus to read the Spanish subtitles. He laughs longer and louder than anyone else when the hero bites off and spits out a chunk of an enemy's ear.

We approach Higüey with the first glow of dawn; the fog lifts and dissipates, and in this, too, the pilgrims see an unknowable hand. We are on the outskirts, marked initially by the walled compound of the cabanas, rooms booked to couples committing the sins of adultery or pre-marital sex. Next comes the cockfighting club, like a miniature coliseum. As the first small barrios appear, so does the first "car wash," which might actually be a car wash but is almost always also an outdoor drinking hall and dance club. The clusters of concrete-and-plaster homes thicken into neighbourhoods and finally a city. The people of Higüey stare up at the guaguas as though at the troops of an occupying force.

"The cathedral!" shouts the driver, knowing that today no one cares about any other stop. I follow the pilgrims out onto the asphalt. Air conditioning had allowed me to forget the fire that consumes heaven and earth from the moment the sun shoulders over the horizon. The light turns the world into glare and black shadows. Ahead, I can make out the line; hundreds of people in the withering dawn, figures strung like rosary beads along the great lane that leads to the cathedral's open doors. The cathedral itself is not what I expected, but then, it's rare that a Roman Catholic shrine dates only from 1956. The building has that look of the future as imagined in the global mind of the mid-twentieth century—sleek, industrial, homogenous, a factory for the production of faith. The front is cross-hatched with square-cut columns and capped with a series of concrete arches, one of which soars above the rest into the sky, where its peak just touches the fading mist. The Latin inscription HAIL MARY, FULL OF GRACE, THE LORD IS WITH THEE is spelled out in large gold letters above an entrance porch that seems designed to suggest an open Bible.

I compose my too-formal Spanish and approach a cluster of people near the end of the line. "How long does one have to wait?" I ask.

"Three hours. Four. Later it will be five or more."

It is decided, then. Though I'm not a Catholic, not even a Christian, I have always allowed myself my moments of symbol and rite. I am here to mark some kind of beginning, to seek my own omens. But I would die under this sun.

I quit the line and walk the roadway that leads to the cathedral. People are setting up chairs and blankets, as though for a market. Each person, though, is missing an arm or is blind, has a single, grotesquely swollen leg or is a shrivelled figure in a wheelchair. Some have partially caved-in faces; others are plainly insane, constantly petted and calmed by companions. It is a beggars' gauntlet, the wounded and rejected demanding mercy on this day of passing piety. Beyond the bronze doors, I can see that the church is teeming, the rumble of chatter and prayer and laughter rising up through the arches. The atmosphere is of a fair, or an audience waiting for a performance to begin. There are people in sunglasses and cycling shorts, in dresses of the purest white, in baseball caps, in suits, in sackcloth. They shoot video, eat fried bread, kneel around votive candles, hang dozens of rosaries around their necks. Odours waft in from the makeshift camp that surrounds the church: goat meat and boiled green bananas, sweat and old clothes, smoke, feces. Cylinders of light cut in from the oblongs of stained glass that fill the towering wall behind the altar.

I push my way forward, stepping over the bodies of families who arrived days earlier to camp on blankets along the inside walls. The altar is enormous, and as I draw close I see that its dark wood is carved into a cascade of polished leaves lit by winking stars of electric light. The icon of Mary, they say, appeared in the limbs of an orange tree to a girl in the sixteenth century. And now I can see the sacred artifact. It is on a raised platform, separated from the congregation by guard railings and a transparent pane. I can just make out the silhouette of the mother of Jesus in her mantle. It is exactly the shape of the arches that carry the church to the sky.

Those who have lined up for hours file past the altar of the icon from a side door that allows them, at last, to escape the sun. The pilgrims have waited for hours, and now they have just a few moments in the presence of the holy. They touch a palm to the pane, or press a rosary against it, or pass a scarf or a shawl through the air in front of it. Some hold out photos of loved ones, or raise wax figurines of babies or cattle. The supplicants' mouths are moving, muttering prayers and asking favours; only a few begin to weep. They are speaking directly to the Virgin, and most seem startled when a cleric seizes their right arm at the wrist and mechanically leads them through the sign of the cross. The most earnest of the pilgrims—those who linger in Mary's presence, their hands whirling in the air to gather her—need the firmest guidance. I study the faces and see desperation, joy, craving, hope. But I am certain I sense something more, some background emotion out of which the others spring. It confuses their expressions. Is it faith?

Now a stranger is standing in front of me. His eyes are black and implacable, the pupils motionless. In the instant before he moves on, the man presses something into my hand. It's a novena booklet, with an image of the icon on the cover. Now that I can see Mary clearly, her power is immediate. Her face is bright in the velvet darkness that surrounds her; even the baby Jesus in his manger, tiny, like a true newborn, is more shadowed than her gaze. Her mantle is twilight blue and covered with stars, so that the boundary between her and the night sky is invisible, except at her head, which is surrounded by a crown of light and corona of fire. There is something honestly virginal in the image, something mesmeric. This is not the wan and pious Mary who seems to know that her son is born to suffer; this Mary's face is full, like that of a girl who is suddenly a woman, a fat little girl who knows, now, she is a princess. She has spoken with the angel Gabriel and she is immortal, cupped in the hands of God, blessed and protected. She looks as if she wants to laugh out loud in delight.

I glance back toward the altar, where the white oval of Mary's visage stands out in the muted light. The seekers pass before her in their steady stream, and suddenly it comes to me, the expression that dissembles every face. It is faith, yes. But it is also fear.

YANIRA OFFERS her cheek to my kiss. "Tell me. How did it go in Higüey?"

The pilgrimage was Yanira's idea. She grew up in Higüey from the age of nine, and still goes to see her mother and sisters there, and to eat the sacred city's famous knots of white cheese, its yuca-root empanadas. Never, however, on the saint's day. Our Lady of Grace brings with her mountains of garbage and a stench from every dark corner.

Yanira is patient with my Spanish as I struggle to say what I've seen. People devout enough to wait five hours to pass a hand in front of an icon, but not devout enough to know the sign of the cross. Pilgrims who will stand in endless lineups to buy the image of Our Lady on paperweights, stickers, T-shirts, candles, amulets and ointments, but so few people waiting for confession that the priest gave up and shut it down. Just off the main street, I had seen the temple, completed in 1572, that stands on the site of the original Sanctuary of Mary in Higüey. There, I had watched groups of women—always women—as they used broom handles to reach past the gates that protect a small orange tree and beat the tree's frail limbs. Every leaf, every twig that falls is kept and carried as a talisman. The tree, of course, is not the one in which the icon is said to have appeared. That tree was long ago picked apart by devotion. I had also seen, on my return to the capital city of Santo Domingo, a news report about a starlet who'd chosen the celebration of the Madonna to debut a plunging bustier printed with the image of the icon of Higüey. She earned a public reprimand from the church.

"Most Dominicans are 'Catholics,'" says Yanira, making quote marks in the air. "Did you see the president?"

Yes. He had arrived by helicopter on the grounds of the basilica, and barefoot children had run across the lawns toward him. The president vanished into a convoy of vehicles, then reappeared on the stairs of the church in a crowd of men holding machine guns. The area had been cordoned off with a temporary metal fence, and inside it were uniformed corps of the air force, army and navy, along with a tattered military band. They were joined by generals, colonels, politicians, sycophants, a fraternity that yawned and gossiped and flashed their teeth in the sun. Then a pariah dog, a chestnut bitch with her belly sagging to the tips of her long, grey, overworked teats, came trotting out into the centre of the pomp, sniffing polished boots and staring with her tongue-wagging smile into rigid faces. Outside the fences people roared with laughter and there was, for a moment, a feeling of divine providence. The presidential election is only months away.

"If the president doesn't make an appearance in Higüey, it means he isn't Catholic," Yanira says. "It would be a political disaster. It's a compromise between church and state."

We are sitting at what has become our regular spot, a park bench to one side of the National Library on the grounds of the Plaza of Culture. It was Yanira's choice, a fenced and gated compound of gardens and museums that is clean and calm—everything that the rest of Santo Domingo is not. I had answered her ad offering Spanish instruction, not to learn the language so much as to cure a peculiar affliction: it seemed I could not speak or even understand the Dominican Spanish without beading all over with sweat. The language is a breakneck eruption of slang and abbreviation peppered with colonial archaisms and indigenous, Haitian and African words. Straining to keep up, I would stand still and inscrutable while great wet patches spread beneath my arms and down my back, soaking even through my pants. My face ran as if with tears, my hair matted to my head, and so I came to Yanira. I remember that she shook my damp hand with a slight disdain for that custom, and then proffered her cheek. Her face was moon-shaped and slightly concave, its features at once small and full—full lips on a round mouth; a button nose that was also broad. Her hair was straightened but without duress. She considered herself a *negra*, though her skin had a cinnamon luminescence. She was serious and punctual, and she crossed her arms against the chill of the Dominican winter. It was twenty-five degrees Celsius in the shade.

Yanira is pleased by the miracle of the pariah dog of Higüey. The president is not popular. The republic has tumbled into an economic crisis, with electricity blackouts as a constant reminder. The only solution, as always, seems to be more foreign debt, which can only mean more political marching orders from the creditors in Paris, London, Bern and, above all, Washington, D.C. "I have a double enemy," says Yanira. "My government, and the government of the United States. I can raise my voice, I can raise my arms in protest, but it's like David and Goliath. It's like impotence."

A hummingbird whirls overhead. *"Picaflor."* Yanira has become the professor once again. "The seasons are changing," she says. "The leaves fall from the trees in the spring." Her laughter comes without restraint.

"Have you started your work?" she asks.

The question irritates me for a moment, because the answer is no. Instead, I've been swallowed by Santo Domingo. I've ended up, too often, drinking tall bottles of beer on the Malecón, the seawall, watching surfers carve past the mats of garbage that wash steadily to shore. At night, in a bland third-storey rental in the university district, I sort through a sheaf of papers hoping to find the missing fact, the passed-over sentence, that will illuminate a path into the life of a man who is forty years dead.

Father James Arthur MacKinnon, an uncle who died before I was born. I can't recall a time when I wasn't aware he was a martyr, shot and killed in a place called the Dominican Republic. My family was church-less, atheist even, and it was duly noted that Arthur was not the kind of missionary who disappeared into Africa or Polynesia, converting the naked heathens. Father Art had been a Catholic missionary to a nominally Roman Catholic nation, bringing the institutional church to a country struggling to support its own clergy. My brothers and I were told that he spoke out against injustice. The precise nature of the injustice wasn't clear to me then, but the Dominican Republic seemed to have the litany: poverty, dictatorship, corruption, and occasional invasions by the United States Marine Corps. Arthur died under the American occupation of the Dominican Republic in 1965. He was killed on America's watch. This fact, I remember, had a particular gilded weight.

Arthur was a presence. He was manifest at the family dinner table, where talk groped inexorably—at times oppressively—toward some higher human ideal. He haunted the lecture halls and church basements where my brothers and I would sit hushed beside our father as a touring speaker showed, in concentric rings, how much of our hometown would be vaporized, or merely destroyed, or only poisoned, by a single megaton nuclear warhead; or while a journalist clicked through slides of El Salvadoran unionists slaughtered by military death squads. I understood that Arthur had died for these sins. The New Testament language was unavoidable. Others had Che Guevara: they wore his red star like a crucifix; his execution was their Golgotha; the United States would forever be their Pontius Pilate. We had Father Art. I knew there were people who believed that my father had lost his religion from the pain of his brother's murder. It wasn't true, but sometimes a story is more convincing than the truth.

In my childhood vision, Arthur's death was like a scene from a western movie. Father Art lived in a place called Monte Plata, in a country torn by revolution. Men in dusty uniforms walked the streets with submachine guns. Father Art spoke out for the rebels, for the poor, and one afternoon two Dominican soldiers picked him up and drove him to the outskirts of town. They told him to get out and walk. What I pictured was a priest in a pure white cassock walking tall into a desert wilderness, and suddenly he is staggering forward, his head thrown back, his body bowed, red stars appearing through his immaculate robe. A dozen bloody asterisks, and he tumbles to the ground, a dead man. The soldiers would have climbed back into their jeep and steered off to report that they had carried out their orders. A general would have rubbed his hands together. The Americans would have issued a statement of sympathy and concern.

There was a real story, too, and in time it pulled apart my vision of the high-noon drama. First to go were the simplest details, like the fact that Arthur hadn't died in his cassock but in civilian clothes, that the land around Monte Plata isn't desert but muddy, subtropical slash. The men who picked Arthur up were not soldiers but policemen, and they were not faceless killers but human beings whose names I might speak aloud. They did not drive away to report to some scheming general, as I had imagined. Their bullet-riddled bodies were found alongside Father Art's.

I can't say when I first thought to myself, *It would be good to know.* It had never been proved that Father Art had died in an orchestrated assassination. How had he come to be the only foreign civilian put to death in a Dominican war? A priest making noise in a backwater town: Would they kill for that? Could that really be enough? Maybe the two policemen hadn't meant to kill Arthur at all. Maybe it was like, "Go give that priest a scare," and something had gone wrong. A fight. They wouldn't have expected a priest to fight, but Arthur was a blue-collar boy from Cape Breton Island, the seventh of nine sons in a coal miner's family. Arthur's death began to seem like a kind of fable, a story from a world where people spoke of "truth" and "good" and "evil" without suppressing an ironic smile. But one day I could no longer simply accept that Arthur was a martyr. I needed to know the conditions of his sacrifice. It is possible to be a martyr to justice or ideology, conviction or dogma; it is possible, even, to be a martyr to chance. To sheer bad luck.

I was suffering the symptoms of a loss of faith.

This much I could hang on to: begin with what had happened. There were concrete questions, immutable facts. How many bullets? Whose gun? At what vector? On whose orders? Find those truths and perhaps make room for others.

In all of this, too, there was a fear: that in any case, it didn't matter. And now I am in Santo Domingo. I go out into the streets and see people angry at the price of onions, checking their hair in shop windows, making overseas calls to loved ones in New York City. I feel every one of the forty years that have passed since Father Art's death, and it's a paralysis. One morning, I suppose, I will get up the nerve to stutter my way into some police archive, and the officer in charge will laugh lightly at my request and step into a back room and, a few minutes later, return with a manila folder. *It's all here*, he will say, patting a file marked SECRETO. And I will learn exactly how Arthur was killed, why and by whom, and it will only take a minute, all of it done with a shrug that says, *Mists of time, Señor MacKinnon. Mists of time.*

"I'm thinking to start with the police," I say to Yanira.

She looks at me thoughtfully for a moment. Then she makes a motion, as though to draw her purse in close to her body. "When I see a policeman, I'm a little bit afraid," she says. Her words have a careful, freighted tone. "Everyone has a revulsion toward the police. They're dangerous. They're unruly. There are a lot of laws to control and oversee them, but the laws . . . the laws . . ."

"The laws don't work."

"They don't work." The problems with the police are an affront to her, she says, a throwback to the days of her parents and grandparents, the decades of dictatorship and secret police and quiet, unsolvable murders. To pick up a newspaper and read about a man shot down, or a woman disappeared—it's a constant reminder of history, the abnegation of the here and now. It's the past leaving its bloody handprints in the present.

Then she really does gather her purse. Our time is up. Class is dismissed.

2

OCTOBER 6, 1960. IN A FEW HOURS,
Father Arthur MacKinnon would
enter a world so unlike the one he'd
known that it followed a different calendar. There it would be year 30,
Era of Trujillo. He already knew that he must not roll his eyes or joke
about these calendars. They were the least of what he'd have to get
used to.

He said an early morning Mass in Our Lady of the Skies Chapel in
New York International Airport, then boarded for a nine o'clock flight.
An hour passed before the plane took off, shuddering up into thickening
clouds. No matter. It was only the second flight of his life, and Arthur
had patience and faith. He had been preparing for this moment since the
winter of 1954, when, at age twenty-one, he sent his first letter to the
Scarboro Foreign Mission Society asking for information. A year later
he crossed the brownstone commons of St. Francis Xavier University in
Antigonish, Nova Scotia, to mail a formal application for the novitiate
year of spiritual training. "I have always considered being a priest," he
had written. His fear that his tuberculosis would put him out of the running had been eased by the medical report. "Well stabilized," said the
doctor, and "fit for gainful employment." Arthur didn't indicate on the
application that the tuberculosis had been the start of it all, that he had
made the decision to be a missionary during two years and ten months
of sucking breath in the sanitorium of Glace Bay General Hospital near
his family home in Low Point, Cape Breton Island.

The weather softened as Arthur's plane travelled south, and it was
clear over the Caribbean. There were the Bahamas, like a glistening net

cast over deep water. The island of Hispaniola was sudden and immense, a knot of verdant mountains that dispelled the sea. The tiny roads seemed to gather, and the minuscule cubes of campesino houses, until finally he saw the chockablock mass of the city itself. Santo Domingo de Guzmán, the oldest colonial city in the Americas, founded in 1496 at the mouth of the Ozama River. He would need to use the new name: Ciudad Trujillo. Trujillo City.

He was more than ready to arrive. At the departure ceremony, held three days earlier in the seminary that perched on the Scarborough Bluffs above Lake Ontario, he had felt an inner cool, no hint of the "hero emotions" his companions sang about in their old hymns. In his mind he had already made his goodbyes. "All this, I suppose, just to go down there and get shot," he had said to a friend.

Art could taste his new country even before he reached the tarmac. The air was heavy, heavier still in lungs scarred by tubercles. Well, he had no complaints for the two waiting Scarboro priests, Leonard Hudswell and Bud Smith. He was alive, and that was enough. He had never been so alive.

The road into town hugged the coast, and Art stared out the car window at the natural beauty—aquamarine waters colliding with an endless band of dark limestone, worn here and there into blowholes that fired geysers of salt spray to the heights of the coconut palms. There was no way for him to know that this was "the swimming pool," the broad bay where Rafael Leonidas Trujillo Molina, the dictator of the Dominican Republic, the man always spoken of only as Trujillo, had the enemies of his regime fed to the sharks.

The fathers didn't stop but traversed the city. The expanding slums on the east bank of the Ozama River led to the Duarte Bridge and the rough, chaotic downtown, which pressed against the narrow streets and ruins and venerable cafés of the Zona Colonial. This was Ciudad Nueva, the New City, founded on the west bank of the Ozama in 1502 after a hurricane destroyed the original colony. Finally came the embassy district and the wealthy neighbourhoods, and then the city faded. The Scarboro Central House was here in the countryside, a green gap to the west of the capital. The only neighbour was the Jesuit retreat, Manresa Loyola, which shared the same crescent of Haina Beach, its perfect rollers breaking up the coast to the Port of Haina. Art was surprised that the Scarboro "house" was more like a dormitory block. He gazed up at the high, airy ceilings. A Dominican woman was serving a stew with rice and salad—the meal known as *la bandera*, the flag.

Father Art was restless. That afternoon, watching as Father Hudswell heard confessions, he winced that he had arrived without a word of training in Spanish. A group of children taught him his first words then and there, but he was embarrassed even with them. Then came his first *chubasco*, a Caribbean squall like the storms that had sometimes come hard off the Great Lakes during his seminary years in Canada. Here, though, every raindrop was warmer than blood.

He went to bed beneath a mosquito net for the first time that night, in heat and humidity like nothing he had known in his twenty-eight years of life.

The new day was taken up with a morning Mass and a walk on the beach with two other young priests. They talked about Fidel Castro. Every generation of Scarboro men seemed to have its own earthly cross to bear. The order was founded in 1918 as the China Mission Seminary by John Mary Fraser, who in 1902 had been the first English-speaking missionary to China from North America. Canada's first Catholic foreign missionaries cut deeper paths into China until 1953, when they were expelled during the purges of Mao Zedong. The first Scarboro priests to the Dominican Republic had touched down in 1943, the thirteenth year of *trujillismo*. Now the world had witnessed the Cuban Revolution. Castro had yet to celebrate even his first year in power, but the priests on the beach at Haina agreed: communism was the leading global threat to Christianity.

Art didn't take that afternoon's siesta. Instead, he began his first attempt to keep a journal.

I hope to be able to record my first impressions and experiences as faithfully as possible and as honestly as possible. Therefore this is strictly personal so (should foreign eyes fall upon this book) I ask them to please not waste their time by reading this. But—if you do insist on reading this—do not expect perfect English as many times this will be rushed. Do not expect pious exhortations (this is not a sermon). Above all—do

not be scandalized, as Fr. Kelly once said: on the missions your every
human fault is magnified beyond calculation.

He didn't write again for three days. He tried to get used to walking the streets, entering shops, even seeing a movie—*The Mouse That Roared*, starring Peter Sellers—in his soutane, a Scarboro policy here. He bristled with anger as he heard the complaints of Father Basil Kirby, who was trying to organize a co-op movement in the country but was forbidden by both church and state from speaking publicly of social ills. Father Art was already forming his own sharp view of his new land, the República Dominicana.

R.D. is a police state pure and simple—guards at every crossroad and
soldiers everywhere. Life is cheap and freedom of speech practically nil.

He visited the immigration offices that day. He was fingerprinted, photographed; the bureaucrats seemed to ask every question they could imagine and took down his answers carefully. He had requested a permanent visa. For a Scarboro priest, the missionary life was exactly that. He could expect to live and die in a place he might never call home.

3

I HAVE DECIDED TO BEGIN AT THE national graveyard. It's far up Máximo Gómez Avenue, almost to the bridge over the easy, swampy waters of the Isabela River, which curls over Santo Domingo from the north. In the cemetery there is a ghost, the one I think of simply as "the lieutenant." Almost nothing is known about him, which seems to make him the guardian of some deep mystery. Second Lieutenant Evangelista Martínez Rodríguez materialized in Monte Plata perhaps a day before he was seen heading out of town in a jeep with Father Art. What more is known of the lieutenant comes only from his corpse. Eleven days after he was found dead alongside the priest, a team of criminologists with the Organization of American States exhumed the body. Laid out on a surgical table, Martínez was five feet, five inches tall, trim, barrel-chested and evidently physically powerful. He had been hit in the left eye by a single bullet, and his head was like a ruined piñata. The OAS team noted a black-ink tattoo on the cadaver's right forearm that read, in Spanish, REMEMBER QUEZADA. A hero? A lover? A friend he had sworn to avenge?

Another ghost, anyway.

The guaguas in their ranks along Máximo Gómez jostle and charge like enormous herd animals. They have none of the order, none of the discipline, of machinery. They leap or stop suddenly, aggressive, angling in and out of traffic. A sign on the windshield might promise a destination, but the sign isn't always correct, and not every person is able to read, and so there is the *cobrador*, the conductor, hanging out the doorway and calling the route. There are few official stops. The guaguas will halt anywhere, and it is not uncommon to see a bus pull over to pick up a passenger, then drive forward only a few feet to the next person, who has decided that this, exactly this point, is where she will come aboard. No one complains, just as no one complains when a man at the very back of the impossibly crowded guagua shouts out to be dropped off, and the people pressed into the fold-down aisle seats, two or even three per seat, must stand and attempt to make way. The cobrador is keening, exhorting, goading, cajoling. If he does his job poorly, the guagua creeps down the road, pausing endlessly, lingering at every crowd, greedy for fares. But the best cobrador is a matador of gridlock, leaping off the moving bus to wade into a crowd, calling, warning that the bus is moving on, it's leaving, it's a split second from departure, and then his hand is on a woman's back, he calls her *doña* and stops two lanes of traffic to bring her aboard, and then the bus really is rolling, jerking back into midstream with the cobrador loping behind, his face calm as he springs onto the running board. The bus veers into the traffic with no regard for lanes. No one hangs so much as a finger out of the open windows.

My guagua crosses the city. Beyond John F. Kennedy Avenue, it enters a jumble of dirty plaster and breeze-block, fronds of rebar wagging like parodies of palm trees out of the tops of unfinished buildings. These are the *barrios altos*, enormous, hard-working neighbourhoods that spread to the eastern and northern flanks of the city, where they fade into the seething shanty towns nicknamed the *zonas apache*, a term borrowed from the forbidden territories in the movie westerns beamed in from the United States. There has always been an official fear of the barrios altos.

I call my stop when I see the first stalls selling fruit, sandals, leatherwork; the graveyard wall runs alongside an open-air market. The world within the cemetery isn't so different: there are carts selling orange juice and peeled sugar cane; hawkers with cookies and balls of salt cheese; there are motorcycle taxis, gossips and layabouts, even a parked guagua. Oddly, no one is selling flowers, though one carunculated old woman has candles laid out on a blanket.

I had imagined that I might walk through the graveyard and find the crypt of Evangelista Martínez. His birthdate would be on the headstone, and around him his dead mother and father, his brothers and sisters. These clues would lead to living relatives, and I imagined them speaking hesitantly at first, then forcefully, finally cracking open photo albums and sharing the dark secret of their family. The ghost would begin to take form.

Already the idea is laughable. The cemetery is like a walled city, with a broad main street that passes whole neighbourhoods of tombs, all in the same rebar and breeze-block, even the same painted plaster, of the world of the living. The grass and the walls are teeming with lizards, one other form of life that seems to thrive in Santo Domingo. There are flies, and as long as there are flies, there will be lizards.

The afternoon sun is indulging its fire. Back at the cemetery gate, an official-looking man recommends the graveyard archive. He leads me to a building indistinguishable from a mausoleum, but with an open door. The room inside is the colour of dry mustard. An ancient desk fills the corner facing the door, and behind it sits a woman in a dark-blue suit with a face like a skull. No: a mummy. She doesn't look up, and though others in the room are chattering, she doesn't speak. Instead, she makes a gesture with a curled finger. Another woman, pear-shaped and slightly hostile, sets upon me with impatience.

"Talk to me," she says, her Spanish barely forming on her lips.

Sweat prickles my skin as I begin to explain.

"Who was he?" she snaps. What interest could this gringo possibly have in this dead man, a set of bones that lost their flesh almost forty years ago?

"He is a friend of the family."

She stares at me for a moment, flushed with an unexplained anger, then disappears into a doorway. A sheet of paper taped to the lintel reads ARCHIVE in black marker. I stick my head into the room and see her opening dusty books onto a desk.

"There is nothing," she says finally.

"There is nothing?"

"We will need more information. If we knew who was at the funeral. Who was at the funeral? Who are his family?"

"That's what I'm trying to find out," I reply, and she scowls and shakes her head.

ON ANOTHER MORNING I walk to the National Library. It is almost cool, and the traffic is only a white-noise mumble. I can hear, for once, the eccentric music of insects and roosters. Then the sun comes aloft with its tropical suddenness, and the air goes still. The noise of the daytime city is rising. Ten thousand ruined mufflers, ten thousand horns honking, ten thousand cobradors shouting from the doors of the guaguas. Every shop turns up the merengue, the rap, the salsa, the Cuban son, and a coconut vendor wheels past with his pushcart, calling out his wares. A mule's hooves clop against the asphalt, and the sounds of work, of machines that grind and whine, sing out over the barrio. The pigeons begin to cry, and in every home the families shout, trying to be heard over the din that surrounds them, and their voices echo off tile floors and bare walls and out through open shutters to overwhelm the city. The madness grows and grows until the first power outage of the day takes place with a sudden shout—*ah!*—and the city is silent. Then, a few seconds later, the hum of ten thousand generators.

Inside the library, the serenity is unnerving. The periodicals section is an upper floor, a ruddy-tiled vastness impeded only by seven tables and as many patrons, who sit like wallflowers at the edge of a dance floor. The librarian is the kind of young man who has opinions about foreign novels. He squints when I speak, as though he could better understand my accent if only his vision were clearer.

"Do you have the newspaper *El Caribe* for the summer of 1965?"

He nods and wanders into the stacks, heavy metal shelves in bureaucracy green. He returns with an apologetic look. "We don't have it."

"Do you have *La Opinión?*"

He returns empty-handed. "No."

It is the same with *La Información* and *El Nacional,* though neither of us is sure whether these were printed in that year of revolution; some papers, like the venerable *Listín Diario,* suspended publication amid the chaos of the rebel uprising that began on April 24, 1965.

"Are there *any* newspapers from that summer?"

At this, he disappears for some time. "No."

"Do you have anything at all from that era?"

His face betrays some irritation, and he is gone so long that I wonder if the search has segued into a lunch break. Finally he reappears, looking pleased. He has a single copy of a magazine; the title translates as *Now*. To my astonishment, it contains an article on the death of Father Art, THE CRIME OF MONTE PLATA. There is also a photo feature, images of dead civilians and revolutionaries with a caption that reads simply, "To save lives." With those three words, U.S. president Lyndon Johnson justified the American invasion and occupation that quashed the Dominican rebellion.

"Is there a photocopier?"

"Ah, there is a photocopier," says the librarian. "Unfortunately, there is no electricity. Also, the photocopier isn't working."

I consider the situation. If *Now* is still publishing, I could visit its offices and arrange to make a copy.

"Does *Now* exist now?" I ask.

"What?"

"*Now*. Does it exist—now?"

He gives me a puzzled look. "*Sí*, now is now—"

"No, no. The magazine, *Now*. Does it exist, today?"

The librarian looks at me with bafflement. Besides *Now*, there is a newspaper called *Today*. I try again: "Does *Now* publish today?" My shirt peels away from my underarms, heavy with salt damp.

"No, sir. *Now* is *Now* and *Today* is *Today*."

"But does *Now* publish on this day, today?"

"Ah! I understand. No, sir. *Now* is published only once a month. It does not publish today."

And this is the way our yesterdays die: in lost documents and broken-down copiers; in comic misunderstandings and selective silences; in books that no one can afford and nights blacked out so that no one can read. Another possibility: that we allow these lapses because we prefer to believe we can live outside time.

I retreat into the Zona Colonial, the warren of stone buildings that date from the first decades of the European invasion of the New World. The main boulevard, El Conde, is now a pedestrian mall, with restaurants selling American pizza and Dominican fried chicken, with shops selling gift-box cigars and blue larimar stone and prehistoric flies revealed in amber. On the side streets, in rooms where high society once debated the rectitude of the Spanish Inquisition, the new elite gathers in nightclubs to introduce one another to American street drugs.

Near the bottom of El Conde, in the heart of the Zona Colonial, stands the Fortress of Santo Domingo. Better known as the Fortress Ozama, it looks down on that great river where it bends into the sea. Construction began a decade after Christopher Columbus, on his first Atlantic crossing in 1492, declared the island to have the most beautiful meadows in the world. Finding them reminiscent of his adopted homeland of Spain, he named the island Isla Española, later known as Hispaniola. The fortress appears at a glance to be the last parapet of some fallen Spanish castle, but in fact it has always been only this, a single battlement rising above a small stone edifice. The Dominican limestone is queerly beautiful, a rock so gently compressed that whorls of shell and coral still decorate its face. It angles steeply three storeys to the top, broken only by rifle embrasures, niches that show the walls to be more than a metre thick.

The fortress was a statement of what would be. Put another way, it declared against all that had come before. It was almost certainly built in part by the Taínos, the indigenes whose ancestors had colonized the island more than 250 years before the Christian era, replacing earlier cultures that likewise had risen through the Antilles from continental South America. Slave labour for the Spanish killed many of the Taínos; others died from disease or slaughter at the hands of the colonists. As Taíno life became a holocaust, as the people died in the tens of thousands, mothers chose abortion; whole families poisoned themselves by eating raw cassava. The Dominican Republic is a place of New World firsts: the first colonial capital, cathedral, hospital and university, but also this, the first genocide. As many as five hundred thousand people, possibly more, died as the Taínos were driven to extinction, and the Fortress of Santo Domingo went on to salute almost every expedition into the Americas in the sixteenth century. The nation became "the Axis of Conquest," a title that acquired irony as Hispaniola spiralled into a series of invasions, surrenders, liberations, annexations. The tower on the fortress has flown the flags of Spain, England, France, Haiti, Great Colombia, the United States and ultimately the Dominican Republic.

Independence, too, is a gesture against history: a world made suddenly new. In the Dominican Republic, the gesture was not enough. The nation was seventeen years old when, in 1861, a desperate president invited Spain to annex it. Four years later, a provisional army and popular uprising finally ousted the Spanish in the War of Restoration. But this was not the end. From 1916 to 1924, U.S. marines occupied the country to quell political instability and assure repayment of Dominican debt. They established the Dominican National Guard, and among the new officers was a young man named Trujillo.

By February 1930, Trujillo was head of the national army and stationed in the Fortress Ozama. His soldiers forced Horacio Vásquez, the president elected as American occupation troops prepared to withdraw from the country, to resign. The clock had stopped. It was year 1 of the Era of Trujillo.

Trujillo had little time for ruins. During his decades in power, he ordered enormous new walls for the Fortress of Santo Domingo, dead grey slabs of concrete capped with ridiculous crenels and bartizans. The fortress had become a defence against enemies from within. The guns of the firing squad rang out; those who had been inside the walls whispered of a who's who of rebels, conspirators, intellectuals, all crowded into rooms lit only by the slits of the rifle embrasures. Witnesses spoke of solitary confinement in the ancient cistern, a literal hole into which prisoners were lowered from above, a place without day or night.

Today, the Fortress of Santo Domingo is a scenic attraction with an official government pamphlet that presents history as ending with the eighteenth century. Every summer, a festival of merengue is held at the base of its brutalist walls. People dance for ten days straight, and in the pulsing epicentre of the music no one seems to remember how families and friends sat on the east bank of the river, looking for, perhaps, a familiar T-shirt or towel hanging from the black slits of the tower. The celebrants wear Taíno-style jewellery and dance under the stars, and as they stumble to their beds in the thick night air their feet rattle over old manhole covers that still read "Trujillo City."

TWO DAYS LATER I am back at the national graveyard. I have scoured the National Library and the General Archive of the Nation and finally my own collection of reports kept by the Scarboro priests. I have uncovered two narrow avenues into the life and death of Second Lieutenant Evangelista Martínez. The first is a front-page story from *La Hoja*, an iconoclastic newspaper born in the first days of the 1965 revolution. Without sources or byline, *La Hoja* declares that every possible version of the murder of "Arthur McKinson" must be considered alongside a singular fact: Father Art had made public protests to the authorities against the imprisonment of young men and women from Monte Plata.

> One of the most credible versions is that the padre was sent for by the chief of the local police, a lieutenant who had been transferred to that post that same afternoon. Later, his vehicle was found riddled with bullets across the door and windshield of the left side.
>
> Nonetheless, there was no blood inside the vehicle, nor any sign of struggle.

The lieutenant, of course, is Martínez. According to *La Hoja*, three members of the Dominican armed forces were to judge the case. The names mean nothing to me: Major José Ernesto Cruz Brea, Lieutenant Colonel Angel Urbano Matos, Captain Narciso Elio Bautista. They were appointed under order number 70 of the Government of National Reconstruction, the provisional council that existed under the American occupation. In the General Archive, a man in a white laboratory coat and gloves can bring any visitor the two books of collected laws from 1965. In each, the Government of Reconstruction, the period from May 7 to August 30 of that year, is a blind gap. It is as though the provisional government, sworn in with America's blessing in answer to the revolution, had been mute. It is as though the truncated rebellion that forms the root of the contemporary Dominican Republic is best forgotten, as though anarchy is not also history.

There is also a small clipping from *Patria*, a newspaper invented to serve and to speak for the rebels. In it, Martínez is an enigma. He could be an assassin; he might be a victim. He had been the commander of a police detachment in the barrios altos, writes an unknown reporter, and was captured on the first day of the revolution. Known to be a "good guy," he was freed on the word of young rebel supporters. "Later, we are told, he ratted out many of the young people who had given him his freedom." According to *Patria*, the lieutenant arrived in Monte Plata not hours before Arthur was killed but three days earlier, when he was "put on show" as the new head of the local police.

> Versions of the story making the rounds in Monte Plata claim that, without a doubt, Evangelista was 'very religious' and that some ten days before the crime he was a prisoner in La Victoria prison, together with another twenty or thirty officials who had gone to join the side of the people in this Patriotic War.
>
> It's added that on that occasion, he declared himself in favor of the patriots.

Martínez was buried, exhumed and buried again, and all in the National Cemetery on Máximo Gómez Avenue. It is beyond belief that none of it was ever put down on paper.

I arrive to a completely different graveyard. There are no hawkers, no motorcycle taxis, and only a few people mill about, most clustered in pools of morning shade. There are gardeners and sidewalk sweepers. There are flowers for sale.

The office, too, has changed. It's empty except for a young man whose cap declares for the Boston Red Sox. He shouts toward the doorway of the archive room, and a woman emerges—a serious-looking woman with a tight, greying Afro and reading glasses on a gold chain. I tell her the date that Martínez died, and she wades into the same great pile of books. Finally she turns to me; she appears to be apologizing. But no, she is walking toward me with an open book and her finger on an entry. Evangelista Martínez Rodríguez. Cause of death: bullet wounds.

A flicker of the ghost.

It's the right man, no doubt about it—interred on June 24, 1965, not even forty-eight hours after he died alongside Father Art. She is apologizing because, where someone should have filled in the block and plot where Martínez is buried, there are only blanks. There is no record, either, of the family and friends who might have attended the funeral, not even a signature to make the burial official. I glance over the page and see too many names and too many blanks. A lot of people died in June of 1965.

"There is nothing more?"

"Nothing."

"Where he is, nobody knows?" I ask.

"No one knows," she agrees.

I walk out into the cemetery and wander until I'm lost inside the sepulchral walls. I'm hoping for a fluke, an intervening hand of fate, but the dead go on forever. One is remembered with an enormous stone sphinx, another with his name written out with a finger in wet concrete. Some aren't remembered at all, their crypts caved in or sagging to one side. I use the high sun to find my way back to the gate onto Máximo Gómez.

As I walk south, the heat of the day is too much to bear. I see a bus shelter ahead, and within it a chiselled black square of shade. Stepping out of the glare, I am surprised to find myself almost alone. There is only a single other person seated on the bench. I meet his locked gaze. I am in the mood to see portents, and in his eyes I read a warning.

Do not stay too long in this maddening city.

Other than a long beard, the man is completely naked.

4

THEY WERE CHEERING FOR HOT BALLS.
To Arthur, the noise was unbelievable, infernal. The town of Azua
had no traffic controls, and so, at every intersection, the trucks would
blast their horns, and between every blast the people crowded on the
flatbeds would shout and admonish, urging a few more people on board
for the ride. It was a free trip to the capital, as long as you were prepared
to cheer for Hot Balls, to satisfy the Generalissimo's need for an adoring
crowd. And who didn't adore the Chief?

Makes my independent Scottish blood boil.

Art had been in the country not even three weeks, in Azua for ten
days. He had been assigned to work with Father Bob Hymus, one of the
first two Scarboro men to come to the republic and now in his sixteenth
year of service. Under Father Bob's tutelage, Arthur would begin to
comprehend this Dominican culture. He would need, for example, to
adapt to the noise, the endless uproar: engines and horns; children and
stray dogs in the streets; Mexican boleros crackling from gramophones;
radios blaring the good works of the Chief. The clamour was so constant that silence was foreboding, and if a bus driver somehow forgot to
turn on the radio, the passengers would soon remind him. The din was
dissonant, a rupture, an antidote to thought.

There were also those things spoken of only quietly. The priests did
not use the term "Hot Balls" in public. They might, among themselves,
use the abbreviation "H.B." It was their own coded term for the Chief, the
Boss, the Butcher. Trujillo: the omnipresent figure that the Dominicans—
quietly—called *El Chivo,* "the Goat." The nickname could only be ex-

plained obliquely. It was a curse, people said, to raise a daughter in this country and find, as she reached her teenage years, that she was blossoming into a beautiful young woman. Full hips, rising breasts, sympathetic eyes. It was the worst kind of curse.

The trucks moved on past the plaza and the *casa curial*, the parish house that stood alongside the white plaster church with its airy nave and three-storey bell tower. It didn't take a leap of imagination to make the uncomfortable comparison; there were framed plaques in many of the houses: GOD AND TRUJILLO. The Generalissimo had suggested that the order be reversed.

Well, there was always the beach. Art had received his assignment to Azua less than a week after his arrival in the republic and had reached the town at night on October 13, 1960. His room was in the parish house just a few feet from the sacristy, and it wasn't until morning that he could get a sense of Azua itself: a dusty town of farm and ranch workers who walked the streets with pistols or machetes hanging from their belts; of women who sat on stoops, shelling hard beans. Some of the homes were newly built in plaster, following on the modern government buildings that Trujillo had raised around the plaza, where the bootblacks waited for custom. Art had gone to Monte Río Beach with Father Hymus that first day, wheeling in a jeep down the short dirt road. It was like nothing he had ever seen. The lapping waters of Ocoa Bay were ringed by staggered summits, yet the landscape was dry—almost a desert, but almost a jungle, too. The road's edge was an impenetrable snarl of thorny trees and bushy cactuses as wide and tall as the bright-painted palmwood-and-tin-roof shacks, the *bohíos*, that marked the limits of the town. In the dust Art could see the road-killed remnants of desert life, the battlefield corpses of lizards, tarantulas, scorpions. The road ended in sand. The zenith sun washed out every colour, and the beach looked almost like snow. To the west, flashes of light off the waxy leaves of red mangroves, where birds on stilt legs picked through the jags of an ancient reef. To the east, the sand gave way to a stony shore that traced to the base of the mountains, peaks so sharply striped with ridges and valleys that cloud shadows looked ragged across their sparse flanks. Art swam. The water was even warmer than at Haina, and through the cool lens of the sea the true colour of the sand was a pale ochreous brown, firm and fine underfoot. Looking back to shore, he could see the coconut palms where a brook entered the bay.

Lovely. The beach would be his escape and his salve. Underwater, everything disappeared: the heat; the cacaphony; his Spanish professor, with her disordered, immersive, psychological lessons; the invisible pressures of the police state. The ocean was like a second church, and here, too, Art's work was baptism, an act that required not one word of this new language.

He had no complaint against the simplicity of his missionary life. Discipline appealed to him, and he had spartan tastes—he flinched only at so many meals of fish, the perpetual food of a maritime childhood. He joked that he was, at least, "dispensed from the cod." Instead, these were fish fried fresh from Ocoa Bay, their skins sometimes bright pink or blue-green, cooked and served whole. Father Hymus would ask, "What will you have? Heads or tails?"

But simplicity was one thing, poverty another. The religious work here was too often the work of death. Too many funerals, too many babies to baptize before they left this world. On his first hospital sick call, he laid his hand on the body. Warm. He began the sacrament of the sick, sprinkling holy water, reading scripture, saying prayers and pleas for mercy and aid. Only later did it come to him: here in the tropics, every body was warm, including those of the dead. The living weren't much better off. He saw a legless man moving around on his hands, like a walking egg; he saw an insane woman chained to a post outside her home. He looked out on a land where you could throw down a seed and see a foot-tall shoot by the end of the following day; he swam in water where men could lay a net in waist-deep water and bring in fish enough for a village. Yet every person who worked that good earth, who drew from that rich sea, lived in a hellhole shanty, without money, without medicine, without hope. It was a national disgrace, a social sin.

Hot Balls will suffer for this.

The winter storms came. The sheet lightning was something new and beautiful, a luminescent wave through the high labyrinth of cloud, **though somehow it still managed to knock out the electrical lights.**

There was so much that was new. The gentle shock of marriage preparations for a fourteen-year-old girl. Learning to drive a jeep. Discovering that bananas grow upward, defying gravity. Getting caught like a fool in the mosquito net in the scramble to shut off an alarm clock. Saturdays, when the women went around in heaped curlers, straightening their hair against their African blood. The hours before dawn, when he couldn't help but listen as each real-gone lover serenaded his lady to the latest rumba beat. Seeing fights in the streets—never with fists, but stones flying through the air, chunks of concrete, sometimes bullets. A western movie shows in town. *Funny to come out and see almost the same on the streets: gunslingers, poverty, bars.*

And then the news that the Chief was coming to Azua. He would visit the local cathedral, and yes, as always, the Generalissimo would expect to be honoured by the singing of the Salve Regina.

By now, Art was hearing the stories. Even the apologists for Trujillo condemned him in their way. No, padre, they would say, it isn't true that the Chief ordered the slaughter of 20,000 ethnic Haitians along the northwestern frontier in October 1937—only 12,168 dead were counted. It's a lie that the soldiers threw babies into the air and caught them on bayonets—they were merely stabbed or beheaded with machetes, like the others. It's true that thousands of the Haitians had lived for years in the republic, that some carried certificates proving their Dominican births. So how were they found out? They were asked to pronounce the word for parsley. *"Perejil! Perejil!"* the Haitians would shout—but they could never quite pronounce the flattened Spanish *r*. No one could deny that the Chief, at times, was forced to approve the arrest or assassination of enemies of the state. But listen, padre, there was so much that he had done. He had distributed land to tens of thousands of campesinos. He had modernized the cities and the roads. He had built schools and hospitals. You know, he built a lot of churches. It was unfair to label the Generalissimo a fascist. Had he not declared war on Japan, Germany and Italy, all in the week following the attack on Pearl Harbor? Had he not opened the borders to Jewish refugees in 1938, several hundred of them settling on his own gift of land near the north-coast town of Sosúa? The Dominican people had reasons to fear their leader, but that fear could be dispelled by obedience; that fear was not necessarily distinct from admiration, adulation, even love. The Chief had carried the nation into the civilized world. You had only to look at Haiti, with its ravaged landscape and its starving people living in shit and mud. Haiti would never again make war with the fatherland. The Chief had solved the Haitian problem.

And so Trujillo at age sixty-nine arrived in Azua. Arthur saw him among the people. The man's vitality—his presence—was undeniable, but he was also unnervingly human. His hair was silvery white, and the skin of his face was loose with age. The toothbrush moustache, in the style of Hitler, had finally been shaved off. He was a heavy-set man now, but always in the finest suit or a military uniform creased like folded paper. Arthur was more impressed by the people, the flock. It was a crowd possessed. They gave the Salve like an afterthought, because they had already turned the Chief into a god.

It was January when Art learned that he would see Trujillo again. This time the terms would be more personal. Christmas had passed, that long season of religious labour, and then the world bid farewell to the year that had witnessed the election of John F. Kennedy, the u-2 spy-plane scandal, and international condemnation of apartheid in South Africa following the Sharpeville massacre of unarmed black demonstrators. It was 1961, but in the Dominican Republic there was only one subject that mattered: the Generalissimo. Trujillo had agreed to a meeting with the church, the latest step in an uneasy relationship that had exploded almost exactly one year previously.

The schism's roots went back earlier still, to June 14, 1959, when approximately two hundred Dominican exiles, Castroist Cubans and other Latin American revolutionaries launched guerrilla invasions on the north coast of the republic and in the mountains of the interior, the Cordillera Central. The rebels were swiftly killed or captured, but the valiant dream of revolution, however pathetic the reality, served to solidify a middle- and upper-class resistance. Trujillo was furious to receive reports that even the children of families enriched by his regime were joining this 14th of June movement. The subsequent rash of murders, arrests and disappearances suggested a blind rage, and people wondered: might the church make some statement? It was the only institution of any power that was not utterly controlled by Trujillo. The Chief understood that in the Dominican Republic, the one battle you were sure to lose was a battle against God.

The five bishops, led by Bishop Francisco Panal Ramírez of Spain and Bishop Thomas Reilly of the United States, along with the Vatican ambassador to the Dominican Republic, Papal Nuncio Lino Zanini, met and prepared a pastoral letter. Somehow, the letter was kept secret as it went out to every trusted parish, passing through military checkpoints and under the noses of the *caliés*, Trujillo's ubiquitous network of informers. Even the dreaded SIM, the military intelligence service—whose officers drove incongruous black Volkswagen Beetles—failed to intercept the letter as it traversed the nation folded into Bibles, mixed into priests' papers or tucked into the robes of inviolable nuns. The rumour that something unusual would happen in the churches of the country leaked out only in time to fill the pews to standing room on January 31, 1960. The letter declared natural human rights to be higher than the rights of the state; that to place the rights of the state above the rights to freedom of conscience, press and assembly was to commit "a grave offence against God." An official version of the message had been sent, the padres said, to the highest authority in the land. "We have promised special prayers to obtain from God that none of the members of the family of the authority referred to shall ever experience, during his lifetime, the sufferings that afflict today the hearts of so many Dominican fathers of families, of so many children, of so many mothers and so many spouses." The church that had ignored a thousand crimes, that had shut its eyes even to the killing of more than twelve thousand Haitians, had finally found its just war.

Now Arthur would witness the surrender.

The campaign against the church had been fomented from the moment the pastoral letter was read. First came a written response to the bishops, a blunt rejection of their implied accusations. The regime cut off all aid to Catholics and then, slowly: harassment, rumours, threats, kidnappings, attacks, expulsions. The press accused the bishops of communism and anarchism. Trujillo launched a campaign to have himself named "Benefactor of the Church," an embarrassing reminder to the newly rebellious clergy that they had spent years accepting millions in benefits from the Chief.

And so, on January 22, 1961, Arthur found himself stepping into the National Palace in Santo Domingo, the grand, domed building in pink stone that sits on a hill above the Zona Colonial. Priests and bishops lined one wall of an audience chamber, faced by Trujillo alone.

Shook the hand that drips with blood. Hated every moment of it.

The bishops acknowledged that they could have taken other steps before reading the pastoral letter to the people. They admitted that their words had been misinterpreted in ways they had not anticipated. They declared their willingness to instruct their priests to avoid even the slightest suggestion of a lack of confidence in the authorities. It was a humiliation, and Trujillo wanted to seal it with wax and gilt. He renewed his campaign for the title "Benefactor of the Church."

At the regular meetings in Scarboro House on Haina Beach, debate grew increasingly intense. Some priests, shocked and disgusted by the poverty in the republic, were pressing for a co-operative movement like the one that was sweeping parts of Canada. Others felt the co-ops were a step too deep into politics for men whose work was the revivification of faith. The conversations were touched by the expanding fear of international communism. In the United States, that fear had become a monomania. The Americans would see red in a co-op movement, no doubt, but was the alternative a church that kowtowed to this torturer, this butcher—the salves, the blessings, the silent tolerance or open embrace of his visits to cathedrals across the country? What if Trujillo invited the Scarboro fathers to a dinner like the ones attended by the wary staff of the Canadian chancellery or the executives of the Falconbridge mining company? Would the fathers attend? Would they laugh along with the dictator's jokes and compliment him on his choice of wines? Art made himself clear to his colleagues: he was on the side of any rebellion against Trujillo. His personal concerns, however, were more practical. He wanted steps taken to improve the language training for new priests. His professor was driving him crazy.

It was no surprise when the truce between church and state shattered. The bishops bluntly rejected Trujillo's pursuit of the title of "Benefactor." Everyone had heard that the Chief never showed a bead of sweat, not in heavy military dress under the August sun, certainly not in the bedroom. Did he sweat now, calculating his response to these impudent pastors?

The religious life suddenly became dangerous.

There was a flood of accusations: that the churchmen used marijuana; that they "enjoyed" the nuns; that they traded in bombs. Priests' cars vanished, then reappeared in front of brothels, where men in cassocks would be seen revelling. In Azua, Art listened from the casa curial as officers of the regime stood in the plaza and condemned the foreign bishops for their crimes against the fatherland. He didn't find himself afraid; he admired the attitude of a bishop who, while his house was being sacked by *trujillistas,* was seen walking calmly out the front door, one hand on his pectoral cross and the other holding a cigarette. And yet the altar boy in Azua attempted to hang himself, crushed by fear and confusion. God and Trujillo, each capable of delivering blessings or exacting punishment.

The bishops gave their orders: be patient.

Patience be damned.

Two weeks later, the word came down that Hot Balls planned to visit Azua once again. The town began a frenzy of preparations. The men of the casa curial decided, then announced, that they would neither give Trujillo the Salve nor offer absolution to those who had attended a local rally against the foreign bishops. Then they prepared to evacuate, expecting their home to be looted or burned.

Nothing happened. On May 20, Arthur stood on the sidelines to watch the great parade for Trujillo, a level of organization he had not before witnessed in the city.

Only force and fear could do such a job.

Nine days later, Father Hymus was denounced on Radio Caribe, the station where one announcer, Lamela Geler, had launched the "Traitor Bishop Repudiation Contest." A second Scarboro man, Father Bill McNabb, was declared an anarchist; other priests were named as "nunfuckers" and homosexuals. There were suspected caliés—spies—all over the streets of Azua. It was time to clear out of the casa curial.

Arthur joked that Bob Hymus was rushing his breakfast, but he joined the scramble for safer quarters. Still, the religious work continued, and the following day he led a wedding ceremony, his first ever in Spanish. He was no longer Father Arthur, but Padre Arturo.

THAT EVENING, May 30, 1961, at a point on the shoreline highway that ran west out of Santo Domingo, a point where the city seemed to fade and night was caught between the land and the sea, a black Chevrolet Biscayne pulled from the side of the road just as it was passed by another Chevy, a light-blue 1957 Bel Air sedan. The driver of the Biscayne accelerated hard and drew alongside. As he did, his three passengers raised their weapons, a sawed-off twelve-gauge shotgun, a pistol and an M1 semi-automatic rifle issued by the CIA. Gunfire raked the Bel Air as its driver locked the brakes, the attackers roaring past, still firing. Both cars stopped. Staring into their victims' headlights, the four attackers saw the sudden muzzle flash of a submachine gun from the Bel Air driver's seat, and then a rear door swung open and a man, robust in silhouette, stepped out and opened up with a revolver. Two shapes closed in on the Bel Air from one side. A shotgun blast, and a high-pitched, almost ululating cry. The shadow figure turned slightly and fell to the ground.

Hot Balls was dead.

5

THERE IS ONLY ONE SOUND AS I OPEN my eyes. That there is only one is enough to make it eerie. And the sound: sheet metal being dragged across polished concrete? It carries in through the open shutters above the bed, along with a breeze that is unusually cool. Sometime in the night, I realize, I have pulled on a dirty T-shirt.

At last I place the source of the noise. Guinea fowl greeting the dawn.

This isn't Santo Domingo.

Yes. Right. The convent.

I'm in the Padre Arturo Educational Centre in San José de Ocoa, a town spoken of simply as Ocoa. Sister Mary Joseph Mazzerolle, known as *la madre,* the mother, has offered me a bed in the visitors' dorm. Mary Jo is an Acadian from Pointe-Sapin, New Brunswick, where her father was a boat builder on Miramichi Bay, a notch in the Atlantic shore cut by a punishing sea. She remembers splitting wood before dawn in the black-and-white world of the northern winter. It's been thirty-eight years since she last saw snow. People always tell her that one day it will appear on the mountains above Ocoa, the Cordillera Central, where villagers on the high ridges sometimes wake to ice in their wells. But the snow never comes.

"He sees about this place," Mary Jo had said in her accented English when I arrived on the day's final guagua from the capital. "He keeps this place alive." I had laughed a little, because it was strange to me, unexpected, to hear a person speak of Arturo in the present tense, as if he were a neighbour. Mary Jo keeps Arturo's memory, and he does what he can, she says, from the kingdom of heaven.

Mary Jo is eighty-four now, a monumental woman with eyes that can light with laughter or the condemning fire of God. Since the day Arturo died, she said, she has daily lit a candle beside his photograph. Every year, on the anniversary of the killing, she takes the framed picture to the cathedral, and the congregation of Ocoa builds a small shrine. The church is always full that day, and after the Mass Ramón Báez, an old friend of Arturo, reads a poem, each year correcting the time that has passed. *Forty years / like forty leaves / torn from the tree / of honour and justice* . . . Then the lineup forms. The faithful of Ocoa pass before the image of Arturo, gathering blessings, giving thanks, making their private requests of the martyr. Lately, Mary Jo has been talking to Arturo about the outcome of the upcoming presidential election. The price of supplies for the medical clinic and seniors' home has doubled, then tripled, and food for the schoolchildren has never cost so much. The town can keep time by the blackouts. When the lights go out, it is 8:30 AM. When they come back on, it is 8:30 at night.

"He's going to do something for us," she assured me with a smile. "He's going to get that old man out of there."

AT THE CONVENT breakfast table, there is fruit and *arepa*—a fire-baked corn and coconut bread—and a message from Father Louis Quinn. The legendary Padre Luis, one of only two Scarboro priests still on the island, a man who has lived half a century of Dominican history, is not available today. His health isn't the best. He suggests that I start instead with his life's work, the Association for the Development of San José de Ocoa.

The association's office is less than two blocks away. On the street outside it, a guard and his pump-action shotgun take in the morning sun. The man doesn't so much as raise his head as I ease past him through a courtyard gate. But a voice manifests from an outbuilding: *"Buen día!"* A figure emerges, lank, with slicked-back hair and skin the colour of brown-sugar hard sauce, with a Roman nose and a restless Adam's apple. His eyelashes are long. On a guagua I had met a German woman who had lived fifteen years on Hispaniola. "Look closely at the people of San José de Ocoa," she impelled me. "Sit and make an observation for a while. You'll see. There is a difference—in the people and in the dogs. The people all look the same and the dogs all look the same. And the people look the same as the dogs."

I hold out my hand and stammer the longhand greeting. *"Buenos días."*

"I'm Frank," he replies in English. "Like Frank Sinatra, but without the money." It's a practised joke, but it suits him. He looks like a young man from another era. His jeans have been ironed.

"Father Lou told me you will arrive here," he says. "The nephew of Padre Arturo." He pauses, gazing at me. "You know, you look like him. In the face. In the nose. A lot in the smile. I have seen all the photographs."

And that is how the game begins.

Frank has a motorcycle, a town-and-country bike in white and purple. Together, we ride the grid of Ocoa, where the houses wheel past in orange, green, yellow, blue. There is the smack of fresh paint, an impression of order, even from the hang-ass back of Frank's wild machine. Trenches wait to guide storm water at every crossroads; the plaza has the concealing lushness that attracts young lovers; even the farm smoke from the mountains files into the sky in pinstripes. Wherever we go, Frank watches for the men and women who wear history in their faces. When he sees the type he's looking for, he darts to the curb, dismounts and greets the person with some formality. Then he gestures toward me. "Who does he look like?"

The person is always silent, polite, the face pensive.

"One of the Canadian priests," says Frank, hinting.

An epiphany. "Father Curcio!"

"No, no, no! Another one."

And then a dawning. "Ah! The one who died!" A look of dead certainty. "Padre Arturo!"

"He's the nephew."

And the face turns sweet and warm. "Oh, you look like him. In the smile, especially. But his hair was darker."

Frank has a list of names in his head, specific people with memories of Arturo, and we ride from home to workshop, from workshop to storefront. At each, family members and workmates shake their heads and say, "She's in the campo"—the countryside—or "He's gone to the capital for a spare part." Between each stop there is Frank, shouting his questions about the killing over his shoulder and into the wind. We are still young men, faintly embarrassed by our fascination with bloodshed and guns. At the same time, the pattern of Father Art's wounds embodies the mystery. The paths of the bullets are a cryptic recounting of his final moments alive.

"I am thinking!" Frank shouts. "Arturo was killed with two kinds of gun?"

"That's what it looks like!"

"A pistol!"

"Yes! With a pistol in the head! And with a submachine gun! Here—" We have rolled to a stop at the curb of Canada Avenue where it runs along the base of the mountains; I draw a circle in the air that encloses my stomach, bladder and hips. Gut shot.

"The policemen had pistols?"

"One had a pistol, and the other a rifle."

"The soldier had the submachine gun."

"Yes."

"And the soldier said he shot all three men."

"Yes."

Frank Sinatra pauses for effect. "But then, when did Arturo get shot with the pistol?"

"Yes," I say. "There are problems."

There are problems. In fact, none of it makes sense.

On the night that Arturo died, every living soul in Monte Plata heard the crackling of gunfire. A few minutes later, a soldier walked into town from the outskirts, telling anyone along the road that he had just shot and killed Padre Arturo, Second Lieutenant Evangelista Martínez and Constable Ramón Restituyo. He was carrying the lieutenant's rifle and Restituyo's pistol as well as his own gun. The soldier's name was Odulio de los Santos Castillo, and the story he told is impossible.

De los Santos had been returning to Monte Plata from a patrol in the campo, he said, when he heard an argument ahead on the twilit road. Creeping closer, through a field, he saw three silhouettes in the headlights of a jeep. Two men in plain clothes and one in uniform—they seemed to be fighting. He could see guns—it must be two rebels confronting a policeman. De los Santos called out and the men made sudden movements, as if to slip from the bladder of light. He took aim at the men in plain clothes and pulled the trigger of his submachine gun. When he was able to take in what had happened, he knew his aim had not been true. He had killed the rebels, but also the man in uniform. Or, as he claimed to have discovered only as he stood over the bodies, the priest, the new police lieutenant and Constable Ramón Restituyo.

A tragic mistake. A terrible accident. It might have been enough, except that Arturo's body, like the corpse of the lieutenant, was exhumed by the Organization of American States criminologists. They found a bullet wound under Father Art's left jawbone; it seemed to be a pistol shot, fired execution-style. A cluster of wounds around the priest's bladder and thighs suggested the submachine gun, but some of these shots appeared to have been fired from a short distance and the others from a metre away or more.

Two scenarios seem possible. In the first, Evangelista Martínez and Ramón Restituyo kill Padre Arturo with Restituyo's pistol. But if so, why does Odulio de los Santos arrive on the scene with his submachine gun and shoot dead the two policemen? How does Padre Arturo end up with submachine-gun wounds? In the second scenario, De los Santos kills all three men. In that case, though, how does Arturo end up with a lethal pistol shot to the head? Why does he seem to have been hit by submachine-gun rounds fired from both near and far? And where were the police taking Arturo that night? There are layers of confusion and obfuscation. That old chestnut: make it look like an accident.

"Perhaps Padre Arturo was shot by both the police and the soldier at the same time?"

I laugh. "Frank Sinatra is a detective."

"Yes," he says, "there are problems."

We finally find one of the people Frank is searching for. Blanco Sánchez is a stocky man with a salt-and-pepper crewcut, new jeans and a tattersall shirt. He takes my extended hand with an almost mystical look and agrees to meet in an hour at the development association.

We gather in Frank's office, a room with the grey light of bright shadows. Frank makes some kind of joke—a *domicanismo*, something only the two of them can understand—and Blanco laughs, but only for a moment. His seriousness surprises me. It's as though he has been patiently keeping his story, and now, by God, it will be told.

He begins in Mahoma, where he lived when he first met Arturo. Then, people would say that Mahoma was two hours away; today, with the new road, they say it is twenty-five kilometres. The village was in Ocoa parish, and Arturo was the new assistant priest, a Canadian and a Scarboro man like his pastor, Padre Joe "José" Curcio. It was Arturo who would drive the rough jeep trail to Mahoma for masses, baptisms, weddings. It was better, anyway, than having to go by mule.

"I remember one time," says Blanco. He speaks slowly, his Spanish easy to understand. "It was raining a lot and the river was swollen, and there was a person trying to cross through the current of the river. It had just gotten to the point that this guy was going to be taken by the current when Arturo quickly walked in and grabbed him. He saved his life. That's the kind of person he was. Decisive."

It is hard to imagine the days after the assassination of Trujillo. There is a tendency to think of freedom as a dove released from clasped hands, a brilliant flash that explodes into flight. Instead, it can be more like a code, a code that is cautiously and painstakingly revealed. In the campo, in places like Mahoma, families struggled to earn the equivalent of one U.S. dollar a day at a time when local prices had climbed higher than those in the United States. It was worse in the lowland plantations, where sugar cane might pay only fifty-five cents a ton, and few men could hope to cut a ton in a single day. These had been the conditions during the final years of Trujillo. And even this ruined economy, a system yoked to the two million people who lived in subhuman conditions, even this collapsed with the death of its master.

But Ocoa had always been different. It is true that the people look different, paler, more Semitic, the descendants of the Arab immigrants, many of them Christians, who had come in a wave in the late nineteenth century and were called *los turcos,* allegedly because they travelled on documents from the Ottoman Empire. It is no coincidence that Ocoa is famous for its candied figs, or that Frank Sinatra would look a part of the scene in Cairo, Amman or Damascus. Another part of this inheritance was a commitment to progress, above and beyond the rituals of campesino life. Into this Ocoa, this place of inquietudes, this village staring over the brink of history, came a Canadian priest who was himself tasting a kind of liberty. Padre Arturo arrived hungry to set to work, immediately, that instant. He found himself among a people looking cautiously outward, peering into everyday life for a signal that freedom was something they might actually take hold of. They in turn saw this blue-eyed priest who lived in the way that the Dominicans had forgotten—he lived as though he were free. "He accompanied us and animated us," says Blanco. "Art was a missionary with a very clear vision—a vision of justice. And he oriented people to his way of thinking. He gave them the gospel, but a gospel that was in keeping with the moment in which they were living. This bothered, it still bothers, the political leadership. They don't want people to speak the truth, and Arturo spoke the truth. Arturo was consistent with the word of Christ."

Blanco stops speaking and laughs softly at himself, surprised to find he is crying. He dabs tears from his eyes with thick fingers.

"One night I had a vision of Padre Arturo," he says at last. Not a *sueño*, a dream, but a vision. "I was arriving at the steps of the church, and as I started to climb them I saw him stopped in the entranceway, looking out at the plaza, and when he saw me he was very happy, and he had that smile, as always—a face totally full of joy. He came to me with open arms and he hugged me, strongly. I asked him, 'And padre, how are you?' And he said, 'I'm fine, Blanco. I'm as good as can be. Where I am now, everything is just fine.' And then I woke up in my bed. I woke up and I was crying."

He lets the story settle in the air between us. "I think about that a lot. To me, it is evidence of something tremendous."

There is nothing more he wants to say. The story is his final word on the matter, so much so that he seems uncomfortable with saying goodbye. When he has gone, Frank leans back in his chair. We sit in silence for a time.

"I had a little pain in my soul when I saw that he was upset," says Frank. "I think it's difficult for people to talk about this. These men don't talk about those times—maybe they think about it when they're alone and cry sometimes. But it's difficult for the tears to come like that.

In all my life I have never seen my father cry. Maybe one time. For this, I am surprised."

He looks up at the ceiling.

"The tears represent powerlessness."

And then he wants to go out again on the motorcycle.

WHAT CAN ONE PERSON remember of another after forty years? Memory travels two avenues over so much time. There is familiarity, an imprint of the person's face, an impression of his manner, and then there are the anecdotes, the lodestones of recollection. Outside these, the mind gropes into forgetfulness. The memories that remain are far from perfect. The details fall away, rapidly at first. Did the person bite his lower lip as he made a joking remark? Was he last seen in the late morning, or the early afternoon? In the end there is a story, stripped down and damaged, to be repeated over the years. This, too, will change in time, be turned by bias, blurred by the accumulation of similar events.

It is down these uneven paths that we ride the Yamaha for three days. In a century-old palmwood bohío, its walls gently angled by hurricanes and earthquakes, Frank's aunt shows me photos of Arturo performing a marriage. A pharmacist recalls Arturo as a man who spoke his mind, but with a natural authority that precluded harshness or vehemence. Lao Castillo, who worked with Arturo to build the College of Highest Grace, remembers his handshake, a powerful downward pull, like a challenge. Arturo was not a revolutionary, Castillo insists, because he didn't speak of revolution; he was a man of action. A beautiful woman remembers Arturo asking her to dance, then lies and says he was a very good dancer. In the home of Chichí Ramón Castillo, a biology teacher and photographer, the stifling afternoon air is being emptied by the down-valley breezes of dusk. Chichí remembers only that Arturo took him and a group of children to Monte Río beach, and he shows me a photo of Arturo and another young priest in front of the jeep. Art is smiling, shirtless, his arms muscled with work, his stomach rippled.

"He reacted to the world like a child. At heart, he was like a child," says a man named Manolo Féliz, sitting in his front room with a chihuahua that wears a red neckerchief. "It was an era of youth. There were a lot of us—a lot, a lot. We were a bunch of kids with no clear idea of God. We had a much clearer idea of Padre Arturo."

The memories triangulate toward a consistent impression. A young priest in shorts and a button-up shirt, the sleeves pushed up to his elbows, is driving too fast in a ragtop Willys jeep. He projects confidence, clarity and a love of life. Blue eyes sparkle behind black-rimmed glasses. Only the brides remember him in church in his vestments. "He was a padre in the church and an hombre in the streets," says one woman, pounding the counter of her general store.

Did Arturo have a temper? Yes. Or no, he simply spoke his mind. Was he revolutionary? He was, of course—or no, absolutely not. A communist? No. He only brought people together to work with one another.

And always they say, "You look like him." I can't help but smile. There is only one photo in which I see a resemblance, and it's the image of Arturo's corpse on the floor of the morgue. I have seen photos of myself asleep and been surprised by that same soft innocence. But there is more to the Ocoans' descriptions, a dozen fractured similarities. Arturo couldn't roll his *r*'s. He loved to swim underwater. He prized simplicity, didn't care for decoration, had a crooked smile and a slow temper that would finally flash and fade. His sense of right and wrong was so immediate, so strong, that he spoke at times without thinking. He was capable of a childlike joy. He had a heart murmur. It is enough to know that we share blood, he and I, that I might glimpse him in myself as we walk, for a while, this path.

There is only so far I can follow.

Powering across town, Frank declaims his latest theories, bending the words back to me.

"I have been thinking! Lying at night in my bed!"

"Okay!" I yell in return.

"Why only Padre Arturo? There were other priests who caused problems! Like Father Quinn! And he is more violent! I've seen him!"

The houses fly past like prayer flags. We stop at last beneath the rings of Saturn on the sign of the Galaxy Club Bar. We have been tracking Arturo's former barber on a trail that has led from a grocery to a private home to the music academy and now to a sheet-metal gate with a sign reading Beware of Dog. Frank opens the gate without anxiety, and there is José Genao. His shirt is open and his feet are bare, with a toughness that indicates going barefoot is his habit. His clothes are loose, as if he's been shrinking, and his eyes are clouded with early cataracts. There is a wildness to him. Though small, he seizes me in his arms and crushes me against his hollow chest. Yes, he says, he cut Arturo's hair every week, a regular cut and shave for twenty-five centavos. "Oh, you look like him! You have his eyes! Eyes like green peas!"

"And how do you remember Art?" I ask. "What kind of man was he?"

José leaps lightly onto his toes and claps his hands together. "He was like a sweet cake for us," he says, bussing a kiss from his fingertips. It is an irresistible gesture, and Frank and I begin to laugh. I picture José as he must have been, a man of explosive passions, total immediacy—the kind of young man who would be dangerous in whatever time and place he was born, and José Genao had been born into a dictatorship. Suddenly he is acting out the day of Arturo's death.

"We were young then, sitting somewhere in the streets, and one of our group came up and said, 'They killed Padre Arturo!' We didn't believe him! We didn't believe, but he said, 'It's true! It's true! They shot him in Monte Plata.'"

José is no longer acting the story but reliving it. "No!" he shouts. "Oh fuck! Oh fuck!" He raises his arms and clasps his head between his elbows, like a person protecting his skull from a blow. "We didn't know what to do. We wanted to protest in the streets! Somehow we came up with a silent procession. The cops were watching us, with their clubs. It was a black day. It was the blackest day!"

He quiets himself, but there is still an energy coming off him, a crackling heat in the air. There is one question that I have asked every person I have met in Ocoa, a question Frank knows I will ask, and this time he voices it himself.

"Do you think Padre Arturo has become a symbol?"

The answer is always yes.

"No!" shouts José. He sees our wide eyes. "Maybe for some people in this town he is a symbol, but not for me. He's not a symbol. He's still with us."

6

"A MAN WALKS INTO A BAR WITH A monkey on his shoulder."

Father Louis Quinn, the legend. His words tumble from lips that hardly move. At first I don't realize he has started to tell a joke.

"The man orders a beer and starts to drink it, and the monkey looks around and takes an interest in some people playing pool. So he hops over to the pool table, looks around, grabs the black ball and swallows it."

Padre Luis. They'll build a statue of him, for sure, is what they say in Ocoa. They don't say, "They'll build a statue of him when he dies." They refuse even to brace themselves against the pain.

"Well, the man finishes his beer and he and the monkey leave the bar and go home. A few days later, they come back to the bar. This time, the bartender has a bowl of fruit behind the bar, and the monkey reaches out and takes a grape."

Father Lou has his good days and his bad days. Today his handshake is weak, and the muscles in his forearms undulate from Parkinson's disease. Worse, his back is uncomfortable in almost any position. Too many years driving fence posts and lifting bags of rice. His eyes flash blue beneath spikes of white hair like cut straw. He wears a pale blue polo, khakis, plain black shoes. The clothes of a priest.

"Well, the monkey takes the grape and puts it up his ass, and then he pulls it out and eats it."

Not your typical priest.

"'I've never seen anything like that before,' says the bartender. And the man says, 'Well, ever since he swallowed the eight ball, he likes to measure everything before he eats it.'"

We laugh quietly, like Canadians. Lou adds a few words about constipation and old age, then shuffles out of the room to get me a cold beer. It is one of the peculiarities of the Scarboro order that no one needs to be called "father," so it is Lou telling me that not much has changed in the casa curial since the days when Art lived here as assistant to the pastor, Joe Curcio. What is now the office was then Art's bedroom, and the ceiling was replaced in 1979, after Hurricane David made off with the roof. "I slept in my truck for about three months," says Lou. The roads into the mountains were choked with mud and debris, every line of communication was broken, and an international news wire reported that Ocoa had been destroyed. Mourners lit votive candles in Washington Heights, the New York City barrio of expatriate Dominicans. Then a man named Rafael González Caro made his way down the ruined valley and told the world the town had survived.

"We were the ones who opened the road," says Lou. "By the time the government people got here, they thought nothing had happened." It was only then that the officials in the National Palace began to look more kindly on the work of the Association for the Development of San José de Ocoa and on the association's leader, Padre Luis.

Lou arrived in the Dominican Republic in 1953, a Newcastle boy whose grandmother had taken him to Canada and raised him in religious schools. His first years in the Dominican Republic were like Arturo's, spent learning Spanish and baptizing babies and suffering the shock of the overwhelming poverty. He took a year back in Canada to study the co-operative movement, then returned; his first long-term posting, which began in 1960, was in the southern mountain town of Padre Las Casas. "A lot of the revolutionary leaders were from Padre Las Casas," he says, "so I was already a communist then."

A joke, but this time with a sharper meaning. A social activist in 1960 in the Dominican Republic would be labelled a communist. And what did it mean to be a communist? It meant you were an irresolvable problem. To exist as a modern nation, the Dominican Republic had to have good relations with the United States. For years, Trujillo had managed his overseas debt, accepted a certain amount of foreign ownership and investment, and guaranteed public order. Terror and progress. It was a balance the White House could live with in exchange for a staunchly anticommunist ally in the Caribbean. Then came the Cuban Revolution, and in the first hours of New Year's Day, 1959, the Cuban tyrant, Fulgencio Batista, fled directly to Trujillo City. To the Oval Office, the situation in the Dominican Republic suddenly looked to be following a simple formula: resentment, revolution, a second Cuba. The U.S. began to back away, to search for more moderate allies, to detach the image of the *yanqui* from the brutal Era of Trujillo. The paradox baffled and enraged the Generalissimo. Communism was the enemy, and so, too, was anticommunism.

"Thank God Fidel Castro came on the scene, or Latin America would be very different today." Lou's statement shocks me for a moment, if only because the sentiment is so rare. It is a modern convenience to forget there was a time when the dictators of the Americas seemed impossible to threaten, let alone depose; when the leaders of the world's democracies took drinks on breezy terraces with the men from these immutable regimes. Only so much has changed: Latin America still has the widest gap between rich and poor of any region on Earth; voters still pause to consider how the White House will react before they cast their ballots in national elections. But what Castro did was disturb the peace of the cemetery. Without him, would a series of despots still be running Guatemala like a labour camp for the United Fruit Company of Boston? Would the grandchildren of General Anastasio Somoza now be dividing Nicaragua among themselves and their friends? Would the bishops of the Dominican Republic have written their public letter against the Trujillo regime?

"I'm generally not afraid of anything," says Lou, the words too quiet to be bravado. "When I spoke against the dictator, my knees were shaking. And I didn't mention him by name."

Lou never came to know Arthur MacKinnon well; from meetings at Scarboro House in Haina he remembered a man with a hot temper, a good sense of humour, a man as plainly anticommunist as he was opposed to the trujillistas. By the time Lou was transferred to Ocoa in August 1965, the casa curial held the memory of the Scarboro missions' first martyr.

Lou came to know Arthur better then. The work that Arturo and Joe Curcio had begun in Ocoa—the Saint Vincent de Paul Society, the College of Highest Grace, the development association that had counted the two priests among the founding members—had lapsed in the national chaos. Father Lou brought them back, then poured a lifetime's energy into their legacy. Today, you hear it in the streets: "Padre Luis is Ocoa." Under his leadership, the association has constructed more than 1,500 homes and repaired over 7,000; built 140 aqueducts; installed 2,700 latrines in 54 communities; established 11 rural medical clinics, 66 schools and a dozen community centres; constructed or repaired more than 500 kilometres of roadway, and reforested 17,000 acres of land. The people have revived the tradition of *convite*, in which campesinos set aside time to work for each other and the community. There is a slogan: "Self-reliance and mutual aid." Climb the hill to where a crucifix overlooks the city to the southwest, and the valley of Ocoa stands out as distinct from any other Dominican town: more ordered, more diverse, more perceptibly prosperous. It is something beautiful.

Of course, they were opposed. It is one of the legends of Father Lou that he stepped between the soldiers and police and the people they were beating. This could be his statue: the young priest, his eyes locked with a soldier's, his hands holding back the truncheon. Later, fighting to get the day's prisoners released, he faced the generals. Always generals. "There's more generals here than there are foot soldiers," Lou says, his voice beginning to rise. "Everybody seems to be a general."

Padre Luis defended himself against accusations of communism for more than a decade. In 1974, the campaign against him crested. He was accosted in the streets, defamed in the press, and one of the vehicles he used to deliver food to work crews in the campo was set on fire. Finally, a commission of Ocoans travelled to the capital to meet the generals of what was then the National Security Service. Tony Isa, founding president of the development association in the time of Arturo and Joe Curcio, put his life on the line. "If Padre Luis is communist, then so am I, and you can put that in your notes," he is remembered to have said.

Father Lou's voice has trailed off, but his eyes are fixed on me, as if waiting for the question that hangs between us.

"Why didn't they kill you?"

He has given this some thought. The answer, he says, seems to lie in the fact that he was a part of a larger movement. The government was perpetually hesitant to attack a priest or a foreigner, though that person's friends and colleagues might be hounded, imprisoned, harassed, disappeared. Men like Blanco Sánchez, the gentlemanly figure who shed tears as he remembered his dream-vision of Padre Arturo. Blanco had been a vice-president of the development association. "I spent most of my life getting or keeping him out of jail," says Lou. The priest developed a network of houses to keep people in hiding, learned to drive carefully through the potholes for the sake of the men and women in the trunk. The regime didn't need to kill Father Lou and make a martyr. It could target his allies, his organizations. There were different angles into the problem.

I'm reluctant to continue. It is as though Lou has already answered my next question. Arturo, a young man with a flash-in-the-pan temper. A campaign against the radical priests, but an unwillingness to kill. A tragic mistake.

"Do you think Art might have been killed by accident? They intended to give him a scare, and things went wrong?"

"Not at that particular point in history," Lou replies quietly.

Those, he says, were the years of the baseball bat. He kept it beside his door. If the police came, if the dreaded SIM pulled up in front of the casa curial in their Volkswagens, he was prepared to fight for his life. There were only two possibilities: death or arrest. If the agents had orders to kill, you had nothing to lose. And there was nothing to lose if they had orders to bring you in. You might stand them down, you might fight them and escape—no matter how you resisted, they would not kill you without orders to do so. Disobedience is the highest crime in a dictatorship.

Lou still has the baseball bat.

"There's a lot of unsolved murders in this country, a lot of killers. They're still in power, still enjoying complete liberty after all the things they did."

He pauses. "I personally think it was Wessin y Wessin."

"The general in San Isidro?" I say. Brigadier General Elías Wessin y Wessin, infamous for sending the Dominican armed forces against the people of Santo Domingo in 1965. It's the first time I have ever heard anyone put a name to who might have called for Arthur's death.

Lou nods.

"I hear he's still alive."

"Someone has to have ordered it," he says, his final word. "Will you stay for dinner?"

Father Lou rises gingerly from his chair, not quite straightening on the walk to the kitchen. The women who keep his house, who have worked with Lou in Ocoa for as long as he has been here, have prepared a shepherd's pie and a salad of tomatoes and lettuce. It's a simple meal at a table busy with papers, books and tiny ranks of ants. We talk for a time about an American I met in Santo Domingo, a businessman who had closed his waterbed factory in Kentucky and hoped to move the company to the Dominican *zonas francas,* the deregulated, largely tax-free trade zones that are a definitive symbol of globalization. The Dominican Republic was a pioneer of these zones, some of which date from the 1970s. The zones are the second-largest employer in the republic after the government, but it is the now familiar story—workers putting in ten or more hours a day and still having to take on second jobs to raise a family; a monthly minimum wage about the same as the price of a box of cigars. The American entrepreneur had crunched the numbers and realized he could save $100,000 a year for every ten employees.

"They should set up a *paredón,*" Lou says. "What do you call those places where they shoot people? A firing squad. Just eliminate people like that. Or send them to the moon or something."

Not your typical priest.

There are people I need to meet in Santo Domingo, says Lou, and goes for his phone. He switches to Spanish, speaking more softly than before. He reaches a man named Roberto. "The nephew of Padre Arturo . . . an investigation . . . assistance . . ." He looks at me. "His name is Santiago," he says. It's my name in old Spanish. Saint James. I've lost a name, gained a name, suddenly found myself canonized.

Lou puts down the phone. "Roberto Santana," he says, writing out phone numbers. "Call him when you get back to the capital. He used to be the rector at the university. Been in jails all over the country. I used to have to keep him in hiding."

It is time to go, but there is something about Father Lou that makes you linger in his presence. There is a greatness, yes, but a loneliness as well. When he arrived in 1953, he says, there were thirty-two Scarboro priests in the country. He likes to say now that there are one and a half. There is Joe McGuckin, an old man of faith in the desert town of Matanzas, and there is him, the "half," slowed by illness and age. Lou has spent a lifetime outside his homeland, speaking a second language, living the combined sacrifices and isolations of a priest, an expatriate, a rebel. He is the last of a line.

Suddenly, in a photo on the wall, I see a familiar face. "This is Art?"

His eyes shine. "Do you think you look like him?"

"I never thought about it until I came to Ocoa."

"You do. You do so very, very much."

1

THE BIG STORM CLOUD OF 1964 (FOR ME) *is that on December 17—I am to be moved to another parish. I sure hate to go. I love this parish—its climate, its scenery, its people and its possibilities. But—obedience wins again.*

Father Art would send the letter home to Canada tomorrow. For today, there was the *despedida*, his farewell party. And what a job the Catholic Student Youth had done with the small school hall! Crepe paper in the rafters, potted palms, the head table heaped with food, the red and blue of the Dominican flag pinned just a little lower than the Virgin. They were celebrating themselves, surely, as much as him and his work. The Catholics had finally won the student council from the antireligious element. The communist threat, even in the high school.

Almost three years in San José de Ocoa. Had he changed? His face was still a young man's, clean-shaven, pomade in his curls. At thirty-two years old he was thin, perhaps the thinnest he had been since his tuberculosis. It was the work that did it, the sheer physical labour of masses, confessions, salves, baptisms, weddings, last rites, funerals in a town of seven thousand souls, in a parish of fifty thousand. They had the Willys jeep, but there were long trips that could be made only by mule, plodding out into the campo in gumboots and a panama hat, the vestments in a saddlebag. He would be remembered, if for nothing else, for his flares. Send a burning star to hang in the sky above a village, and everyone would be waiting in whatever makeshift church by the time he arrived.

Was there more to his thinness than the hard labour of faith? His chest X-ray hung just outside the dining hall of Scarboro House in Haina. "Typical lungs of a Scarboro missionary," read the caption. The morbid humour of priests. There were so many tiny lesions that it looked as though he had just taken a long pull from a robusto cigar.

He was one of those rare young men who feel the perpetual nearness of death. It was not an abstraction to him; the Sydney Coalfield mines took too many lives each year from a close community. During Art's years in Nova Scotia, the local pits claimed close to 350 men, and many more had died from early old age or lung disease. He had feared for his own life and the lives of his father and brother Francis as they struggled with tuberculosis. All three survived, but in the year following Arthur's recovery his brother Ernie, the nearest to him in age, lost control while driving home from work at the No. 18 Colliery mine. The car slammed into the concrete abutment of a culvert, and Ernie, a leading contender for a welterweight title in boxing, died in hospital the following morning. He was nineteen years old.

Arthur still kept in his diary the notes he had taken down at his first priestly retreat in the Dominican Republic. He had underscored "Lessons of Death."

It's not death that matters but how we live.

Degree of Glory depends on our death.

A priest went to heaven and arrived in time to see a grand procession. Exhausted by his journey into the afterlife, he asked for a chair. They gave him only a small one, and he felt that he had to complain. "Well," the heavenly handlers said, "that's all the wood you sent up."

Don't fear death. Prepare well for it and you don't have to worry. A priest who had done good all his life was asked what it felt like to be dying. "Like a man on third base getting ready to steal home."

Arthur had written those lines in 1961, and death had seemed a ready enough possibility then. The momentous news had reached Azua as rumours. People passed notes that "T" had been killed. They whispered that the Goat was dead. By the time the fact was officially announced over Dominican radio in the late afternoon of May 31, 1961, a Friday, everyone in the country knew exactly what had happened. Soldiers were marching in the streets. There was no one out there but soldiers and dogs.

The following day, a new rumour: there would be an invasion. Dominican exiles were about to attack. Or Cubans. Or American marines. Everyone was confused. Who would kill Trujillo without also overthrowing the government? Who would leave a power vacuum to be filled by the sycophants and murderers who had wet Hot Balls' hand with their sweating palms for all these years? The guagua drivers who had been to Santo Domingo told of a frenzy of trujillista vengeance, house-to-house searches in which anyone might be a suspect and every suspect would be suddenly *desaparecido*. The innocent would be tortured, the guilty would die without peace. There is a saying: To kill a snake you must cut off its head. Whoever had murdered Trujillo had put too much faith in those words.

That Saturday night, all of Azua awaited the invasion. One of the men who drove the shared taxis, the *públicos,* had come from the east, from the little town of Las Charcas, where the people had heard machine-gun fire and then the electricity had shut down. But who were the invaders? How many? Whom would they kill? Then came another report from Las Charcas: There had been this drunk soldier, see, in a bar. He had gone crazy with rum and stress and suddenly said to the bartender, "Here's how I pay my bills." Then he opened fire with a submachine gun, killing eight people and wounding God knows how many more. The mayor heard the gunfire and ordered the town blacked out. That was the "invasion." That was the "revolution."

A misunderstanding.

But the body of the snake did finally die. The sadists and toadeaters turned to fight among themselves. Even the corpse of the old Goat himself left the country for France, first on the tall-ship schooner *Angelita* and then on a chartered Pan American Airlines DC-7. The dictator's eldest son, Ramfis, who had been named a full colonel at the age of four, a brigadier general at nine, and who had chartered a flight from Paris at his father's death to seize control of the armed forces, followed aboard the Dominican navy frigate *Presidente Trujillo.* As a final gesture, Ramfis had personally executed the six remaining prisoners accused of complicity in his father's assassination.

At last the people of Azua felt ready to take to the streets. They tore down the bust of the Generalissimo in the plaza, shouting, "Hang him!

Freedom!" The young men with nothing, no allegiance, no jobs, tore down every street sign that hinted at the Era of Trujillo. *Libertad por Navidad!* Liberty for Christmas!

One month later, in January 1962, Arturo had driven the steep, wild road up the sun-seared ridges to Ocoa. There, in his rare letters home, he could finally write without fear of the censors. The envelopes arrived in Canada stamped The Dominican Republic: Enjoy the Climate of Freedom. What was the country actually like? A paradise. A garden rising to cooling mountains and ringed by sugar beaches and sea cliffs that rang with the roar of the sea. Impossible colours, birds, butterflies, flowers, a world of green, teeming fish in the reefs. All of this, and so much pain.

Naturally the cry of the stomach overwhelms the interest of the soul, no matter how well meaning. And can you morally force one to go to church on Sunday if he is ashamed to go because of the tattered rags he has for clothing?

Is it any surprise there were times when he could not contain his temper? Chasing a dog out of the church. Rolling up his sleeves to fight when one man demanded food ahead of all the other hungry. His pastor, Father Joe Curcio, called him a hardhead. It was fair, in its way. Who else would have chosen battleship grey for the walls of the casa curial? Who else would have stuck the cooking pot down in front of the bishop and told him to serve himself? Something inside Art demanded austerity. How else could he face the people after Hurricane Flora in 1963, the families who had lost everything because they had nowhere to build their homes but the flood plain of a river? How else could he turn away the poor to feed the poorest? How else but to eat a spare meal himself, tuck into his sleeping bag inside a half-built house so he could rise at first light and go immediately to work?

Oh, he was human enough. There had been laughter when he backed into the Mass candles and set himself on fire in front of a visiting bishop. "An overglow from my halo," he joked. *I have come to cast fire upon earth and what will I but that it be enkindled.*—Luke 12:49

He would miss the children of Ocoa. They came to him and he to them—perhaps that was the only way to explain it. Every adult had long hours to work to keep food on the table. Only Padre Arturo had the time to take the young people out to plant trees, to bathe in the river, to sing songs, grind flour, climb mountains, ride into the campo. Once, he took a group to the incredible beaches east of Higüey. There was nothing else there. A few fishermen in their camps. A stretch of immaculate sand and coconut palms nodding over the spume of the breakers.

Together with Father Curcio, Art could say that he had laid a foundation in Ocoa. Nothing more. He would not be there to see what would come of it all. And now the hall was filling for the despedida. It wouldn't be too much to say the room was overflowing—there would be more laughter than tears tonight. And then: away to Monte Plata, dusty and poor.

These were hopeful times, at least. The president of the republic was Donald Reid Cabral, a favourite of the United States, and familiar enough with some American diplomats that they called him "Donny." Two years earlier, in December 1962, Arthur had watched with pride as Dominicans voted in the nation's first democratic election in thirty-eight years. They had elected Juan Bosch Gaviño, a leftist writer and intellectual who in 1939 had been among the founders, in exile, of the Dominican Revolutionary Party. Bosch and his party had each captured more than 55 per cent of the popular vote, almost double the take of the party quietly preferred by the White House. President Bosch had lasted seven months. There was a saying: Bosch needed to make a new country, and he wasn't given even enough time to make a baby. Accused of being soft on communism, he was toppled by a right-wing military coup. Now there was President Reid, a modern businessman and a civilian, and maybe it would be for the best. "Democracy" and "Progress" were the stated White House objectives for the Americas; the U.S. didn't like the way the first had turned out, but there was still some hope for the second.

Back in the Scarboro seminary days, an old Jesuit had come to visit. "One of you could be a martyr some day," he had said. Arthur had believed it at the time, but now, in the Dominican Republic, the days of the martyrs were over.

8

I MAKE THE CALL FROM A PAY PHONE IN THE core of Santo Domingo. Roberto Santana picks up on the second ring.

"Santiago, where are you?" As though he's been waiting for a call from an old friend, as though I've been known as "Santiago" since the day I was born.

"Independence Park."

Santana's voice is toned with authority. "I'll send my driver," he insists. "Watch for a white Toyota Land Cruiser. The driver's name will be Cuevas." *Señor Cuevas.* The name enters my mind in translation: *Mr. Caves.*

I wait in the park for Mr. Caves. I hadn't expected this kind of immediacy; I'm dirty and exhausted from days on the back of Frank's motorcycle, and what I need now is a bath, a nap and some time in my own head. Arthur's story had been distant when I left for Ocoa. Now it seems urgent, intimate, delicate. I feel a need to be circumspect, to step carefully.

Independence Park is a roundabout at the gateway to the Zona Colonial. On the sidewalks, vendors sell green coconuts, enormous papayas, the smooth-skinned *caimito*, star apple, with its milky flesh. Flakes of ash are snowing the city; cane-field chaff is burning across the whole south of the country. Children chase the largest of the falling *cachipas*, exploding them in their hands before the flakes can settle to the ground. It is a season of ashes. I watch the faded and dented cars, the flow of ragged guaguas. Somehow I miss the arrival of the spotless white four-by-four with the silver trim.

"Señor Santiago." The tinted window is rolled down precisely to eye level. Mr. Caves? Yes, Mr. Caves. He hopes I like Chinese food.

He drives with a death wish and full air conditioning. Somewhere in the madness of Santo Domingo gridlock, we disappear into a tunnel, and on the other side open throttle toward the highways out of town. Mr. Caves turns sharply into a parking lot and pulls up at a door. From the outside, Restaurant El Chino Lee looks like any strip-mall takeout anywhere on earth. "Go ahead, he's inside," says Mr. Caves, who stays with the vehicle. The door opens onto a room full of white tablecloths, around which servers in black vests make obsequious gestures. Roberto Santana is unmistakable, even with his back to the room. He presides at the head of a table spread with half-finished plates of noodles and fried fish, everyone dressed for business. I look like a backpacker who took a wrong turn in Jamaica.

Roberto Santana asks the men in black vests to bring me a flan. I follow the conversation just long enough to get the gist: the presidential election.

Twenty minutes later, we're both in the four-by-four with Mr. Caves. Santana calls out an address, and the acceleration pushes us deep into the beige leather. "You met Padre Luis?" Santana asks. "I know him well. I'm from Ocoa. Padre Luis and I have the same . . . we are on the same side." As if he's uncertain how far to take this conversation. Santana is perfectly mannered; beside him I feel uncultured and ham-handed. His tie is red silk. His hair, flecked with grey, is combed back above eyes that capture a netherworld between delight and world-weariness. He exudes power, and there is a frank sensuality in his face, even his gestures. He is gentle with any woman who calls in on his phone.

"Tell me about your project," he says.

I explain, sounding like a simpleton even to my own ears.

"I remember this case of Padre Arturo," he says, though he could only have been a teenager then. I will want to speak to the chief of the police and the head of the armed forces, he declares, and to the most powerful old generals, the aging revolutionaries, the men in charge of the newspapers and the television stations. He can put me in touch with them all. Mr. Caves bumps over a curb into another parking lot. Santana excuses himself and disappears into an apartment. I make conversation with Mr. Caves, but I can see that his heart isn't in it. He spends his life waiting.

Santana is back. "To the Palace of the National Police," he commands.

The nausea is immediate. I have been circling this story, sussing out its edges, seeking safe passage into its sheltered secrets. Now we are hurtling across town into the mystery's dark heart. I am badly dressed, too exhausted to speak Spanish, and my notes are not in order. I'm sweating like cold glass in a heat wave, and I am not at all certain that I want to make myself known to these police who cause women to cling to their purses. Even Mr. Caves seems to drive more carefully as we approach the building. The Palace of the National Police is huge and the colour of cheese mould. Dirty air conditioners vent through nearly windowless walls. The words "Law and Order" span the false battlements, and a ridiculous staircase forces every person who enters to climb one storey to the open front doors. It would be impossible to walk up those stairs without feeling watched.

"The country then and now, it's very different," assures Santana. "Today, the leaders in the army are men of today's government. They're men who fought the trujillistas." At the guard post of the parking lot Santana lowers his window a scintilla. "It's me," he says to the uniformed man inside. We drive directly to an unmarked door at ground level.

Santana leads the way into the belly of the beast. He moves briskly through hallways and doors, calling out greetings, shaking hands. At last we enter a white anteroom that contains a half-dozen policemen in uniform grey. "You see, they are all young," says Santana. "Except for the old man here." He gestures to an officer in, perhaps, his mid-thirties. The men are delighted with the joke, and Santana pushes on through a heavy door. The room beyond is stately, every inch in tasteful wood. The desk, too large to be useful, is perfectly organized—pen holder, ink blotter, black telephone. It sits below a shelf lined with three signed baseballs, probably from Dominican players in the American major leagues.

This is the office of the chief of the National Police, says Santana. Yes, the chief himself. He is out of the country for the moment, but we can simply walk in. You see? Did you notice the private kitchen? The chief prefers steak. As for this forty-year-old murder, we will talk to a police archivist. Tomorrow. We will talk to him tomorrow. He will open the files and, perhaps, every question will be answered.

Ten minutes later I am back in Independence Park, breathless, astonished, surprisingly hopeful.

I HAVE THE ADDRESS for an apartment in the western suburb known as Kilometre Ten, a long ride on the lurching guaguas. Misjudging from the map, I call my stop too late. It's growing dark and I find myself lost, wandering dead-end roads where people stare with neither malice nor kindness. At last I make my way to the Malecón. A blackout has murdered the street lights on the seaside boulevard, and the edge of the ocean is a black roar. Down the road is a restaurant sign lit by a generator. When I can see my map again, I find I'm less than two blocks from my destination. I turn left, turn right, and out of the darkness comes a woman's voice: "Santiago. Welcome. Padre Luis said you would come."

She is Rosa Hernández de Ayala, with a penitent's face and a dancer's legs. In the candlelight her skin shines like the shell of a nut. She draws a feast out of pots and the silent refrigerator: potatoes, eggplant, chicken patties, onions, bread, papaya, beer. As she begins to serve the meal, her husband appears; he's been searching for me in the streets. Juan María Ayala Regalo is small and wiry, with a sugar-cane smile. His shaved grey hair, glasses and sun-darkened skin bring to mind Mahatma Gandhi.

"All my life I've known the Scarboro padres," says Rosa. "Oh, Padre Arturo—I remember him." She says it as much to herself as to me, and her tone is dejected. She is from Yamasá, not an hour by bus from Monte Plata. Padre Arturo stopped in town not long before he died, she says, and asked for a taste of her *sancocho* stew. The Yamasá priests had made her famous.

She seems to hurry away from the memory.

"You look a lot like him," she says. "And how old are you?"

"Thirty-three."

"Oh, benediction! The same age that he was!" She looks at me with Catholic eyes. It is a curious footnote that Arturo is forever remembered as a man of thirty-three, the age at which Christ is traditionally said to have died. In fact, Arturo was three months shy of his thirty-third birthday. It's a piece of mythmaking that I cannot bring myself to correct.

As the three of us talk into the night, I realize that I am speaking too freely, bubbling over with giddy fatigue and the contagious certainty of Roberto Santana. The case of Padre Arturo once again seems a simple matter, perhaps too simple. The past and present are expansive and open. Again I have the feeling that I will make a phone call, maybe two, and somewhere a clerk will pull a sealed envelope from a dusty vault and chuckle to himself at the passage of time. Rosa and Juan listen patiently, politely. They wait until the shadows have narrowed the wider world and there is nothing but the three of us and the circle of light from the candle. Then Juan sits back in his chair and smiles. "When I heard you were looking for the story of your uncle, I was worried," he says. "I thought: Here in this country, the truth costs a lot."

I remind him that I was, just this afternoon, in the office of the chief of police himself.

Juan continues as if he hasn't heard me. "In this country, a hard, narrow search will go nowhere. The truth doesn't travel a straight line. It travels the way of the serpent."

IT IS A SEASON of *bachata*. Sometimes the mood is for merengue, the famously upbeat rhythm of the republic, but for the moment it is bachata, the music of the shanties and bohíos, of a homemade guitar, a bongo, a stick scratching across a grater, everyone drinking all night, a bowl of *mondongo* tripe soup to bring in the dawn. A singer wailing, now cajoling, pleading, slipping in a dirty joke, winding up almost sobbing. *La fiebre de amargue*, a bittersweet fever. When the nation is looking inward, when the family is hungry and the winter is wet and cool, when the blackouts last for hours, it's a season of bachata.

I am waiting for Roberto Santana. I wait for him in his office in the Piantini business district, on the eighth floor of a tower where American brand-name suits are for sale at ground level. I wait for him in his tasteful apartment in La Esperilla, a neighbourhood of embassies and smart restaurants on a hill above the Autonomous University of Santo

Domingo. I spend some time in the studios of his television program, *Roberto Live*. He is always somewhere just out of sight.

Time passes in increments. On the north coast, the humpback whales have come again to the Bay of Samaná, where liberated slaves from the United States once settled the coconut forests. Now the tourists arrive. They pile into covered boats and swallow seasickness pills, returning to shore a few hours later with memories of fifty-foot-long animals hurling themselves out of the sea, so immense that the speed of their flight and fall seems unnatural. The fishermen on the bay have stowed their motors, waiting for gas prices to drop. Instead they row their *yolas,* the high prows splitting the Atlantic chop. At sundown, other yolas appear. These are crowded, filled with anxious faces turned toward the Mona Passage, the black-market crossing to Puerto Rico, stepping stone into the United States of America.

It is a season of squalls.

I wait, too, by the phone at Kilometre Ten. The apartment, on the second storey of Juan and Rosa's home, is the only remaining headquarters of the Scarboro Missions in Santo Domingo. It is almost always empty. Father Lou has given me the run of the place: a main room and kitchen, three small bedrooms, a bathroom with cold water drawn down from a cistern. Everything is simple, decorated here and there by the figure of Jesus on the cross. "You know how the rich have their ranches?" says Juan with a hiccuping giggle. "Well, this is *el rancho de los pobres.*" The ranch of the poor. Heat pools in every room. I have never even thought about unfolding the U.S. Army–surplus wool blanket.

From the bedroom, I hear the apartment's front door swing open. Stepping out, I see a lean, pale figure with a tall man's stoop. His hair is thin, but he looks powerful, with veins that rise off the sides of his temple. He fixes me with glacial eyes. "I was told you were around," he says in English, and as I extend my hand, he takes it, moves swiftly to pin it behind my back, then suddenly lets it go and laughs lightly. He's all in blue: blue guayabera, navy pants, blue socks in a pair of sandals the colour of tar. He hasn't introduced himself, but he must be Father Joe McGuckin, the only other Scarboro priest still alive in the republic.

"You know there's beer in the fridge," he says, taking a seat in one of the four rocking chairs set out around a table. He starts to fill his pipe, cutting a cheap Dominican cigar into Number 7 Supercut from Canada.

Joe McGuckin arrived in the Dominican Republic in 1959 and has lived here much of his life. He is not a soft man. His parents emigrated from Ireland like so many others, climbing aboard a boat that would take them to New Zealand, Australia or Canada—they didn't know which. It turned out they were sailing for Montreal, where the Canadian Pacific Railway was offering settlement land in exchange for a one-third share of any future crop. "It was slavery, really, is what it was," he says. "It was like something you'd see down here."

Joe McGuckin grew up in Clandonald, Alberta, far above the latitude of gentle souls. Once, the Royal Canadian Mounted Police sent to the nearby town of Vermilion an officer who wore spurs and wasn't shy about putting them to the young and rebellious. A group of them jumped the cop one night, and the spurs went back into storage. Father Joe is the first priest I have met who can remember outrunning the police in a car chase.

He is tapping his pipe to prepare for a refill when he says, "You know I was the last one to see him alive." He can only mean Arthur. "He came in from Monte Plata and I was in Haina. I don't remember what we talked about." Of course, he was not the last person to see Art alive, but the last of the Scarboro men, the last of his colleagues. "I think it was that evening," he says. He doesn't finish the sentence. *I think it was that evening that they killed him.*

McGuckin suspected, still suspects, a conspiracy borrowed from the time of Trujillo: the policemen were sent for Arturo, and the soldier was sent to kill the policemen. A cover-up. "That's the tendency of the rich, the powerful—to kill a person, and to think they'll become irrelevant. Spill some blood. But if the people keep it alive, the blood never dries. It never dries."

"How do people live with this?" I ask him as he tamps the bowl of the pipe, lights the plug. "All these people who died, and all these killers still alive. There must be neighbourhoods where informers live next door to the families of their victims, or the old trujillistas live next door to the old rebels. How can people live like that?"

"They live in their memories," says Father Joe. "They're like

Mary—they keep it in their heart, they keep it in their heart. She watched her kid die on the cross, but she didn't wail and cry. She kept it in her heart."

His voice warms with his mention of the Mother of God.

"But how can you be sure? How can you tell what people keep in their hearts?"

"By their quietness," he replies, his steely eyes unblinking. "They don't talk about people, they don't talk about what people have done. Not even now."

Except that, sometimes, the silence is suddenly broken: an eruption of violence. The priest remembers a feud that exploded, finally, in a cockfighting ring. They carried out five corpses. Over a rooster. To hear the people tell it, five men died over a rooster. "Revenge is serious business here," he says.

There is a saying: Against the dead, prayers; against the living, your revolver.

The evening wind is building and hissing through the shutters. It will push up the seas, I know, and along the Malecón young couples will sit together at open-air bars and share tall bottles of beer. They will watch the surf, or the children who play where the street lamps light a pocket beach choked with the garbage that spills from the mouth of the Ozama River. The lovers and the children have learned not to see the garbage. They prefer to see the moon, the palms wagging over the breakers, to feel the breeze lift the sweat from their arms.

It is always a season of illusions.

TWO DAYS LATER, in the evening, Roberto Santana calls. He is coming to see me. He will arrive in a matter of minutes, he says.

Not much more than an hour later, the white four-by-four appears in the dark of the street. I can't see Mr. Caves through the tinted windows, but Santana is in the back seat, the window rolled down. As he steps out, he looks younger than before, less exhausted, in jeans, a tattersall shirt and a baseball cap. He takes a moment to greet Rosa and Juan—his perfect manners—and then follows me to the apartment. He has been in the interior, he says; today he is campesino Santana. He takes a seat in one of the rocking chairs arranged around a table, huge things that, when you lean back, whisk your feet off the ground like a child's. As he sits holding a red soda from the refrigerator, it is impossible not to see him as a precocious little boy.

This is a different Roberto Santana from the one who showed me into the private kitchen of the chief of the National Police. Then, he was a man with power and connections, a man thoroughly of the moment. Tonight, he slips on his reading glasses and sorts carefully through my collection of notes, clippings, autopsy reports. His eyebrows rise and fall. Once, he makes a long, soft, whistling noise.

Finally, he looks up at me over his glasses, a professor ready to speak. He holds a closed fist in the air between us. "In this case, this case of Padre Arturo, a lot of time has passed," he says, gently shaking the fist. "It is possible that no one will have a problem. Maybe." He snaps his hand open. "Maybe not." He snaps it shut. "This is a dark thing, a *cosa mala*. There are people involved who are still alive. In whatever you do, be careful."

He lowers his hand and draws the clippings and documents into the space between us at the table. "For example," he says. A finger traces silently to the name of Elías Wessin y Wessin, the man whom Father Lou had named as his suspect. "He is alive." At the time of Arturo's death, Wessin y Wessin was the most powerful military man in the country, says Santana. The finger moves on to the name of Brigadier General Antonio Imbert Barreras. Imbert, he says, is a national legend; he was one of the men who shot and killed Trujillo. In the summer of 1965, however, he was the president of the provisional government under the American occupation. It was Imbert who ordered the three-person military tribunal that investigated the death of Padre Arturo. "Imbert is alive," says Santana.

Now he taps at the name of one of the tribunal members, José Ernesto Cruz Brea. "Still alive," he hisses. Cruz Brea wasn't well known in that era, says Santana, but this would change. He would go on to be a leading figure in the military and police, a symbol of the 1970s, the years of the *dictablanda,* the soft dictatorship, that rose from the ruins of revolution and occupation. He would be alleged to have links with the antiterrorist and anticommunist Democratic Front, better known as the Banda Colorá, an unofficial paramilitary force that harassed, disappeared and murdered opponents of the government. Most infamously, Cruz Brea is among the accused "intellectual authors" of the assassination of Orlando Martínez Howley, an outspoken journalist, in 1975. Santana hesitates, as though there is more that he wants to say, but he moves on.

Angel Urbano Matos—another member of the tribunal ordered to investigate the shooting of Padre Arturo, another name connected with the Banda Colorá. "Dead," says Santana. The final tribunalist, Narciso Elio Bautista, was trained in military intelligence by the United States armed forces at their Caribbean School in Fort Gulick, Panama. Then there is a man named Salvador Montás Guerrero, listed in one report as the first military investigator to reach the scene of Art's death in Monte Plata. A notorious trujillista, says Santana. "He might be alive, he might be dead."

All these dark figures, gathered around the corpse of a priest.

Santana has begun to look smaller and smaller in his rocking chair. He has hunched his shoulders, and his voice, almost a whisper, has the tenor of a man sharing confidences in a public place. When he glances over his shoulder, my eyes follow. He's looking at the black rectangle of the doorway where it opens into the night. *In whatever you do, be careful.*

Santana rises. "I have my homework," he says with a smile, but his bearing of total confidence does not completely return. The past troubles his voice and his face. I feel as if I have begun to understand.

I have begun to understand, at least, a story people tell. They tell it almost like a joke. It is a tale of Fulano, the name people use to speak of anyone and no one. "Who told you that?" a person might say as they hear a piece of gossip, and the storyteller might reply, "Fulano told me." But in the story I'm thinking of, a group of boys are on their way to school. Suddenly, at the side of the road, they see a dead body. It has obviously been dumped there, murdered. It is lying in plain sight; in fact, you almost have to step over it to keep walking up the road toward the schoolhouse. Even if you were blind, you could smell the cloying, sweet-and-sour odour of death. It is impossible to ignore, and yet no one seems to look at it, and no one says a word. Finally, as they arrive at the school, one of the boys can't hold it in any longer. His head is throbbing, he will burst if he doesn't say something.

"Hey," he whispers to his friends, "did you see Fulano there at the side of the road?"

The boys' faces grow cloudy. Only one of them replies.

"Bigmouth," he says.

9

YANIRA SUGGESTS WE MEET AT THE *colmado*. "Have you done the colmado?" she asks, and I admit that I have not.

There are two on Yanira's street in the University district. The first is a traditional streetside grocery: oil, salt, bread, eggs, olives, cheese, tiny coconut cakes—staple goods to complement the fresh foods from the markets. The doorway of the colmado is built on the remains of some colonial portal; the ruins of a fort, they say. The threshold of Yanira's corner store might be four centuries old.

The second colmado, two blocks away, is what some now call a *colmadón*. They will sell you beer at a corner-store price, and there will be baseball on the television. Only the rich and the pointedly stylish go to the American- or European-style bars, with their marked-up prices and air conditioning. The life of the city is in the colmados, and the second one on Yanira's street has awnings and a canopy of trees to give cover from any weather but the hurricanes. The colmadón has its own generator, so even in the blackouts—especially in the blackouts—the street is filled with people smoking, drinking, flirting, debating. That's how I finally find the place, stumbling through the barrio by starlight until I see the white glow, hear the laughter.

Yanira has taken two plastic chairs near the edge of the darkness. She is known here. "A woman of the colmadón," she says in a scandalized tone. This is a kind of liberation for her; she rents her apartment from a family who will not tolerate vice. Gentleman visitors are forbidden to pass beyond the front door.

Yanira loves the night. These are her hours of *alegría*, that untranslatable emotion that is neither happiness nor cheerfulness, but something more like a total and hopeful engagement with life. I have a different distraction. I want to hear what she knows about the Banda Colorá.

The 1970s, she says, with a wave of her hand. She is not in the mood for the Banda Colorá.

But have I seen the trinitaria? The flower is everywhere at this time of year, a bougainvillea named for thé secret society, organized into cells of three, that began meeting in the Zona Colonial in 1838 to plot Dominican independence from Haiti. The name refers, too, to the three Fathers of the Republic who are at rest in Independence Park. Foremost among them was Juan Pablo Duarte, who had returned from three years in Europe to build a rebel organization bound by passwords, blood oaths, numerology and mysticism. Duarte had been driven into exile by the time his two loyalists, Francisco del Rosario Sánchez and Ramón Mella, led a strange, bloodless, largely middle-class coup on February 27, 1844. They formed a government, but independence lasted less than a month before Haiti again invaded. The *trinitarios* were forced to ally with the nation's large landowners, who had little interest in revolutionary ideals. One of them, a man named Pedro Santana Familias, was appointed leader of the independent Dominican army. Mere months later, Santana branded Duarte, Mella and Sánchez traitors as they worked toward a democratic election, and the general himself assumed dictatorial authority. Civil government has never since been entirely free of the threat of its own armed forces.

The trinitaria bloom purple, red, magenta.

"Have you seen the white one?" asks Yanira.

I haven't.

"No, it's very rare," she says. "Very beautiful." There is a famous play, *The White Trinitaria,* in which a thief climbs the flowered vines to break into a home, where he finds an aging and unmarried woman, alone. Confrontation gives way to discussion, and terror transforms into love.

Like a metaphor for dictatorship. Yanira rolls her eyes, and I drop the subject. She looks out into the night. Ash is still falling on the city.

"Do you know how I got interested in astronomy?"

Yanira had once told me that if everything were possible, if, for example, she had not been born in the Dominican Republic, she would have become an astronomer.

"I saw a UFO," she explains. "It looked like a star, but a star that would move and then stop, change direction, move and then stop again." It was a childhood experience, but one that had never come to make sense, not even when American satellites became a common sight, trailing across the sky like the lights of offshore cargo ships moving steadily into the wind.

"It's a good city for astronomy," I say. "The power is always out."

At last we are both smiling.

Then she begins to talk about Joaquín Balaguer. He was a strange politician, soft-spoken, devout and slightly effete. A man of incarnations. In the first, he was a puppet president under Trujillo. He even looked the role, like a marionette, a jumble of sticks and twine stuffed into a suit. Somehow, though, he stood apart from the servants and sycophants who surrounded the petulant tyrant. From the moment of Trujillo's death, Balaguer schemed toward power, even as he was cast into exile with the rest of the old guard. In 1965, he returned in a second incarnation. In a republic still wounded by revolution and occupation, Balaguer emerged as a White House favourite and, therefore, the one person who might guarantee an end to U.S. interference. He won the presidential election of 1966, and a third incarnation began. To some, it was the "Dominican miracle," an era of unparalleled economic growth, largely financed by the United States and an extraordinary market for sugar. For most, it was the Twelve Years of Balaguer. For those dozen years, every suspected communist, every opponent of the regime who dared to speak out, was harassed, attacked, disappeared or murdered. Every four years the people would cast their ballots, the outcome already decided by force and by fraud.

Then came the final incarnation. In 1978, after trying and failing to fix the elections, Balaguer was unseated. He ran again and again until, in 1986, when the country was crippled by recession and violent protests against austerity measures taken to guarantee the republic's international credit, he won. Nearly eighty years old and going blind, he went on to rule for ten more years. He died in 2002 at the age of ninety-five, somehow to be remembered as a pious intellectual, faintly disgusted with the blood on the hands of his military men. He had outlived the national memory.

"You know, Balaguer wrote a book that was published with a blank page," says Yanira. She pauses to remember the title. "*Memories of a Courtesan in the Era of Trujillo.* He promised that after he died, the blank page would be filled in with the name of whoever it was that killed Orlando Martínez, the journalist."

On March 17, 1975, Martínez, a controversial newspaper columnist and director of *Ahora* magazine, was shot to death in his car while stopped alongside the university campus. It was the height of the Twelve Years of Balaguer.

"He actually published a book with a blank page?" I ask. The story sounds apocryphal.

"He wrote the page and gave it to someone who could publish it after he died."

"Did it happen?"

"No. It's been two years since he died. But you know, the people who did it, who killed Orlando Martínez—maybe they're still alive. Maybe everyone will need to die before we can know the truth." She looks again into the darkness, crosses her bare arms and hugs herself against the deepening night.

She has answered, after all, my question about the Banda Colorá.

NOTHING NOW IS the same as a month ago, a week ago. How did it happen? It is the nature of change that we notice it after the fact. For example: lizards run across my bedclothes in the night. The first time one leaped onto my bare chest I shouted out loud; now their weight on the sheets is familiar, anticipated, curiously comforting. How long, I wonder, was the New World "new" to Columbus? When he first saw the dark smudge of an unknown island he must have heard the trumpets of angels and his own beating heart. Soon enough, though, the sand underfoot would have been real, and the odour of leaf rot, the irrepressible heat, the stirrings of greed. It would no longer have been possible for him to remember the shape of his hopes and fears in the hour before his discovery.

Was there really a time when I believed Arturo might have been forgotten and the restless dead were not my constant companions? Was there a time when I looked into the mirror and failed to see these traces? A little in the crooked smile, yes. In the chin. I put on my black-rimmed glasses and there it is, too, in the eyes. His hair was darker, but the heart murmur is the same.

Rosa is preparing breakfast, as though there has always been a gringo, the nephew of a martyr, who lived upstairs and was fond of *mangú,* a mash of boiled green bananas. "Who are you going to vote for?" the people ask on the streets, and the sly ones reply, "The one who'll give me my mangú."

Rosa bustles in the kitchen. She has the oddly charming habit of dropping knives, spoons, lids, even food on its way to the plate. Her hands are not always steady—she has trouble with her blood sugar. Sometimes her heartbeat is irregular and she will suddenly take a seat. One day her heart was fine; the next moment it was not. On doctor's orders, she gets up with the sun to go for a walk.

"Did you go to see the Chief today?" I ask her.

"Every day that I can," she says, "I go to see Trujillo."

It's a joke between us. She walks an hour east along the Malecón, toward town, always turning back just a little beyond the shining black monument that marks the place where Trujillo was killed. Rosa has admitted that the first vote she ever cast was for the dictator. She was a young woman then in Yamasá, a town she remembers as a church and a plaza rising out of a green jungle and endless rain. She had never known any leader but Trujillo, and he was like a godfather. It is important to Rosa that I understand people didn't live for thirty years in fear of a cartoon tyrant. There were reasons Trujillo survived. In his first decades, he crushed the power of the *caudillos,* the land barons with their thousand fiefdoms, and created a sense of nation. He provided hospitals, free medical clinics and campaigns against disease, enough that the mortality rate in the republic steadily declined. He gave women the vote, though he offered only his chosen candidates. By the end of his era, he had redistributed almost a quarter of the country's farmland, often to families who had lost everything to the U.S. sugar companies that had staked vast plantations during the eight-year American occupation, which began in 1916. In Santo Domingo, the Chief provided garbage pickup, clean streets. There was a culture of *respeto*, of honour and responsibility; men wore dress jackets on El Conde. Addicts and drunks did not rage on the sidewalks. You could sleep on a plaza bench with your pockets full of money, and a woman could take the siesta alone with her doors unlocked. Until one day the only crime left in the country was that of speaking against the regime.

There is a saying: In the past, no freedom, and today, too much.

Rosa is across from me at the breakfast table, remembering Yamasá. A quiet place, she says. Even when Trujillo died: quiet. Even during the revolution: a church and a plaza, a green jungle. Then she is remembering a day when the rain was preparing to burst from the sky. That was the day that she heard, she says. She was on the street, going to see her father, when a young man from the church came running toward her, shouting. "They've killed Padre Arturo!"

"Oh!" Rosa cries out now, taking her head in her hands. I'm frozen in place, witnessing her pain, and when she lifts her eyes the tears surprise me. It is too far to go on this morning, with the sun coming in through the doorway.

"Do you have a photo of the padre?" she asks.

I climb the stairs to find one, and I leave it with her, her fingertips careful on the edge of the print.

A day goes by in Santo Domingo, completely unextraordinary.

That night I am sitting again with Rosa, our faces lit by a candle lantern. "Tomorrow, I will go to Bonao," I announce, as though the decision was something we had discussed at length, weighing the pros and the cons.

Rosa looks at me with concern. "And? What is in Bonao?"

Perhaps: the grave of Ramón Restituyo Santiago, the constable. He was buried in the town of Bonao and exhumed July 3, 1965, one day later than his lieutenant. Five feet, four inches tall, paunchy and thick through the chest. A bull. The forensic examiners found twelve bullet holes in his body; six entrance wounds ran down his left side, piercing his thigh, buttock, abdomen, chest and shoulder. The force of the bullets in his body was extreme, shattering ribs, vertebrae, a femur, a collarbone, his hips. He would have lost consciousness almost immediately. His damaged lungs would have flooded, and he would have died.

Perhaps also: the Restituyo family and their story of forty years ago.

"How will take care of yourself?" demands Rosa.

"I'll just—"

"Never tell anyone that you are from the same family, that it is your uncle you are writing about. Never say that you're looking for the people who killed a member of your family. Never trust anyone who says they're going to help you." Her voice is plangent and anxious, strengthening, tightening. "Look around you, listen, think, always, before you do anything." She casts a hand across the table toward me. "Be careful. Be careful, Santiago! But have confidence in the Lord, trust in the Lord for your protection, for your safety, for your success. Let the Lord bless you," she says. Her head is falling and her eyes squeeze shut and I realize that she is praying, praying in all earnestness, for my shelter in his love, for my success by his hand, for my salvation from nameless enemies, speaking no longer to me but to her God.

No one has ever prayed for me in my presence. It's a strange sensation. It makes me feel as if I need to be prayed for.

Rosa looks up, and now she is smiling. Then the lights come on in the barrio. Juan comes to the table to say that the government must be worried about the effects of too much moonlight.

10

RAMÓN RESTITUYO IS NOT AT REST IN THE cemetery of Bonao. It is a custom at the old cemetery to rub, for good luck, the polished ears of the statue of a dog that stands guard over one tomb, but I do not find Restituyo. The gravedigger leans on his sore hip and says the archives have been moved to the local office of the national government. There, three women shake their heads, no, and suggest the civil office of Bonao. At the civil office one of the world's most beautiful women, pregnant, with a single mole on a high forehead above towers of blue eyeshadow, a tattoo across her lower back, waits among a crowd of mortals for the bureaucrats to retrieve some fact of her life from their endless dusty tomes. She is in the civil office of Bonao, but there is no trace of the dead policeman, Ramón Restituyo.

It is a strange place, Bonao, folded within mountains that can look bracing or gothic. The wind carries black smoke from the Falconbridge ferronickel mine and smelter, then, in the next gust, the scent of citrus orchards and rice paddies. The rest of the country still remembers Bonao as the unwholesome domain of Petán Trujillo, the dictator's brother, who ran the town and its campo like a kind of mad king, complete with a private army called the Fireflies of the Mountains. The driver of a *motoconcho,* a motorcycle taxi, tells me that Petán's men would cut off the head of anyone who spoke against the regime; a grave-keeper says that the heads were put on public display. I ask them: Is it true? They reply: It's what they say. But the town is known, too, for its groundbreaking battle against Falconbridge in the 1980s, for fair wages and safer work and a cleaner environment. Government housing is expanding into every fallow field. Young couples wait in shanties under patchwork roofs, refusing to unpack the belongings they have stuffed into sugar sacks. *You can see we are all packed,* they say. *We are going to have our own home.*

"Hello there, how are you?" I stop in the street and turn toward the voice. The man behind me is a skeletal figure; his clothes hang on him loosely, and his jeans gather under his belt. His hair is shorn almost to his scalp, which is nearly translucent. His eyes pop in their sockets. "You're a tourist?"

"No."

"A Mormon?"

"A journalist."

"I thought that you must not be a Mormon. They always travel in pairs," he says, too polite to make the joke about *las pelotas de Dios.* God's balls, always in a pair. "Perhaps I can be of some assistance? My name is José Almonte. My friends call me José Luis."

José Luis grew up in Bonao. These days he lives in the capital, where he works in the Zona Colonial building shuttered doors for an Italian boss. It is good work that pays a reasonable wage, but when he can, he returns to his hometown. For him, it is a moment of relief and pleasure to see out of the window of the bus the cat's tail of grey smoke from the mine.

He's a young man, and he doesn't know the story of Padre Arturo. The name Restituyo, however—that he knows well. It's an old family name in Bonao, he says. He suggests we look them up in the local library, an idea that seems hopeful until we arrive there. It's a box of a room staffed by a woman with amphibian eyes. "There's nothing," she says. "All I might suggest is that you talk to a woman who works at the secondary school. Her husband is a Restituyo." She writes a name down on a tab of paper and hands it to José Luis.

Well, it is something. We walk across town to the school, where a guard is standing at the front doors, blocking a group of girls who want to go outside. We distract the guard with introductions, and the girls pour past him on either side in a torrent of giggling. Unflappable, the man nods seriously, takes our slip of paper and disappears into the hallways.

"I must warn you, there are many Restituyos," says José Luis. "It is a very big family."

A minute passes, and then a small, stout woman appears, dressed in a creamy beige skirt and jacket that match the walls of the school. She has a sweet, smooth face, but her eyes are wary. I explain who I am, a journalist, dispassionate, interested only in knowing the truth about this situation that involved, somehow, both a Canadian priest and a police constable named Restituyo, a good son of Bonao. Her face betrays not the faintest reaction, a mask so perfect that at last I ask, "Do you know the case?"

"I do," she says. "My husband is the brother of the constable."

I actually gasp.

"He is in Mexico for a conference, but his sister also lives here in Bonao. We can call her." She turns and leads us into an administration office, where she waits her turn to use the single phone. As before, I have the sensation of a search that was moving too slowly suddenly moving too fast. Now the woman is dialling; now someone has answered her call. Their conversation is indistinct, lost in the echo of children's voices in the halls, the hum of fans, the noises of town life drifting through the shutters. Abruptly the woman holds the phone toward me. "Her name is Ramona," she says. "Go ahead."

Instantly, the sweat.

"Hello?"

"Hello." The voice is hard, hard as a hammer kicking back off a nail. I start talking.

"I know the whole story!" she booms. "I can tell you exactly what happened. Because I went to the police. I went to the army. I went to the parish in Monte Plata."

"Yes, señora, I want to hear your story. I am very interested in your story. I have a lot of information about the Canadian priest, but no one knows the story of the Restituyo family—"

"No one."

"No one knows exactly what happened and—"

"I will tell you exactly what happened."

And yet she still makes no suggestion that we meet, that we get together and talk. Visible moons of moisture are waxing beneath my arms and across my chest. I don't have to look down to know it.

"Señora, I do not speak Spanish very well. It is very difficult to talk on the telephone for me."

"Put my sister-in-law back on."

The two of them talk for an unnervingly long time. I can hear Ramona clearly now, the voice of a woman who is angry and unsure of what it is she wants to do. The sister-in-law cups the receiver in her hand. "What was your name?" she asks.

"Santiago," I say.

"Your last name."

"Santiago MacKinnon." I can't bring myself to lie, so this is it. Ramona will suspect a trick, her hard voice will go silent and the story of her brother, the constable, that ghost, that killer, will be sealed from me forever.

"I'll show you the way to her house," says the sister-in-law.

We leave immediately. The sister-in-law—in all the excitement I have not learned her name—makes workaday conversation with José Luis, who has abandoned whatever errand brought him to town. I walk a pace behind, trying to absorb the calm of the mountains. I can see the fires on the slopes as farmers clear the underbrush. In between them are valleys filled with flame trees, all of them ferociously in bloom. The canopy of flowers is the same colour as the embers that glow from the earth.

At a crossroads, we turn onto a track that seems to fade into the campo, pass an enormous burgundy trinitaria and then walk through the gate of a concrete home in white and muted green. Every other detail is lost at once in Ramona's glare. It is a relief to break from her gaze as she introduces her older brother, Demetrio. He looks like too many years of hard work. The pores of his face are deep, the lines sad, the eyes cautious. His nose is dramatic: wide, with flaring nostrils. His lips are broad and hard. A baseball cap sits high, farmer-style, on a short Afro flecked with grey. The two don't look like brother and sister except that they share an identical, resonant anger.

The house is large. Ramona leads us through a sitting room crowded with porcelain figurines—white buttermaids, princesses, ballerinas—that exude a peculiar lifelessness, like that of a funeral home or a modern church. We continue onto a caged patio, where electric-green anoles commute up and down the bars. As we perch on patio furniture, there is a quiet moment to take a closer look at Ramona. Her skin is mestizo and smooth. Despite slender arms and legs, she gives an impression of robustness. She is wearing capri pants and a sleeveless floral blouse. Then she erupts.

"I went to Monte Plata three times. I took my investigation to the capital, and I went to Monte Plata, too, because what had happened to my brother was very strange. I went to the Palace of the National Police, I went everywhere and I investigated everything, I talked to all the neighbours where my brother lived. With that woman, you know? And the neighbours told me that the soldier used to live with her. The soldier used to live with that same woman. What was she called?"

Demetrio, looking at his big hands, says, "She was *morena*." The word means "dark brown," and it could be a description or the woman's name. Morena is probably the most common nickname in the republic.

"The fact is that she had lived with the soldier. That's what I found out when I talked to the neighbours."

I stare down at my list of prepared questions and find myself dislocated. Not one of them makes any sense. Each is based on a single assumption: that the figure at the centre of this puzzle is Padre Arturo MacKinnon. For the Restituyo family, the matter is equally simple: someone conspired to kill their beloved son and brother, Constable Ramón Restituyo. And why? Why murder a man who every month sent twenty-three pesos from his meagre salary to support his widowed mother? He died alongside a priest and a lieutenant, but the connection is not at all clear. It is possible there was a plot against the priest, and so the two men who were with him had also been killed. It is also possible that someone wanted to kill Ramón, and so had to kill the priest and the lieutenant. The one certainty is the eternal innocence, the victimhood, of Ramón Restituyo. It is necessary only to determine who is guilty.

The two invite me to consider the facts. The padre had been working toward clemency for young prisoners taken from Monte Plata. He needed to travel to Santo Domingo to meet with officials at the Palace of the National Police. He would be accompanied, of course, by the new lieutenant Evangelista Martínez and by that good officer, that honest keeper of the peace, Constable Ramón Restituyo. Three upstanding men of Monte Plata, going to make inquiries on a matter of justice. They are found, dead, on the road outside town beside a bullet-riddled jeep. A soldier claims to have killed the three men in a tragic misunderstanding. More likely, though, this soldier, this Odulio de los Santos Castillo—he was waiting in the fields outside town, and he ambushed the jeep, and then, as the men scrambled to escape, he gunned them all down. Perhaps he killed three men just to take his revenge on Ramón Restituyo, the man who was living with his morena. Or perhaps the target was this Padre Arturo, and Odulio de los Santos was selected for the job because it would be easier for a man who could also kill his cuckold. The facts cannot be ignored.

I say quietly: "And what do you think of the articles that say it was your brother and the lieutenant who killed the padre?"

It is Demetrio who recovers most quickly. "There are articles that say this?"

"Yes."

"It's a defence of the *matador*," he snorts.

"It's a defence of the matador!" roars Ramona. A defence of the murderer, then, but I can't ignore the double meaning. The image of a bullfighter manifests itself in my mind, a figure whirling, calculating, choosing his moment to sink the sword through the heart. The master of the game. "If you look in the autopsy papers, it was clear that the three were killed by the same kind of bullet."

"And that they were fired by a machine gun, not a pistol," says Demetrio.

"Not a pistol. My brother had a pistol—"

"A .38. And the lieutenant had a pistol—"

"—and the lieutenant had a pistol, and all three men were killed—"

"—with the same kind of projectile."

There is a sudden pause. "It was very clear," says Demetrio with finality.

I, too, have read the autopsy report. I have a copy of it, I explain. In fact, it's in my shoulder bag. It's true that the Organization of American States criminologists concluded all three men had been struck with the same kind of bullet. But they said something more, as well.

Demetrio gestures for the report. I open it to a marked page, with shaking hands. He reads, his face clouded and intense, while Ramona tells me how Ramón died without children, how eight months passed between his final contact with the family—a telegram, more reliable than the uncertain mail service—and the day soldiers showed up to tell her mother that her son was dead.

"Maybe you were given the wrong information, because they didn't want you to know exactly what happened," she says to me. There is some butter now in her brassy voice.

Demetrio has finished reading the document, but his eyes remain fixed on the page, on the words that do not fit with the Restituyo family's story.

> This foreign priest was killed under suspicious and equivocal circumstances, which could not conceal the fact that this might have been another summary execution on a public thoroughfare. His murderers in turn met immediate death at the very scene of the crime. The priest bore wounds from at least two different arms, evidence of strong pressure on his neck and a deep bruise from a blow to the chest. His clothes, with bullet holes, showed impregnation with gun powder when examined under ultraviolet light, which indicates that some shots were fired from a short distance.

"He had a pistol wound," I say softly, "right here." I place a finger beneath my jawbone, pointing upward through the top of my head.

But Demetrio has begun to conjure a new truth, a scenario still rooted in the foundation of his brother's unshakeable innocence. He builds the story in fractured sentences. Well. The man who committed this massacre. He has shot the three men. It is an easy thing—no?—for him to take up the pistol. He can take up the pistol, he can take up any gun of the three men and he can shoot the padre's dead body. He can make it look like the padre was killed by the policemen. It is easy for him. There are no witnesses. No one can know.

We are all thankful for this possibility; a chill had begun to permeate the Caribbean afternoon. "And you never heard more about a tribunal or an investigation?" I say at last.

"No, nothing, nothing, nothing!" says Ramona.

"Never!" says Demetrio. No one ever came to talk to the Restituyo family until this strange day, four decades too late, when their sister-in-law called from the school.

"What you need to do is look for the matador," says Demetrio. His face is fierce with accusations.

Ramona nods. "The only one who knows why they killed the three is Odulio de los Santos Castillo," she says. "He's the only one who can say who sent him, how it happened, who gave the order, where all of this came from. And he's alive. He's alive."

Her voice breaks and a pair of tears gather along her lower eyelids. Demetrio shoots me an angry look. *Now look what you've done, you and your questions.*

"They killed my brother as if it was nothing," she continues. "This Padre Arturo—he was killed as if it was nothing. The lieutenant was killed like a dog. Thirty-nine years have passed, and they've never told us of any reason. Three dogs. They were killed like three dogs."

We stand to say our goodbyes, and I am jarred by the realization that José Luis is still with me, sitting back in a chair to my left. Now he pulls alongside me as we walk back through the porcelain princesses and out to the street, feeling the faint discomfort that follows an intimacy. I can see that Ramona and Demetrio feel some relief at having told their story, but they are anxious, as well. The story no longer belongs only to them. It is exposed, open to be picked apart and attacked. They promise any other help they can give, but it is hard to say whether they want to know the truth.

In the street, the sun is punishing, everything made raw. I can't hide my excitement, but José Luis is disturbed. We have transgressed; we are strangers who have broken a silence. He asks sharply, "Why are you do-ing this?"

What can I reply? That I am beginning to see the urgency of truth? That in its absence form myths with the power to shape the past, cleanse the conscience, transform the guilty into the innocent? That it seems important Arturo be more than another one of these myths, that his story be plain-spoken, as he would tell it of himself? And what then? Will the living be punished? Will the dead be despised in their graves?

I say something about how the truth can set us free.

José Luis nods, willing to accept this out of politeness. He laughs a little at himself. Five hours earlier he had said to his sister that he was stepping out to pick up some groceries. He'll go home now and tell her that he spent the afternoon with the dead. It can be a strange country.

IT'S NIGHTFALL IN Santo Domingo. I call Yanira from a telephone on Máximo Gómez.

"Guess where I've been?" I say.

"Bahía de las Águilas."

I have to laugh. She has insisted that I visit this place, the "bay of the eagles." There is no other way to understand the paradise that Padre Arturo found when he arrived four decades ago, she says. Then, there were no tourists. It is something, she says, to stand on an empty, wild beach of white sand, no one to tell you if there are sharks or jellyfish or a riptide, no one to mix you a rum caipirinha, no one to sell you a coral necklace. To see Bahía de las Águilas is to glimpse the island through the eyes of the Taínos, or Columbus. To miss it is to fail to grasp something essential, something primordial, about the country. And yes, she admits, it is almost impossible to get there.

"I went to Bonao," I say.

She agrees to meet on the porch of her landlord's home, only a few minutes' walk away. On a side street, the blossoms of a trinitaria stand out above a high garden wall. A white trinitaria. I pick a single flower and enfold it in my hands to show to her. She takes it gently when I arrive, then listens to the story of Bonao.

"I believe them," she says.

I can't hide my surprise. And yet I have to concede that the story the Restituyo family tells is not impossible. The lieutenant and the constable could have been ordered to bring Arturo to Santo Domingo to talk about the rebel prisoners. All three of them could have been ambushed and shot by the soldier. In a country still malignant with the heritage of Trujillo, it is far from inconceivable that the assassin would pick up Ramón Restituyo's .38 revolver and shoot the priest for a second time, confusing the facts of the slaughter. Yanira likes the story of the soldier with a jealous heart, sent to kill his cuckold and with him the priest. What is hard for me to accept is that there could be a place like this one, a place where a simple explanation is always suspicious, where the grandest conspiracy is believable.

The evening seems to linger, an endless hour between lightness and dark. "The night has a clear light," says Yanira, the woman who watches the stars. "The moon is full."

IT WAS APRIL 24, 1965, AND TIME FOR THE five o'clock news. William Tapley "Tap" Bennett Jr., the U.S. ambassador to the Dominican Republic, was driving through the hills of his home state, Georgia. He had meetings in Washington, D.C., on Sunday, but that was still a day away, and for the moment he was not a career diplomat but a sandy-haired Southern boy come home to see his "ma," whom he feared might not be much longer for this world. Driving southeast from Atlanta to the family property in Longview, he snapped to attention. A coup attempt had been reported in Santo Domingo. He was surprised—just two days earlier, his friend Donald Reid Cabral, the president of the republic, had said to him, "I believe it is safe for you to go now." Reid had not been able to suppress a wry smile; there had been at least ten significant plots against his government since the turn of the New Year. Now one of them had proved to be more than empty whispers. The Dominican revolution had begun.

. . .

At exactly that time, in Santo Domingo, the streets were emptying. Only an hour earlier they had been swarming; it had seemed as though every living soul in the capital was out, celebrating, shouting slogans. Rebels had captured the state broadcaster, Radio Santo Domingo, and they were bragging that a band of valiant young officers had arrested the army chief of staff. The government of Donald Reid would fall. The military coup that in 1963 had thrown out Juan Bosch, the first elected president in thirty-eight years, had finally been answered. Coup and counter-coup. Bosch would return. He was in Puerto Rico, packing his bags to come home. Freedom! Democracy!

But then the tank squad came, and the *cascos blancos,* shock troops that had been trained by riot-squad detectives from the Los Angeles police. Radio Santo Domingo changed hands again, and police with machine guns were clearing the streets. In the barrios the word was out: the revolution was over.

. . .

The following morning, Blanco Sánchez, the man who would later have his powerful dream-vision of Padre Arturo, was driving through the Cibao Valley, that shirt-sleeve campo of farmers and ranchers. He heard horns blaring, and then the caravan rumbled into view, men and women, even soldiers, hanging out of car windows or crowded into trucks, and every voice chanting, *"Libertad! Libertad! Libertad!"* He knew then that the lastest rumours were true. Overnight, whole army divisions had joined the insurgency and moved in to recapture the capital. The revolution was real.

. . .

In San José de Ocoa, the nuns at the convent prepared for a day of Sunday masses and work in the medical clinic. Illness and poverty didn't rest on the Sabbath. The sisters traded jokes about the farewell party that Sister Mary Joseph Mazzerolle had prepared two days earlier for a Peace Corps volunteer. Mary Jo had eaten a wiener, and she was still recovering from the shock. It was the first time she had eaten meat on a Friday—forbidden by papal edict, though not in hungry nations like the Dominican Republic—in forty-five years. Voice of America radio played in the background as they went about their Sunday tasks, but there was no news on it about the Dominican Republic.

. . .

That same Sunday morning, April 25, Constable Ramón Restituyo put on his uniform and presented himself at the barracks in Monte Plata. There were reports of a coup by rebels in Santo Domingo, and police and loyalist soldiers were anxious about the day to come. The PRD—the Partido Revolucionario Dominicano, the Dominican Revolutionary Party of Juan Bosch—was behind the uprising, and the town's young rebels would need to be watched. Monte Plata was the second place in the country where a PRD group had formed. That Canadian priest, Padre José Ramón Moriarty—he let them meet in the parish hall. The new assistant pastor, this Padre Arturo MacKinnon, was no improvement. He had been in Monte Plata for just four months, and what had he done? Made friends with the kids who threw rocks in the park. He seemed to like nothing better than to hang around with the *tígueres,* the young and rebellious.

The men at the barracks tried to get news over the radio, but there were no broadcasts out of Santo Domingo.

· · ·

At around eleven o'clock that morning, Father Paul Ouellette, regional superior for Scarboro in the Dominican Republic, heard Radio Santo Domingo crackle back to life in the mission house in Haina. The rebels had retaken the airwaves. Donald Reid had fallen, the broadcast said, and rebel soldiers had captured the National Palace. The radio was exhorting the people of the city to go to the palace or to gather at the Duarte Bridge over the Ozama River. Across the bridge was San Isidro, where the old generals still refused to support the rebellion. The strongman was Brigadier General Elías Wessin y Wessin, the tank commander and head of the armed forces who had led the overthrow of Juan Bosch. Now he sat in San Isidro with his tanks and troops, along with Juan de los Santos Céspedes, the general of the air force. Would they fight the insurgency? If they did, their troops would have to cross the Duarte Bridge.

Father Ouellette drove his jeep into town. He stayed away from the seething core of the city, because he didn't like the tone of the talk on Radio Santo Domingo; it had a communist flavour. He did get to within a few blocks of the National Palace. As he watched the crowds, four air force planes appeared above the rose-coloured dome. Then an explosion shook the air, the sonic blast and the smoke fading off over the city. A warning. The word in the streets was that San Isidro would bomb the palace and Radio Santo Domingo that night. Father Ouellette decided to return to Haina, driving George Washington Boulevard along the sea. Communism, he thought, was about to topple its second domino in the Americas.

· · ·

In his headquarters on the great plain of San Isidro, Elías Wessin y Wessin was ruminating. In front of him stood a trusted lieutenant colonel and a major, both in a state of some excitement. The capital was overrun by communists and traitors, and these officers wanted action. Specifically, they were requesting an x100 tank, which they would drive to the air force base for a meeting with Juan de los Santos.

If he refused, Wessin y Wessin knew, the submachine guns might soon be trained on him. He was famously anticommunist, but for all his bluster, he, too, had failed to take action against this sudden insurgency, now in its second day. He needed the support of the air force, but De los Santos believed he could negotiate a power-sharing deal with the rebels. That wouldn't work for Brigadier General Wessin y Wessin. Half the traitors were mewling for the return of Juan Bosch, that "liberal democrat," that "social reformer," that godless communist he had chased out of office exactly nineteen months earlier. The other half might accept a military junta, but with a new balance of power. Neither side wanted to see the name Wessin y Wessin anywhere but on the mailbox of an exile house in Miami.

Did the sons of bitches imagine he would surrender? Any subordinate could recite the three principles that motivated the life of their brigadier general. First, he was an honest soldier; let the others corrupt themselves into millionaires, let them cover their chests with the bullshit decorations handed out by Trujillo—he would not. Second, he was a man of the Father, the Son and the Holy Ghost. And third, he hated every communist and fellow traveller on God's green earth.

Crush the rebellion, or move to Miami.

The lieutenant and the major were awaiting his decision.

· · ·

Just before four o'clock that afternoon, air force planes appeared again over the National Palace. Their machine guns raked the walls, the dome, the windows. So: it would be war.

· · ·

Second Lieutenant Evangelista Martínez Rodríguez was in danger. He was the police commander of the Santo Domingo barrio known as Villa Agrícolas, Fifth Precinct, the barrios altos. What did that mean on this evening of April 25, in a city occupied by rebel soldiers—a city without law, where men in uniform had begun to hand out guns to civilians, where you could learn how to make a Molotov cocktail from masked guerrillas on the government television station? The answer wasn't clear. He had been commander of his detachment for not even two months. This morning, the chief of the National Police had declared that his forces would be "neutral." That lie had held for exactly as long as the stalemate between the rebels in Santo Domingo and the generals in San Isidro. Now San Isidro had attacked. What did it mean that the police were "neutral" now? It meant that three thousand armed men in Santo Domingo had not yet chosen sides. Now the people would remember that the police had been agents of torture and imprisonment, perpetrators of a thousand casual abuses. Now they would remember the informers, the caliés still unpunished from the days of Trujillo.

Could he flee? Abandon his uniform and melt into the city? Evangelista Martínez wasn't a deserter. He had been in the armed forces since 1957, a soldier trained in the Era of Trujillo. But he was in danger of losing his life. He could feel the hatred rising in the barrios altos.

. . .

Five o'clock. The U.S. State Department in Washington, D.C., where ambassador Tap Bennett had arrived by air that day, received a telegram from its Santo Domingo embassy:

> Situation extremely confused and no identifiable authority is exercising any effective control over the government.
>
> All members of the country team feel Bosch's return and resumption of control of the government is against U.S. interests in view of extremists in the coup and communist advocacy of Bosch return.

. . .

A waning crescent moon rose over the north coast, over the southwest headlands, over the Bay of Samaná, over every camp where fishermen sat near their hauled-up yolas, talking late. They grilled reef fish over coals and, with quick, angled strokes of their machetes, opened green coconuts to drink themselves full. They slept in thatch huts on white sand or in caves of water-smoothed limestone, oblivious to the bloodshed in their capital, news they wouldn't hear for a day, maybe two, maybe more.

· · ·

Morning in San José de Ocoa, April 26, 1965. Outside the convent, a commotion. Sister Mary Joseph, making doughnuts, felt a surge of excitement: it had to be a wedding. Everyone had told her that to see her first Dominican wedding—well, that would be something to remember. The noise! The celebration! The people in the streets! She threw open a window to cheer with the people. And someone said, "Sister, that's no wedding. That's a revolution starting."

· · ·

Father Lou Quinn drove hard from the quiet mountain town of Padre Las Casas. He had two radio stations to keep tabs on now, the rebel Radio Santo Domingo and the new Radio San Isidro. Between them he could piece together the news. The planes had renewed their attack just before dawn, striking the radio tower, the palace and the crowds that had gathered to block the western gate of the Duarte Bridge. The Dominican air force was slaughtering the Dominican people; the Dominican people were murdering the Dominican police. Entering the capital, he drove onward to the bridge. There were hundreds of people there, almost all of them young men. San Isidro was blasting them as communists, but he knew many of these faces; he counted some of these people as friends. They were social activists who fought for better housing, fairer wages, land redistribution, human rights. Some, too, were tígueres, young men with no hope, no future, nothing better to do than revolt. No one seemed to be in charge, but they had already sustained aerial bombardment and were prepared, even, to fight the tanks of San Isidro.

· · ·

In the campo, a colony of weaver birds. The males perched beside the nests they'd created out of twigs, reeds, twine and hair, chattering wheezily to the females. It was hard to say which was more beautiful, the nests, as round as Christmas ornaments, dozens of them hanging in a single tree, or the birds themselves, with their heads like black hoods above their deep-yellow bodies.

Another day passed.

• • •

In morning light, a nun in the sugar-refinery town of Ingenio Consuelo, two hours east of the capital, saw a group of young men preparing to leave town to fight in the revolution. "For which side?" she asked, and they replied, "Whichever one gives us the guns."

• • •

The first hours of Tuesday, April 27, were quiet at Scarboro House in Haina. Over the radio, Father Ouellette heard that a morning ceasefire had been declared to allow the American government to evacuate its citizens; a civil war waited on consuls' wives, the Michigan Jazz Band, businessmen in town for a brewers' convention. Father Ouellette decided to drive again from Haina into the city. He made it less than half a mile before he saw a blockade of more than a hundred tígueres and turned around. Then, just after eleven o'clock, he heard San Isidro attack: the roar of strafing airplanes, the hollow boom of bombing. Hundreds would die, but he laid the blame on the insurgents. It was clear that San Isidro would not cede power to the revolution, and so the revolution would fail. The rebels ignored that failure at a price that would be paid in blood.

At two o'clock, cars, buses and trucks began to pour into Haina: the American evacuees. They had gathered that morning just west of the city at the Ambassador Hotel, and now they would be shuttled to U.S. Navy boats offshore. More than a thousand people filled Haina, and Scarboro House offered a ringside seat. It was three hours of mad scramble. People had been prepared initially to be orderly; at the Ambassador Hotel, they had patiently lined up for documents, tagged their bags, checked the blackboards for bulletins. Then a group of insurgents ran through the hotel lobby and gardens and opened fire with submachine guns and rifles. The Americans cowered on the ground, terrorized, while the rebels searched the crowd for a single man, Bonilla Aybar, a hated right-wing journalist. They didn't find him.s

It had been pandemonium ever since. The Americans wanted out. Father Ouellette couldn't help but feel a pang of longing to join them.

• • •

In Monte Plata, Father Joe Moriarty and Father Arthur MacKinnon took in the news in bits and pieces. People were trickling into town from the capital, looking for peace and quiet. Monte Plata had its toughs, and some of the more eager would-be revolutionaries had painted their machetes a communist red, but there wasn't much fuss. In the casa curial, a more important realization was dawning: a civil war would leave the poor of Monte Plata without much to show for food. Already, the handful of street lights that ran each night until midnight on a diesel generator had been blacked out. Everyone felt the absence, because the electric lights had come to Monte Plata only a few months earlier.

For now, it was a wait-and-see game. Over the radio came the news of the ceasefire and the American evacuation—the United States, always ready to take care of its own. Arthur decided to drive to Bayaguana, half an hour to the east, to visit the Spanish priest who was living there alone. It was a time for small mercies.

. . .

Tap Bennett had been back in Santo Domingo for just over three hours when the various leaders of both the Dominican Revolutionary Party and the rebel armed forces appeared at the U.S. embassy. He asked that they disarm, and they joined him in the office where he sat with the thick wooden storm shutters closed—the embassy had been under fire periodically since that morning. The men seemed sullen and defeated, and the meeting was bound to be pointless. The insurgents were outraged by San Isidro's violence; Bennett reminded them that it was not San Isidro that had opened this conflict. The United States, he said, was alarmed by the communists who had rallied to the revolt; the rebels dismissed them as "details." The rebels believed the U.S. ambassador should mediate a peace agreement; he disagreed. The White House wanted Dominicans to talk to Dominicans.

Bennett felt he had been direct but diplomatic, always the Southern gentleman. Yet the rebel leaders lingered, as though uncertain what to do next or unwilling to rejoin the cold, hard world. Terms of surrender would not be kind to the insurgents. They would be forced into hiding, or exile. Some had already declared that they would rather die fighting.

. . .

And then: a miracle.

From the east bank of the Ozama River, artillery cannons pounded the western gate of the Duarte Bridge, scrambling the human blockade.

Aircraft raked the zone, and Wessin y Wessin's tanks rumbled to the front. This was the hour that the city had feared for three days. Now the armoured units crossed the river, filling the four lanes of the span. They seized the western bridgehead, the infantry falling in behind them. But they had fought their way into a hornets' nest. There was gunfire, true, but also stones, chunks of iron, flaming jars of gasoline. Thousands of civilians, untrained but armed with whatever they could find—the whole lunatic armoury of everyday life—were attacking in the streets or from the windows above. The tanks fought forward and retreated, fought forward and retreated. The dead littered the streets. But the army of San Isidro could not defeat the people of Santo Domingo.

· · ·

President Lyndon B. Johnson did not need this problem in the Dominican Republic. He had Vietnam to worry about. He had the Cold War. He had, really, a global war on communism, and it was literally troubling his sleep. The conflict boiled beneath surfaces and threatened even the peace on American soil. It required new thinking—pre-emptive thinking. He had already seen the alternative: watching a few dozen shitty little reds, beardy bastards like Fidel Castro, take over an entire country that you could skip a pebble to from South Beach, Miami.

Now he had this telegram from his ambassador in Santo Domingo, a man he knew and trusted. Tap Bennett wanted the president to know that a U.S. military adviser had gone that morning to San Isidro and found grown men weeping, a senior officer urging retreat from the Duarte Bridge and a Dominican general formally requesting American troops.

> The country team is unanimous that the time has come to land the Marines. American lives are in danger. Proposes Marine beachhead at the Ambassador Hotel. If Washington wishes they can be landed for the purpose of protecting evacuation of American citizens. I recommend immediate landing.

Well, landing the marines would be controversial. The United States had signed agreements against intervention among the sovereign nations of the Americas. Johnson could wait and consult with the Organization of American States, but what had he said about the OAS? "It couldn't pour piss out of a boot if the instructions were written on the heel." Since day one of this latest tin-pot war he'd been hearing that the communists were ready to make Santo Domingo a new Havana. Emergency and long-range plans for anticommunist intervention in the Dominican Republic had been quietly on the books for almost four years. If he ordered an invasion, however, his critics would rush to call him a knee-jerk anticommunist who had launched an illegal war. It was 5:30 PM, April 28, 1965. The hump day of the week, a Wednesday. The sun would set on Santo Domingo in one half hour.

·   ·   ·

Just before seven o'clock that evening, Father Ouellette watched as 405 American soldiers of the Third Battalion, Sixth Marines set foot on Dominican soil, the first U.S. military invasion in the Americas since Nicaragua in 1926. The troops were landing, said President Johnson on U.S. television, for one reason and one only: to protect American lives.

·   ·   ·

And on the beaches that line the eastern seaboard of the republic, the sea turtles hauled themselves ashore beneath a sliver of April moon, dug nests, laid eggs and returned to the sea, just as they had done for more years than the idea of time can make meaningful.

12

SO: I'M LOOKING FOR THE MATADOR, AND I have only two fragments of useful information. The first, that he is rumoured to be alive. The second, that he may have been born in a place called Los Jobillos. Los Jobillos is a minuscule dot on my map, not far from Yamasá and on the banks of that town's eponymous river. There appears to be no road.

In the past, such places were accessible only by foot or by mule; today, there is the motoconcho. As I join the other passengers stepping down from the guagua in Yamasá, the men on their motorcycles circle, shouting for our attention. I lock eyes with an older man and explain that I want to go to Los Jobillos. He shakes his head, points to the wire and twine that hold together his tiny engine, then flags down a younger driver with a dirt bike. Neither man finds it strange that I'm looking for someone in Los Jobillos but know nothing more than his name.

There is a road to Los Jobillos after all, but the map-makers were right to make no mention. It's rutted and ruined; in places, the mud and loose, naked stones push us off the road and onto the footpaths that still cross the campo. We move not much faster than a mule at a trot, and I have a chance to take in the Yamasá that Rosa had described to me that morning. The land is a rolling plateau, here and there punctuated by a whaleback hill, everything as green as if it were here, exactly here, that life itself began. The people we pass are on mules, or they walk. There are half-collapsed houses, children wearing dirty shirts but no pants, men doubled over in fields. Everyone seems to carry a machete.

Los Jobillos is nothing, a few plaster houses along the road. Still, three men sit beneath a cluster of taller trees, as if the pool of shade were a fine old town plaza. The driver rolls to a stop. "Talk to them," he says.

"I'm looking for a man named Odulio de los Santos Castillo."

The men consider the question carefully, appreciating this contribution to the passage of time this morning. There is no doubt, they agree, that the De los Santos name is an old one, and the family is large. But the name Odulio—this is not at all familiar. They weigh the issue a while longer, then suggest that we ask at the house beside the church, which we had passed on the way into town. We wheel around, and already a woman in a bright, yellow-flowered shirt has her eyes on us. As we approach, I can see a single braid wound over her forehead, the rest of her hair covered with a kerchief. She has hard, bare feet and a baby at her hip.

"Odulio de los Santos Castillo," she says, drawing the name out with care. "There is no Odulio de los Santos Castillo here. But maybe in Los Jobillos."

"We just asked in Los Jobillos," says the driver.

"No, the Los Jobillos that is a little farther along."

"There are two?" I say. The driver nods as if I've asked the most painfully obvious question. We ride onward, waving again to the three men beneath the trees, and break out into the campo. The sun has turned the horizon into a trembling mirage. Now the road is two shallow ruts darkened by recent rain and busy with donkeys, oxen, goats, dogs, roosters. We pass a sign: BATEY DE LOS JOBILLOS. This other Los Jobillos is a village of men and women who work on the large plantations and live on the owners' land. The term "batey" is a Taíno word that once described the clearings people cut for a game, also called batey, that involved bouncing a rubber ball off any part of the body but the hands or feet. Today, the word is synonymous with the poverty of Haitian immigrant workers, some of the poorest people in the hemisphere. We pull up alongside a woman with the umbral skin of the Haitians; a baby nurses at her breast.

"I don't think there is any Odulio here," she says in Spanish that suggests at least a generation in the republic. A white-haired man takes an interest and walks closer to the discussion.

"He was a soldier," I say.

"There are more soldiers in Los Jobillos," says the man.

"We've just come from Los Jobillos," says my driver.

"No, there is a Los Jobillos farther along."

This time the driver laughs.

The two of them give us directions: a crossroads, a bridge, a hilltop, a blue house. Tracks and small roads stretch out in every direction. At the house, a man says the name Odulio is familiar, and perhaps we need to travel just a little farther down the road. My driver is getting impatient, and we are both saddle-sore from the potholed road and the midday heat, but we go on and come to a group of men pulling beams and breeze-block from an abandoned house. A young man walks down to meet us at the roadside.

"Odulio." He turns the word over in his mouth, his eyes fixed on mine. "No." But then another man, small, bullish, mustachioed, a Dominican among the Haitians, shouts down from the rubble, "Odulio de los Santos?"

"Yes!"

"A soldier?"

"Yes!"

Then he, too, becomes pensive and watchful. "I don't know him," he says, shaking his head.

As we retreat toward Yamasá, the driver can sense my disappointment. "Many people don't like to give information," he explains. As if in reply, a woman in a widow's dress, her hair wild from too many years of straightening, walks toward us from her bohío, waving a square of white cloth. When we stop, she stands and stares, saying nothing.

"I'm looking for a man named Odulio," I say to her. I can hear the weariness in my voice.

She gives a start. "Odulio de los Santos!"

"Yes." A tiny boy has appeared at my feet, snapping flies off my boots with flicks of a rag.

She begins to speak quickly, too quickly, then stops and says simply, "He is dead. They killed him."

"Who killed him?"

She shakes her head, turns, and begins to move back toward her tiny plaster house.

"Does his family live here?"

But she has said all that she has to say.

We make our way back, the road seeming longer than it did in the morning. "It is always best to talk to the old women," says my driver, as though this were a lesson that he himself would need to remember. As we approach the first Los Jobillos, he drives hard through the holes and dips, eager to return to the asphalt and colmados of Yamasá. When the woman with the spiral braid on her forehead comes running toward us, shouting that we should stop, he hesitates, hesitates, then angrily squeezes the brakes.

"Odulio de los Santos Castillo!" she says, her face flushed with the excitement of memory. "I can't be sure, but there are De los Santos Castillos in La Mina! He must have lived there! Ask in La Mina!"

My driver turns his head so that I can see the corner of his right eye. "You want to go to La Mina?" he asks.

"Is it far?"

"Yes," he says.

"No," she insists.

In fact, it takes only a few minutes. The route to La Mina quickly opens up on a good gravel road, and the village is a busy cluster of houses. The driver pulls up in front of two old women, one with white hair in a neat bun, the other with a gold-rimmed incisor. Chicken scatter as I cross the yard to reach them.

"I know of an Odulio de los Santos, but he is dead," says the white-haired woman. "It's been some time now."

"He was a soldier?"

"I think so."

"Does his family still live here?"

"I don't think so. What do you want with them?"

As I explain, she is silent; it is impossible to tell whether she is studying my face or staring into the air. "I remember the story of the priest in Monte Plata," she says with a note of finality, and the two women go mum, a neutral, inscrutable silence.

As I walk back to the motorcycle, I see the driver is talking to a young man with a thin moustache. "Odulio de los Santos is dead," the young man confirms. "He died after Hurricane George. But there is a woman who knew him and his family, and you can talk to her." Her name is Juana Heredia; she lives in La Cuaba. It's in the hills on the other side of Yamasá—a village, he says, a *campito*.

My driver has had enough. He pulls the motorcycle around and rides for Yamasá. He has earned several days' worth of wages, and now he is going to enjoy it. I'm left standing on the grey-brown main road of Yamasá, watching men and women duck in and out of doorways that lead to every conceivable service. It is early afternoon now, with the sun blazing up the street so that the shadows of the awnings don't even touch the ground. I am giving up on La Cuaba when a motoconcho pulls alongside. The driver is a crafty-looking young man with a beetled Afro and mottled skin. He introduces himself as Daniel Berroa. He has a wife and one son. La Cuaba is not so very far away, he says. As for the afternoon heat, it is cooler in La Cuaba.

From the moment we leave Yamasá we are climbing, weaving up a band of asphalt between jungly slopes. In the distance are shining hillsides too sheer for trees. We follow, for a time, a robust little brook—the headwaters of the mighty Ozama River. There seems to be a village in every saddle of every ridge, but we are high in the hill country when Daniel announces La Cuaba and stops to ask a man doing roadwork about this woman named Juana Heredia. There is no Juana Heredia in his town. "Try La Cuaba," he says, and I have to explain to Daniel why I laugh out loud.

From La Cuaba we go to La Cuaba, and then to La Cuaba Arriba. At a hilltop fry-house, a woman and a nearly toothless older man bend their heads to the question. When the man begins to speak, it is in English. "I live here forty years," he says. "I know everyone. I see everything. Juana Heredia." He shakes his head, no.

"I understand," says Daniel in Spanish. "Some people don't like to give information." He shrugs and turns to me, but makes no move to leave. He has made the man uncomfortable, and now the woman is taking up the challenge. "I think there *is* a Juana Heredia," she says, as though it were nothing more than a matter of faith. "I think she could live up that road." It's a steep dirt path just across the shattered tarmac. We have barely begun the climb, however, when we see a woman in fuchsia, with a kerchief on her head, sweeping a small garden alcove.

Her name is Juana Heredia, and if she is lying when she says she never knew an Odulio de los Santos, then she is the best liar on earth.

"There is another Juana Heredia," she says, "in La Cuaba."

We follow Juana Heredia's directions to the home of Juana Heredia. As she promised, the house is unmistakable. Set back from the road, it looks like a miniature colonial fortress. Its breeze-block bricks have been carefully masoned but left unpainted, and a concrete cross faces the front door from the yard beneath the trees. A girl and a boy, perfectly mannered, both in their early teens, both in their blue-and-beige school uniforms, step out to greet Daniel and me as we walk to the door. They seem utterly unsurprised to be receiving a gringo here in the mountains. Yes, says the girl, Juana Heredia is her mother, but she is working at the church up the road in La Jina. Her mother has always worked with the Catholic church; for years she was the cook for a priest in La Cuaba. A Canadian priest.

"A Canadian priest?"

"Would you like to see our photos?" the girl asks, gesturing into the main room and a corkboard on the wall. On the board is a collection of images of a big-bearded man working, building the strange house, talking with campesinos in the street. "Padre Rodríguez," the girl tells me. I see a small plaque that reads FATHER ROD MACNEIL. The name is familiar, and then I recognize a face in another photograph. It's Paul Ouellette, the late regional superior of the Scarboro Foreign Missions in the Dominican Republic.

I feel a dizziness, a spangling of awe, but there isn't time to put anything into words. An older woman is striding into the room from the front door. "Hello. How are you? Are you hungry?" she says in hardworking English. "Would you like a hoo-eese?"

"A hoo-eese?"

"A hoo-eese." She's smiling with a trained, deliberate politeness, but it's hard to meet her gaze—one eye looks steadily three inches to one side of my head and the other toward the ground. She turns suddenly on the boy and girl and barks, in Spanish, "Get these men juice! Get them bread!" It is clear from the hesitancy of the children that there is neither bread nor hoo-eese in the house. I see the boy take Daniel by the elbow and step out the front door; they begin a hushed conversation.

"Why don't you stay the night and speak with my mother?" the woman says, again in English. "Where did you come from?"

"From Yamasá. I am—"

"I have four sons," she says. "Two daughters and two sons. Four sons."

"Congratulations." As she flushes with pride, I manage to ask, "Did your mother know a man named Odulio de los Santos?"

"Of course. He lives in Monte Plata?"

"You know him?"

"He is my uncle."

"Your uncle!" The fizzing sensation expands behind my eyes, a crackling excitement at the powers of chance. "And he's alive now?"

"Yes."

"He lives in Monte Plata right now?"

"As always."

Daniel is making hand signals from the front door. "We can go to La Jina now," he interrupts. "We can meet Juana Heredia there." His gestures have some urgency, but I'm reluctant to tear myself away. The day has been long and largely hopeless, and now there is this connection, this breakthrough. "Right now," says Daniel, with the look of a person who is keeping some secret knowledge. He kick-starts the motorcycle, we say hurried goodbyes, and the two of us pull away up the road. When we are clear of the house, he slows down to look at me over a shoulder. He turns a finger in a circle at his temple. "That woman is crazy," he says.

WE DO RIDE TO La Jina, deep in emerald hummocks, and we do find Juana Heredia. She did indeed cook for Father Rod MacNeil of the Scarboro priests for many years, but she never knew Odulio de los Santos. The uncle in Monte Plata is another man with a similar name, Dionisio de los Santos. I will want to talk with Dionisio, she says, but he is very old now, an ancient, and marked for life, surely, by the death of Padre Arturo. Dionisio was the catechist in Monte Plata. He was the last of Arturo's friends to see him alive.

There is nothing more to do but return to Santo Domingo. I have lost the trail of the matador, and instead found my moment to turn toward Monte Plata.

13

IN THE NARROW SACRISTY OF THE MONTE Plata cathedral, Padre Arturo donned his vestments. Even this, the least of rituals, was meditative. Father Art was known for his dedication to the liturgy, but it would be a mistake to call his devotion orthodoxy—he was at least as well known for his impatience with Rome and with the posturing of the bishops. Yet in ceremony he found grace and humility, and in these he found his God.

Today, of all days, he would need him.

It was June 17, 1965, the day of Corpus Christi, the ancient sacrament of the Eucharist as the body and blood of Christ. He could hear the scuffing feet on the cathedral floor, worn concrete with a crack that ran straight up the aisle like the torn veil in the Temple of Jerusalem. The pews would fill for the morning Mass. Corpus Christi was a central solemnity of Catholicism, a celebration of a divine presence that the people could reach out for and taste and touch, but that was not the only reason they would attend today. The revolution—the civil war—had come to Monte Plata.

The first ripples had been felt weeks before, of course. In the first days, saboteurs had burned a bridge on the route to the capital, and the road itself was soon closed by the battles in the barrios altos. In Santo Domingo there was debate, protest, conflict, outrage. And here in the campo—a wall of silence. Silence and hunger. For almost two months, all the highest powers of the nation had delivered was the propaganda and invective of Radio San Isidro.

Looking back, it had been decided before the revolution was even a week old. The first few hundred U.S. marines, observed by Father Paul Ouellette from Scarboro House on April 28, had proved to be only a beachhead. The marines kept coming and coming, and then, on April 30, the paratroopers of the Third Brigade, Eighty-second Airborne Division touched down in San Isidro. There was no longer any doubt about why the Americans had sent in the troops. "There are signs that people trained outside the Dominican Republic are seeking to gain control," President Johnson had said in an address that day heard around the world. "Thus, the legitimate aspirations of the Dominican people, and most of their leaders, for progress, democracy and social justice are threatened." The crisis couldn't wait for the jaded bureaucracy of a multinational response, said the president. "Loss of time may mean that it's too late to preserve the freedom which alone can lead to the establishment of true democracy."

The paratroopers attacked along a narrow corridor from the Duarte Bridge to an "international security zone" established by the marines who had landed in Haina. On the morning of May 3, Santo Domingo woke to a city divided. The armed rebel leaders were isolated in Ciudad Nueva, while most of the civilian insurgents were on the other side of town in the barrios altos. "The Berlin of the Americas," people said in the streets, and the U.S. soldiers nicknamed their major crossing point Checkpoint Charlie. In little more than a week, the Americans had deployed an overwhelming force of 42,412 troops. They had turned a rebel victory—call it what it was, a people's revolution, men and women, armed more often with hammers and shovels than guns, turning back the tanks of San Isidro—into a surrender.

One week after the invasion, Lyndon Johnson won the support of the Organization of American States. Still, only six other nations, five of them ruled by military regimes, contributed troops to the intervention. The White House brokered a Government of National Reconstruction under President Antonio "Tony" Imbert Barreras, one of the two surviving assassins of Trujillo.

Then came Operation Mop-up. On May 14, the Government of Reconstruction and the military leaders of San Isidro, neither trustful of the other, came together in a total assault on the barrios altos. Eight days of house-to-house fighting followed, and no one bothered to deny that the number of civilian deaths was high. Even the U.S. joined in a unanimous United Nations Security Council vote to demand a ceasefire. But American troops did nothing to stop the slaughter.

It was only then that the war really came to Monte Plata. The police and soldiers at the local barracks had been tentative in the first weeks of the revolution. Now they could see that the old order would prevail. Everyone knew who had been talking revolution, who had painted his machete red, who had tuned in to Cuban radio. Soldiers and policemen picked their neighbours from the streets or from their homes. The terror was worse for its familiarity, a total extinguishment of hope.

What is the work of a priest in such times? For Joe Moriarty and for Arthur, the answer was stark. They had a duty to mercy and to justice. Both men began to argue at the barracks for clemency for the prisoners, but for Arthur it was a mission.

And then, on June 16, the day before Corpus Christi, the local police lieutenant had arrested thirty-seven people, most of them young men. The town was in an uproar, but it was the mothers, the wives, the girl-friends who came to the casa curial, weeping, asking for help. Arturo went that afternoon to the barracks but was bluntly turned away. That night, four prisoners were released while thirty-three were loaded into trucks and taken—where? To San Isidro, their families were told, or the Palace of the National Police. No one knew what to believe, but everyone knew the rumours. Everyone had heard that shots rang out along the Yuca River at night, after the curfew, and that in the morning fresh graves would appear. Everyone knew the Yuca River. The main road from Monte Plata to the capital passed over it.

How many days had it been since Teresa Roedán de Andujar, a woman who felt Christ to the marrow of her bones, had appeared in the doorway of the casa curial? She had asked for Padre José Ramón Moriarty, and Father Art explained that the pastor had been sent home to Canada on furlough, along with half of the Scarboro priests in the republic. She had appeared uncomfortable then, as if embarrassed. "I don't believe in dreams," she had said plainly, "but last night I had a dream, and in it I was told that you needed to be very careful, because they are planning to kill you."

What had he felt then?

"There are people who have this power," he had said to her. "That when something is going to happen, it will be revealed to them and through them."

"*Ay,* padre, be careful!"

He managed a smile. "Don't worry yourself," he had said. Then he had held up the permit that would allow him to leave on his own furlough just as soon as Joe Moriarty returned.

It was time to begin the Mass. Father Art had never been one of the great preachers, the men who gave the gospel as though seized by the Holy Spirit; normally, he spoke from notes. Today, he would do without. He stepped out of the sacristy to stand at the altar, the congregation always so handsome in the church, the girls and women in their dresses with their straightened hair, the men in their guayaberas, the poorest children barefoot and shirtless. When there was no sound but the people breathing, he began. He was disgusted by the arrests, he said, his face calm. He had cancelled the sacred procession of Corpus Christi. It was a celebration of love for the human life of Christ, and that day in Monte Plata there was no love for human life.

Then he proceeded with the liturgy.

In the congregation a woman began to weep. She was sobbing, shaking. It was Aída Flores de Santana, the wife of the army lieutenant in Monte Plata, and it was as though there was something in the homily that she could not bear. She was losing control, slipping into hysteria. Comforting hands took hold of her, helped her to stand and led her from the church. Padre Arturo continued.

14

I HAVE COME TO MONTE PLATA AS AN ascetic. I am fasting, refusing all food and even water. I have decided that this is for the best, a way of cleansing body and mind for the pilgrimage. More honestly, it's accidental. One day ago in the Zona Colonial, I ate rancid cashews from a street vendor. Now my stomach feels like a swallowed object of delicate, hand-blown glass, trembling in time to the shuddering guagua. It doesn't help that Monte Plata is in the newspapers this week for torture. A nineteen-year-old, arrested for a break-and-enter robbery, had been taken to the town's prison, where he fought with another inmate. The guards put him in handcuffs—the word in Spanish is the plural of the word for "wife"—and hung him by his wrists in the sun for seven hours. I am trying to forget the image of the young man's swollen hands, the raw burns across his knuckles, the fingers black with the same pooled blood, the lividity, that appears in the flesh of the dead.

The road, at least, is beautiful. Pastures dappled with sheltering trees. Here and there a monadnock looms, or the hidden channel of a river snarled with orchids and strangulating vines. In places the road is lined with bamboo, and the sound of the hollow stalks in the wind is like bone tips touching under the skin.

More than an hour outside Santo Domingo, the road arcs toward the foothills of the island's eastern mountains, the Cordillera Oriental, and abruptly comes to a crossroads. As we turn south, the first bohíos of Monte Plata appear. The town takes form, its centre marked by a sharp corner onto the main street. The road is suddenly lined with crowds, and in my delirium I imagine they must be waiting for me, the nephew of the martyr. But no. Everything is purple: purple pennants and purple placards, purple shirts and purple caps. It's the colour of the Democratic Liberation Party, the opposition to the government. A convoy of supporters is circling the town, led by a truck that blares a partisan merengue from a wall of speakers. Everyone is drinking, the women glistening, the young men stripping off their shirts, politics indivisible from dancing, rum, sex. The crowd chants in time: *"E' pa' fuera que van!"* It's out they go!

It takes me a few minutes just to cross the street from the plaza to the Hotel El Toro. They give me a corner room, where I can feel the rhythms of the main street in my intestines.

I lie on the bed. Outside there is a party, a decadent optimism. For me, a day of sickness. Sickness and an unsettling mystery. Rosa at the bottom of the stairs this morning, her voice singing out, "Santiago! Excuse me! Excuse me!" I had rinsed the fever from my face and gone to meet her, attempting a smile. A man had called just after dawn, she said. He was from La Mina in the hills of Yamasá. He understood that I was looking for one Odulio de los Santos Castillo, a soldier. The man gave his name as Wilson, and he didn't leave a number.

I hadn't met anyone called Wilson in the hills of Yamasá, and I didn't leave a phone number with anyone in La Mina. "Thank you," I said to Rosa, but I choked on the words.

A NEW DAY, and there is only one place to begin. Stepping out of the hotel, I turn and walk the road out of town.

I have the aching, hollowed-out feeling of illness, and the people who stare from their stoops make me glower. "Such a caring people," Joe McGuckin had said with his wry smile. "Always looking out for one another." It's a relief to step into the cemetery with its labyrinth of crypts. I explore the empty passages until I lose track of time, until I feel eyes on my back once again. A man—he must be the gravekeeper—is watching from the shadow of the gate. His skin stands out black against a cap and shirt in bright white, the campaign colour of the governing party. He has graveyard mud on his boots, and his name is Juan de los Santos. It's a large family, De los Santos.

"Do you know where Padre Arturo is buried?"

"Ah yes," he says, immediately in motion. We have walked only a few paces when he stops and bows his head.

The grave is a low plinth surrounded by red and white tiles and a chain. The marble tombstone is crusted with lichen, and without thinking I am on my knees, pressing my fingers into the carved stone, tracing the forms. "You . . . are . . . a priest . . . in eternity," I read aloud. Juan is beside me now, and together we draw out the meanings, letter by letter: Reverend Padre Arturo MacKinnon, born September 30, 1932. Died June 22, 1965. A passage from scripture, Matthew 5:10: BLESSED ARE THOSE WHO ARE PERSECUTED IN THE CAUSE OF JUSTICE, FOR THEIRS IS THE KINGDOM OF HEAVEN.

"I remember him," says Juan. "A fighter for the poor."

"It's true," I reply. A fighter for the poor, and persecuted in the cause. Yet there is something uncertain about this ragged tomb. In my walk through the cemetery I had seen crypts in perfect glory and others long forgotten, and the grave of Padre Arturo is neither of these. I might point to the way grass fills every crack but the tiles are freshly swept, or to the corner of broken stone that is carefully set to one side. In fact, though, my reaction is instinctual, a sensation. There is something deeply humble, even furtive, about the wax from a simple candle, the hint of green in the tired flowers knocked down in their plastic bucket. The grave has the feel of contested ground.

Juan asks if I've seen the monument at the place where Arturo died.

I follow his directions back to the roadway, past a fading mural of Arthur's face on an abandoned building— *"Arturo Vive!"*—and onward toward the first fields of the campo and a whiff of wet soil. The small houses that line the road are full of people doing not a lot: watching a gringo walk down the highway.

The monument is nearly as far as the crossroads to Santo Domingo. It's fenced with a low, locked gate, and I've barely glanced at it before a young mother across the road is shouting out a name and another woman appears in a doorway and calls back into her house. A boy of six or seven comes running toward me with a key. Together we open the gate and then I am standing in front of another cenotaph of tile and stone. I pick up a piece of garbage tossed into the enclosure from the highway, but again there are flowers, some still with colour in the petals.

This is the place. On this stretch of road Arturo lay murdered, his blood seeping into the earth, the bodies of Evangelista Martínez and Ramón Restituyo fallen beside him. I am trying to reach into that moment, to fall back through time toward some epiphany, but no tears come to my eyes and no visions fill my head. Monuments have always left me cold. What I feel, instead, is a strange impatience.

"HERE, AT THIS POINT HERE." Jesús Nicolás de los Santos is striding away from his motorcycle toward a magenta trinitaria that bursts beneath two palms, one of them hung with passion fruit vines. "At this exact point." He studies his feet and shuffles in the gravel until he is convinced that he has found precisely the spot. "This was the last place Arturo spoke to anyone."

It is late afternoon, the end of another day spent clinging to the back of a motorcycle. Jesús drives a Yamaha. We have been in workshops, sitting rooms, kitchens sweet with the smell of yuca-root dumplings. Padre Arturo was everywhere, drawn in recollections from the lacquered boxes of memory. Jesús had listened carefully, sometimes nodding his agreement or adding a detail in his booming baritone. Each person held a piece of the puzzle; what remained was to put it together, said Jesús. That was the way to keep the martyr's blood from fading. "I keep the memory of Arturo alive!"

He leads me on toward a house, its blue plaster scorched by the sun. In 1965, says Jesús, there was only a wooden bohío; this patch of earth has been the De los Santos family home since some whim of Trujillo dispossessed them of their land in the campo. Inside the open door, a woman with the smooth hair of endless Sundays at church is rising to greet us. She introduces herself as Diodora de los Santos, sister to Jesús, and then she slips out the back door and I can hear her coaxing someone to come inside. The man who appears is bent like a comma, shuffling forward a few inches at a time, his fingers fussing with the top buttons of his shirt. When he has done up three, he stops, his eyes searching mine from a fallen face. This is Dionisio de los Santos, veteran catechist of Monte Plata and the last person to see Arturo before he was shot at the side of the road. He has lost his powers of memory. Dionisio can listen, but he no longer can tell.

Jesús guides his father to a chair, explaining to him who I am and why I've come to the family home. Dionisio seems to smile slightly, but once he is seated he only gapes. Even with the separation of years, the similarity between father and son is unmistakable: the same lean, tall build—tall even in the head. Then Jesús leans toward me, lays a huge hand on mine and presses a single long finger against the pulse of my left wrist. "Okay," he says. "I will tell you the story."

It is impossible to begin with the day that Arturo died, he says, his barrelhouse voice ringing round the room. You have first to understand Trujillo. You have to understand that when they killed the Goat, the Goat didn't die. This is why the people didn't rush into the streets that very hour. They waited patiently for democracy, and when it came in 1962 they stood in orderly ranks and cast their votes for Juan Bosch, the professor—and then watched as he was toppled by a coup after seven months. Half a year of democracy, and then a military junta. Who could say that Trujillo had died?

So: It is 1964. Power is gathering around two men. The first is the military strongman Elías Wessin y Wessin, an Era of Trujillo soldier and architect of the coup against Bosch. The other is the president of the junta, Donald Reid Cabral. Reid began as a figurehead, leading only by the whim of the armed forces, but he was also a friend to the Americans. In his single full year in government, he received $132 million in foreign loans, mostly from the United States. It was nine times as much as the elected government of Bosch was given, but then, Reid was willing to allow foreign influence on the economy, to guarantee his international credit with austerity programs, to criminalize the communists. He was an ally in the United States' global war.

None of which is the way the era is remembered. What people remember is the first day they saw the ad hoc currency, printed on newspaper, that was issued to combat inflation. There was the "political freedom" of applying to the government for a permit to protest, with demonstrations to be held on the runways of an abandoned airport.

There was a country so rich with loans that the people had to be fed by international aid agencies like CARE and CARITAS.

"They say the food that arrived here was, above all, left over in the United States from the Second World War," says Jesús. "There was powdered milk and cheese, butter, flour, more." It was hard in those years to find anything like these American products. Everyone wanted a share. Much of the aid was distributed by the Catholic church, however, and in 1964 that meant Padre José Ramón Moriarty. The pastor had one simple rule: the food would go to the poorest. Anyone else he turned away. Soldiers and policemen—he refused them. They were poor, yes, but each had a small salary, and many had lousy barracks to sleep in, the slop in the mess hall to ward off starvation.

Jesús pauses, and his voice becomes slightly breathless. The day is dimming, and his face in the shadows is like a new moon.

"Monte Plata had its dominant families," he says. "Monte Plata was almost feudal, with these families that controlled the economic power because they owned the ranches and farms, the land. They were the owners of the principal businesses. They had joined together, and together they were very close to the Trujillo regime. Very close to the Trujillo regime. So much so that when Trujillo came to Monte Plata, it was their houses that he went to visit."

From the moment of Trujillo's assassination, these wealthy families were in danger. To them, democracy was a threat. Democracy had put Juan Bosch in the National Palace, a man who made land redistribution a constitutional requirement and derided the ones he called the *tutumpotes,* the all-powerful. It was class warfare. And when the priest in Monte Plata gave food only to the very poor—that, too, had the blush of communism.

"Do you see?" Jesús is pressing again on my arm, as if to feel whether his truth has made its way into my blood. You can't begin the story of Arturo with the last hour of his life. Maybe going back as far as Trujillo is not enough. Maybe the story begins with Columbus, with the very first Hail Mary spoken on the soil of the Americas. But a bitterness had surfaced in Monte Plata in 1964. It was like some great fungus breathing spores into the wind, invisible and poisonous. A visitor would see a small town with more mules than cars, where the people still met at day's end beneath the trees in a plaza that smelled of jasmine. The visitor wouldn't hear the rumour carried voice to voice, house to house: that a priest might soon hang from those trees.

On December 17, 1964, a new priest, Padre Arturo MacKinnon, came to Monte Plata from San José de Ocoa.

"A very tense situation," I say.

"Very tense," agrees Jesús. "But Arturo—I've been told that his father was a miner, a coal miner in Canada. He was, yes? So we can see where Arturo is coming from. He's from the class of the poor, miners, workers. But the most important thing was that he continued the line of Padre José Ramón. Arturo continued bringing food to Monte Plata, and he used the same policy as Padre José Ramón to deliver the food to the poor. But he is new, and he's a young man. He connected with the young people in the population. He had a young man's thoughts of freedom, of a new society, of struggles like the Cuban Revolution that had such an impact on these ideas, of the death of Trujillo. He had felt the struggle for freedom, for freedom, for freedom. The longing to see a free Dominican Republic."

It was an image that had been recalled again and again as Jesús and I circled the town. Padre Arturo, driving too fast in his Land Rover or hammering fence posts in the midday sun, but always surrounded by young men and women. The poor, the workers, the students and children—it wasn't only that he worked with them, but that he seemed to prefer their company. It was as though the powerful ones, the families who ran the ranches and the colmados—it was as though they had a lesser grace. But the tutumpotes had friends they talked to, as well. Their friends worked in the National Palace and the military command.

Dionisio appears to be nearly asleep; Jesús eases back in his chair. "Then, as you know, they began to take prisoner many of the young men," says Jesús. "They seized them from their beds, took them out of the town by night, tortured them. And then, the only person who had the authority, who had any kind of power to defend them, is Arturo. Arturo!" His voice fails under a sudden downdraft of sadness.

"They planned the death of Arturo," says Jesús quietly. "It was not only planned in the military sector, but also in the civic sector of Monte Plata."

The army and the tutumpotes. The idea sinks into me like a venom. It seems too dark a secret for these pretty streets with their century-old Victorian houses, their rusty water tower like a tattered Chinese firecracker.

"How do you know all this?" I ask.

"Ah!" Now Jesús has been thrown off balance. He has the expression of a person who has been asked a question so obvious he has never given it a moment's thought. "How do I know it? Because this is a small town."

The truth travels the way of the serpent.

"So it was planned here," he continues. "Here and in San Isidro."

"At the highest levels in San Isidro?"

"Yes, the highest levels. This kind of thing, an act that will bring international consequences—this wouldn't take a low form. That wouldn't happen in this country."

On the morning that Arturo cancelled the sacred procession of Corpus Christi, not long after Aída Flores de Santana had collapsed in the pews, two soldiers appeared at the door of the church. They carried submachine guns, Jesús says. They looked inside for long enough to let their eyes adjust to the shadows, and then they disappeared. The Mass was ending, and as the faithful filed out, they saw the soldiers on a bench in the plaza in front of the church. The two men were still there as Arturo walked across the road to the casa curial.

I feel myself jump in my seat: Dionisio is speaking. Jesús turns toward his father in surprise. The old man is reaching into the air, speaking urgently in almost unintelligible words. "Yes, Papa, yes," Jesús says. "Be calm, Papa." Dionisio falls silent, but his eyes have a momentary sharpness.

"When we left the Mass," says Jesús, "Papa said to Arturo in the terrace of the casa curial, 'Arturo, I think you'd better lower the tone of your sermon, because things are not good and you could put yourself in danger.' And Padre Arturo said to Papa, 'Dionisio, I know what I'm doing. If I don't do it, no one is going to do it.' That's what he said to Papa on the terrace of the casa curial. He had taken a firm position, okay?"

During the afternoon Mass, Arturo had nothing more to say. There was message enough in the abandoned Corpus Christi, the absence of the sacred and the holy.

When the Mass was over, he drove to San Isidro with a group of prisoners' wives. The Land Rover rumbled down the wet roads and through army checkpoints to the military buildings with the huge columns and porticos of some imagined ancient empire. It was an architecture of intimidation; it would have been impossible not to feel fear, just as it is impossible to stand in a great cathedral without sweeping your eyes to the heavens. They parked in front of the offices of Elías Wessin y Wessin, but the general would not meet the priest from Monte Plata.

"Ah," said Wessin's officers when they had listened to Arturo's complaint. "You're a communist."

"Not a communist," he replied. "I'm a man of the church."

The next day, he tried again. Arturo and a group of women drove south through San Isidro, but this time they continued over the Duarte Bridge into the U.S. Army corridor that still divided the capital city. It wasn't far to the ramparts of the Palace of the National Police, where fifteen people from Monte Plata were locked away from the sun. Again the highest officer, Police Chief Hermán Despradel Brache, refused to speak to the visitors. Instead, Arturo met a colonel. The men spoke behind closed doors, but the women could hear the padre's voice rising.

As the delegation left the building, Arturo turned to a woman whose husband was in jail. "They're going to deport me," he said.

"No, padre, that's impossible," she replied.

The colonel, said Arturo, had not been unclear.

Later that day, a Friday, the Monte Plata prisoners were released. Over the weekend, an announcement came down that the lieutenant in charge of the roundup, a man named Julio Gil Reyes, had been transferred to San Juan de la Maguana, far away in the mountain desert that stretched toward the border with Haiti. For a few short hours, there was hope. And then: men roused from their beds, women pulled off the streets. Once more, Arturo stood before the army and police. There was no mistaking his anger now. The words spilled from him freely, of repression, the young people, torture, the mothers' tears.

Jesús pauses, and the sound of traffic outside, the roar of passing motoconchos, is a kind of obliterating silence. "It was Arturo's final act," he says.

That afternoon, the cook in the casa curial set out a lunch and called Arturo to the table. When she returned to clear his plate, his food was untouched and he sat with his head in his hands. Was he crying? She had never seen him look like this, never seen him without an appetite. She spoke to him with care, but he only stood and made his way to his room. That afternoon, when a priest from Bayaguana came to visit, there was no sign of trouble on Arturo's face. The two priests sat swapping stories. The visitor left at 5:50 PM.

Perhaps half an hour earlier, a tailor named Ramón Carreras was sitting with two policemen, friends of his, in a bar just past the corner where the main street turns out of Monte Plata. A lieutenant walked in, a man Ramón Carreras had never seen before. He was Evangelista Martínez Rodríguez, the new lieutenant of the Monte Plata police. Martínez took a seat at the table, and when he had a drink in his hand, he asked one of the other men to find Constable Ramón Restituyo. It took about an hour, and the lieutenant was getting drunk by the time Restituyo appeared. Ramón Carreras couldn't remember ever having seen Restituyo out of uniform, but today the constable was in khaki pants with a checkered yellow shirt. He had hardly sat down when the lieutenant asked to talk to him in the washroom. When they emerged, Restituyo immediately left the bar and the lieutenant went back to his drinks. Then a soldier, a good friend of Ramón Carreras's family, came in off the street and said, "Ramón, your mother was wondering if you might go home."

Ramón said, "Tell her I'll be there in a little while."

"Listen, boy!" hissed the soldier so that only Ramón could hear. "You want them to kill you? Walk!" Outside the bar, the soldier warned Ramón that the lieutenant had been sent to do something bad. When Ramón arrived at his house he saw that his mother was crying, but he was drunk, and he fell asleep at the table. Late that night, he awoke to find himself in bed with a single, crystalline thought in his mind. He didn't need to be told what had happened to Padre Arturo. Somehow, he already knew.

IT WAS THE SUMMER solstice, but the day was fading. June is a wet month, and all day the sky had been flat and grey. It was nearly dark when Arturo's jeep appeared in front of the De los Santos bohío. Dionisio saw the familiar Land Rover and went out to greet his friend. Yes, it was

Padre Arturo in the driver's seat, but there were other men in the car: the new lieutenant on the passenger side, and Constable Ramón Restituyo sitting behind the padre. Dionisio could hear his children gathering behind him. His son Jesús was already a little man, the spitting image of his father.

"Dionisio, have you eaten?" asked Arturo.

"No, I just got home," the catechist replied. He'd been working a patch of land in the campo. "I was going to have a bath," he said.

Arturo let his forehead fall against the backs of his hands where they rested at the top of the steering wheel. Then he lifted his head and said, "That's fine, Dionisio. We'll talk again in five minutes or so."

Those were Padre Arturo's last words to any friend on this earth. He said them just outside the door, where the purpling trinitaria blooms beneath the passion fruit, the palms.

15

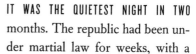

IT WAS THE QUIETEST NIGHT IN TWO months. The republic had been under martial law for weeks, with a curfew from five in the morning until sundown at six, but the night of June 22, 1965, was more unnaturally still. June 22 was meant to be the second day of a general strike called by national labour leaders against the "American imperialists," but then: nothing happened. Exhausted by conflict, the Dominican people went to work or to the market; when the sun went down, they went home and closed their doors. Bands of uneasy police patrolled the streets, waiting for things to explode. It was as though there had been a strike against the strike. At Scarboro House in Haina, Father Paul Ouellette could hear the surf against the beach, the zinging of insects.

At 9:15 PM, the telephone rang. Ouellette picked it up and exchanged greetings with the papal nuncio. The nuncio had just received a call from Hermán Despradel Brache, the chief of the National Police, who reported that the priest in Monte Plata had been shot and killed while driving through a military checkpoint. Two civilians were also dead. A military ambulance was going to collect the priest's body and bring it to Santo Domingo.

The body should stay in Monte Plata, said Ouellette.

The nuncio said he would check with Despradel and rang off. Paul Ouellette waited.

Father Artie.

The phone rang again. It was the nuncio calling to explain that the ambulance had already left the capital, but the police would get a message to Monte Plata that the body should remain there. Ouellette phoned Despradel and listened as the chief told him that Art's jeep had been zigzagging fast toward the Monte Plata army checkpoint until the guards had finally opened fire. That was the official story. There was nothing more Ouellette could do until the curfew was lifted in just over seven hours.

There were only two other Canadian priests in the house, Jack Mc-Carthy and Joe McGuckin. Ouellette broke the news to them in the sitting room. Death is no mystery, no rarity to a priest at work in the Dominican Republic, but this was something else again. One of their own, and with so many questions left hanging through the night. They made plans for the morning, and then Ouellette made his way to the chapel. Tears filled his eyes, and he asked his God: Did I do the right thing? On the fourth day of the revolution, the Canadian chargé d'affaires had called to say there could be an evacuation of Canadian civilians in the republic; U.S. President Lyndon Johnson had officially offered evacuation to any foreign citizen. It became a bitter joke. The president had ordered the marines to land "in order to protect American lives," but by the time the soldiers hit the sand, most of the civilians were already gone. On the first day of the intervention, troops could find only a few hundred American citizens to save—even the consular staff called them "stragglers." In the two weeks that followed, it was Spaniards, Britons, Chinese, Romanians, anticommunist Cubans. Art Buchwald captured it exactly in his column for the *Washington Post*. He wrote about "Sidney," a tourist in Santo Domingo who shows up for evacuation and is told that he can't leave.

"Why not?" says Sidney.

"Because we've been sent here to protect Americans and you're the only American left," says a Marine Corps colonel. "If you leave, we have to pull out."

They evacuated ninety-one Canadians, not one of them a Scarboro priest.

FATHER JOHN GOMES arrived at Scarboro House and found it empty. Well, Paul Ouellette and the rest must be out on business. Gomes himself was in from Baní, about half an hour to the west, to run errands in the capital. He was still getting organized when Father Antonio Sánchez, a Spanish Jesuit, appeared at the door in his white cassock, a large pectoral cross dangling from his neck. He must have come over from Manresa Loyola, the Jesuit house on the neighbouring property. Gomes knew Sánchez to be a chaplain to the Dominican military, so it was no surprise when he told Gomes that he had just been called by the armed forces hospital known as the Marion. They needed someone to identify the body of a Scarboro priest believed to be Father Arthur MacKinnon. He'd been shot when he failed to stop at a military checkpoint.

Something turned in John Gomes at that moment. He had arrived in the republic in 1962, and in three years he had witnessed the death throes of the Era of Trujillo, an election and democratic government, the inevitable coup, a junta, a revolution, civil war, the American occupation. Now the last of his naïveté was gone, a candle flame pinched into darkness.

Gomes and Sánchez drove the seashore road to the Marion, near the university campus in Santo Domingo. It was midmorning, the clearest hour of the Caribbean day, but the horizon was hung with monsoon clouds. They found the hospital overwhelmed, a full house of the wounded and dead. Finally an elderly nurse recognized Sánchez. "I think, padre, you'll find him downstairs," she said. They made their way to the base-ment morgue. Someone pulled the body from cold storage, and then—there he was. Arthur MacKinnon, frozen on a tray on the floor. Gomes knew it was dangerous to read too much in the face of a dead man, but still, there was no sense of peace on Art's face. His fists were clenched. There had been a struggle, a violent death. Gomes could feel it.

The two priests squatted alongside the corpse and began to take in the details. Art's eyes were softly closed. His hair was caked with gore, and a single dark rivulet crossed from his hairline to the tip of his left eyebrow. His skin, his clothes were spattered and stained with blood, sand and the ochreous mud of the campo. Ruined bones stood out under the flesh of his left cheek. There was a bullet wound on that side, a small hole behind the jaw. Art's grey checkered shirt was unbuttoned over what had been a white undershirt, and both were drenched with blood across the right shoulder. The only wound there, though, was a ragged cut where the ribs roll under the arm. It was hard not to think of the wound from the lance thrust into Christ on the cross. So went the prophecy: "They shall look on him whom they pierced."

But the waist. Art's undershirt was pulled up slightly, and Gomes could see the highest of the bullet wounds that had torn across his body at the level of the bladder. Shattered. It was strange to look at a human body and think: *Shattered.*

He and Sánchez began to pray.

That's when Paul Ouellette arrived at the morgue with Jack McCarthy. Gomes and Sánchez had thought nothing of the two other caskets in the morgue, but Ouellette took careful note. They contained two dead policemen from Monte Plata, washed and in uniform. A new story, different from the official version, was forming in Paul Ouellette's mind. He and McCarthy had reached Monte Plata at seven o'clock in the morning, stopping first at the military barracks. Art's Land Rover was there. Even at a glance it didn't look like a vehicle that had been raked with submachine-gun fire as it raced toward a checkpoint. The windshield was intact. The bullet holes, a half-dozen of them, were arrayed across the driver's-side panels, and the shots had plainly been fired at an angle from the rear. There was not a trace of blood inside or on the outside of the jeep.

A group of locals wanted to show the two priests where the bodies had fallen. It was back—four hundred, maybe five hundred yards—on the road toward the capital. Here, the people said. This is where the padre died, and the new lieutenant, and the constable Ramón Restituyo. An empty road between sodden fields of yuca and corn. The military checkpoint wasn't even in sight. The two priests drove onward into the centre of Monte Plata. The day was muggy and hot, and yet it was as though the night's curfew had never been lifted—an eerie silence, a sense of life behind closed doors. The casa curial was padlocked. Finally they found someone on the street who told them that Padre Arturo had been sent to the Marion.

There was nothing to do but make double time back to the capital. And what about these new suspicions? The nunciature, on Máximo

Gómez not far from the hospital, seemed to be the place to begin. The nuncio received them immediately, listened carefully, then mentioned that the American ambassador, Tap Bennett, was scheduled to arrive within half an hour.

Bennett arrived at 9:30 AM, and he was the next to hear Ouellette explain his doubts. Bennett readily agreed to provide a U.S. Army Red Cross helicopter to return the body to Monte Plata for burial. Just a week earlier, Art had mentioned how much he'd like to take a ride in a chopper. That same week he had made his final visit to Ocoa. He'd told friends that "they were after him" in Monte Plata, but with a smile that said, *So what?*

Father Artie. Now, in the morgue of the Marion, Ouellette's tears came freely. It is one thing to suspect a murder and another to know, at a glance, that your suspicions are correct.

FATHER LIONEL WALSH was standing beside his bed that morning of June 23, and who should appear behind him but Father Jim Burns. The two Scarboro men worked together in El Seibo, on the baking eastern plains of *los hatos*, the cattle country. Burns had left an hour ago and had not been expected back for a day or more, but now here he was. He seemed to be holding something back.

"Artie's been shot," he said.

"What?"

"They say he went through a military checkpoint and didn't stop." Burns paused and turned to leave Lionel's bedroom. "We'd better get ready. Funeral's going to be this evening."

There wasn't much more to say. The men gathered their cassocks and prepared for the trip. They were on the road within half an hour, and the roar of the Land Rover's engine was soothing. It was more than two hours to Monte Plata, a long southward bend almost as far as San Isidro and north again into the plateau. The eastern entrance to the town is abrupt—fields and pasture, then suddenly the church and the plaza. They turned onto the main road, empty and wet with rain, and parked in front of the casa curial. Lionel knew the place. He had lived here for a time. Nineteen sixty-one? Sixty-two? He wandered into the old bedroom. Well. Artie was certainly living a Christian life. There wasn't much in the room, hardly a sign that a person was staying here. Lionel saw the familiar bed and the desk. A day calendar lay open, and Art had written something in the space for July 1, 1965.

"Going home."

Eight more days, and Art would have been back on Cape Breton Island.

16

MY FINAL CONVERSATION IN MONTE PLATA
takes place on an empty sidewalk
with the sun just flattening on the
horizon. Rain threatens over tin roofs to the south, and a man is speaking to me in code. We've been talking for some time. This man, people told me, knows the story of Arturo. *He knows.* But all the man will talk about is "silent forces" and "dark acts," and no one seems to have a name. There's only "the lieutenant" or "that woman" or "Fulano."

He can see that I don't think much of it.

"You want names?" he says finally. As though I've called him a liar.

He's holding out his hand for my pencil and notepad. "For your personal archive," he says, and, carefully, pausing at times to stare into the clouds, he makes marks across two pages.

"Quickly," he says as he hands me his work.

He has written a list. At the top is the heading "Military and Police Involved at the Local Level in the Death of Arturo." A second section lists "Civilians." As I scan the ranks of the accused, he reaches again for the pencil and marks a series of slashes beside ten of the fourteen names.

"The dead," he says meaningfully.

How many times had I heard it said in my tours of the town? Ten times? A dozen? "A lot of cancer in Monte Plata." Always with a weighty nod, loaded eyes, perhaps a finger pointing to heaven. "They say," said one woman, "that if a person kills a priest, a curse falls on his family for generations."

The man is eager to go now. We shake hands and he walks away quickly, and I think of Jesús in the instant that I asked him how he could know there had been a plot against Arturo in Monte Plata. His strange smile. *Because this is a small town.* And then I think of the most famous of Dominican proverbs: Voice of the people, voice of God.

THE GUAGUA OUT OF Monte Plata starts from the base of the water tower, a muddy pullout where the kids are playing baseball. It's stickball, really, the batter swinging a piece of a two-by-four at a flattened water bottle. Ask them, though: it is the bottom of the ninth, two men on base, and these are the major leagues. The kids are always playing in the major leagues.

The bus fills and the cobrador leaps aboard and the engine rumbles to life. It takes me only a moment to realize we will pass the casa curial and then turn onto the Santo Domingo road. It's exactly the route Arturo drove on the night that he was killed. As we pass the parish house, I check the second-hand on my watch.

What is it like in that moment? The police are standing on your doorstep, and you know you are going to die. What do you think of then? Of yourself? Of your mother and father, your loved ones, receiving the phone call? Of the letters you had planned to write that evening and the appointments you will miss in the morning? Well, you stand up and you go. There's no time for grand gestures. You push your chair in at the table. You close the door of the casa curial. The walk from the house to the Land Rover. The electric lights on the plaza. The silent church. The fading sun.

The guagua rumbles through the bend, past the military checkpoint, the cemetery and finally the monument. I check my watch: three minutes. That's how long—a minute more, a minute less—it would have taken to drive from the casa curial to the killing field. The process that Jesús described, in which all of history resolves itself into a discrete moment in time, can also be seen in reverse. Those three minutes contain the secrets of Arthur's death. What happened within them decides questions of guilt and innocence, degrees of conspiracy and impunity, eternal mysteries of fate and consequence.

So little time.

The bus rattles and bumps through the familiar landscape and down to Santo Domingo, where I switch at sunset for the long ride to Kilometre Ten. The route, along Independence Avenue, is an undiffer-entiated backdrop of pharmacies, plaster apartment blocks, one-room shops, fast-food outlets, endless colmados. They are there, glittering, pumping with music and life, and then they are gone. Another blackout. Look for the star, Rosa told me. It's the logo of an American oil com-pany, illuminated even when everything around it is dark. It towers into the night sky, fixed, visible for miles. My stop is *la bomba,* the word that means both "gas station" and "bomb," and when I call it out, something in my pronunciation always seems to sow confusion. I try to sit near the driver and say the word softly.

The barrio is murmuring in the cool evening air, men playing domi-noes, a group watching Mexican soap operas in the corner colmado. I turn into my street, and Rosa calls out from the sitting room.

She asks about Monte Plata. All I can think to say is that I finally stood at the edge of the grave.

"Oh, I remember that day that Padre Arturo died," she says. "It was a black day. Black! Rain came down like someone had opened a seam in the sky." In her face I can see that she is there again, a young woman on the streets of Yamasá, and here comes the young man from the church, running, shouting the news. "*Ay!* My God!" she cries, and her face is drawn with the pain, but I can see, too, that she is concentrating. "I re-member I went not too far. To the plaza, and then I had to sit down."

She pauses, and her face has the same sad expression as when I gave her the photo of Padre Arturo. Once again I have the feeling there is something more she wants to say, some memory that is formless and just out of reach. "It meant something to me, you know," she says. "It meant something."

A few minutes later, she calls me from the bottom of the stairs. "San-tiago! Excuse me! Santiago!" The gracious voice of Rosa.

"I almost forgot to mention," she says as I appear in the open door-way above. "That man Wilson called again."

I step down to take a note from her hand, and I can feel her watching my eyes as I read. There's a phone number and a name. The mysterious Wilson. Sergeant Wilson of the National Police.

Part
TWO

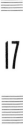

17

SOMEONE KEPT KNOCKING OVER THE crosses. The first had been a wooden crucifix propped in a jumble of rocks and flowers on the roadside, but the second was set in a block of cement. It, too, was broken apart. The crowbar was found discarded across the road from the house of Dionisio de los Santos, as if in defiance.

The midnight desecrations troubled Paul Ouellette. They were a reminder of things unspoken that surrounded the death of Padre Arturo. The investigation was his duty as regional superior, but there was more to it than obligation. The murder had unsettled his sense of justice, even his sense of the holy.

He had arrived in Monte Plata with the body, whirling down on the baseball diamond beyond the water tower, the people below uncertain whether to gather or scatter beneath the unfamiliar helicopter. All afternoon mourners streamed into town: priests from across the country; the Canadian nuns; caravans from Ocoa; the papal nuncio; even Bishop Tom Reilly, the American cleric who had himself been arrested and faced death in the hours after Trujillo was shot dead. Arthur lay in purple vestments on a U.S. Army stretcher in the sacristy. There, several members of the OAS Human Rights Commission explored the damaged body, even probing a wound with a finger. One of these scientists said, as he left the room, "This death is going to change the path of things."

The little church had filled, the people of Monte Plata looking around the chapel to see who had come to the funeral and who had not. When the service began, Father Antonio Sánchez, the Jesuit who had gone with Father John Gomes to the Marion hospital, stood before the crowd with his cassock cincture still stained with Arturo's blood. "This body brings us a message," he said. "It asks of us unity, peace, love. It asks of the Dominican people more love and less hate, more understanding and less vengeance. God has chosen this young priest as a holocaust, as a pure host to expiate so many crimes, to save each and every one of us." He turned to the Canadian priests and said, "To the Fathers of Scarboro I do not give condolence but congratulations. I congratulate you because you now have a martyr, a saint in heaven." The throng sang its cantos and psalms, and Arturo was lowered into a coffin, the simplest wooden box, really, and hardly wide enough to fit him. It was difficult to find a coffin in June of 1965.

The procession to the cemetery had passed beneath a frowning sky, and then the people of Monte Plata stood patiently on the roadway, out of the mud, as the gravediggers leaped into the hole to empty with buckets the water that had pooled from the rain and the sodden earth.

Finally the first soil was cast over the coffin.

"God will punish us for this," a woman in the crowd had said.

Now six days had passed, and still there was no shortage of mysteries. The side window of the Land Rover, for example, was starred and fractured, but not by a bullet. Did that suggest a struggle in the vehicle? No one who knew Arturo doubted that the young priest might have refused to go quietly. The two policemen could have lured him to the jeep claiming that last rites were needed, a spiritual emergency. Driving out of town, he would have smelled the booze on Martínez's breath; he would have wondered why Restituyo was out of uniform. A family in a house along the road had heard the men arguing as the jeep passed. People who lived near the crossroads, the crossroads that Arturo had never managed to reach, had heard even more—the jeep's engine roaring and then stalling, the raised voices of the men. Some said there was a single burst of gunfire; others thought they heard a blast followed by a single shot. After that, people said, the soldier Odulio de los Santos had appeared, coming in from the campo, running. He had vanished down the road. Moments later, he shouted; some said they had heard the words, "Hands up!" There was another round of gunfire, and then silence. A few minutes later, Odulio de los Santos was seen heading for the barracks.

Many people spoke darkly, too, of what had taken place earlier that day, in the afternoon. There had been gunshots then, as well, ringing out across the campo just ahead of the hours of siesta. Odulio de los Santos had been sent from the barracks to investigate—an investigation that happened to place him, alone and armed with a submachine gun, on the road outside Monte Plata just as Arturo and the two policemen approached in the jeep. Again and again the people of Monte Plata recalled that afternoon, those shots. It didn't seem to enter anyone's mind to dismiss them as coincidence.

Father Ouellette drove from Haina. He had a meeting with Odulio de los Santos. By now, the news reports would have spread the breadth of Canada. The first wire reports had got it wrong, of course. A "Joseph A. MacKinnon" had died, or an "Arthur H."; the priest had been killed for "harboring rebel fugitives" or "en route home on furlough" or in circumstances "not believed to be connected with unrest in the republic." Ouellette's own telegram asking the Scarboro society to deliver the news to the MacKinnon family had declared that Art had been "shot accidentally" by a soldier. At the time it had been all he could say.

How would the family be taking it? There was only one way. The mother, when she could speak, would want to know if her son had suffered. The father would say something like, "He didn't last too long, did he?" That was Cape Breton Island, a place where the deepest pains are felt in private. The brothers and sister, the friends and old colleagues—shock, anger, confusion, helplessness, powerlessness, incomprehension, grief. They would look to the Canadian government for answers. The secretary of state for external affairs, Paul Martin Sr., would stand up in Parliament, express the nation's regrets and promise a thorough investigation. The politicians wouldn't admit that the Canadian chancellery in the old Copello Building in the Zona Colonial had been occupied during the first week of the rebellion in Santo Domingo and was now the seat of the "revolutionary government." Canada's diplomats were meeting in houses and apartments and hotels, and it was a trick for them just to get three meals a day or a functioning phone line. No, the Canadian government was not going to come up with a hard-hitting report.

Paul Ouellette rolled into the capital and made his way to the army barracks known as the Transportation, alongside the baseball stadium.

The stadium was empty these days; the revolutions, the *coups d'état*, they didn't seem to happen in the baseball season.

Ouellette parked. It was never entirely comfortable to meet the secret police—the hated SIM had been renamed the J-2—but the captain who came to greet him was cordial. The officer agreed to let Ouellette see Odulio de los Santos, who was being held prisoner pending the outcome of the military's internal investigation, but said there was no private room in which they could talk. And what would De los Santos say with the J-2 listening in? Nothing. Ouellette suggested the meeting take place in his jeep, and the captain could see no way to refuse.

They brought out Odulio de los Santos.

He was not a hard-faced man; really, he was almost boyish. The armed guard walked the priest and the soldier to the jeep and then retreated out of earshot, but in any case De los Santos told his story readily. He began with the shots that had been heard in the campo. He had been sent to investigate, he said, but didn't find anyone or anything, and as the daylight faded he circled back, ending up on the road from Sabana Grande de Boyá. Beyond the crossroads, he saw a Land Rover heading toward him, fast, with the lights on. The jeep was zigzagging—he had to throw himself into a ditch to avoid being hit. Then the vehicle stopped and the engine roared, as if someone was trying to drive but the jeep was out of gear. It stalled. Two people jumped out on the driver's side, and a third ran around from the back of the jeep. Night was falling, and the headlights were twin bells of light on the road. He recognized the lieutenant, he said, but could see only that the other two men were in civilian dress, one slim and one heavy. The three were arguing, and then one of the civilians grabbed at the lieutenant. Odulio shouted, "What's going on?" and someone shouted back, "I'm the lieutenant!" and another voice cried, "Who cares if it is the lieutenant?" Suddenly the men were moving. If they were rebels, they would be deadly opponents in the dark. His soldier's training, his sense of duty to the lieutenant, told him what he needed to do.

He opened fire—a short round—and the fat man fell. The thin man seemed to be running for the ditch, and the lieutenant, too, was moving for cover. Odulio fired again, aiming for the civilian, and both men dropped to the ground. He realized then that he had emptied his submachine gun, a Cristóbal carbine. He knew the gun's serial number by heart.

He waited a minute, he told Ouellette, thinking that the lieutenant had thrown himself down to avoid the gunfire. Finally he realized that all three of the men were dead. The lieutenant still had his arms caught in the straps of his gun. It was a rifle, Odulio said, "an FAL rifle." The makes and models of the weapons didn't mean much to Paul Ouellette, but they seemed to mean a lot to the young soldier. Odulio picked up the lieutenant's rifle and found a pistol on one of the civilians—he didn't say whether he recognized Constable Ramón Restituyo—and then he walked toward his barracks, only a few hundred metres away. No one seemed to be coming to investigate. He remembered a boy on horseback, and a woman in the dark, and maybe other people, too, each asking what had happened. He told them he had just killed three people. At the barracks, he told his lieutenant what had happened, and they placed him under arrest. He'd been a prisoner now for a week.

Odulio de los Santos seemed frightened. Father Ouellette knew that the soldier was in danger—he could be locked away for good, or disappeared, or his family might hear that he had "died in an attempt to escape." Even if he was set free, he now had the families of three dead men to hunt him down.

De los Santos and Ouellette stepped out of the vehicle, and the priest watched the guard lead his prisoner to the stockade.

Ouellette saw problems with the soldier's story. He said he had told the people who lived along the road into Monte Plata that he had killed three men. Some of those people recalled the soldier saying that he had killed two, and three were dead. De los Santos described only two rounds of submachine-gun fire, fired from a distance, but even with his untrained eye Ouellette had recognized the powder burns around the wounds of Arturo's bladder and upper thighs; he had seen the small hole beneath the jaw.

The most troubling facet of the story was this: it was too perfect, too tidy. It was the only possible way to explain the killings in Monte Plata as nothing more than a regrettable accident. Odulio de los Santos had given Paul Ouellette a version of events that disavowed any hint of conspiracy or of orders being followed. It suggested a tragedy without sin.

Ouellette returned to Haina and typed up his notes for a report to the Scarboro headquarters in Canada. When he was finished, he added a covering note. "The Dominican Armed Forces is investigating, as also is the OAS and when their reports are made known, a prudent action will be taken." He was a man of faith, even in the fairness of the Dominican military and police. More, though, in Odulio de los Santos. He did not believe the soldier's story, but he did believe in the young man's innocence. He believed, even, that the appearance of Odulio de los Santos on that twilit road could be a divine providence, the gesture that would bring an obscured murder to the light.

18

SERGEANT WILSON HAS SOME NEWS about Odulio de los Santos. That, at least, is what he tells me when I call. He says only a few words, reluctantly. I will need to come to the police detachment in Yamasá, where he is stationed, and then he will say what he has to say. I still don't know how he got my phone number.

The morning guagua is making quick time. Holy Week enters its weekend tomorrow with Good Friday, and already the outbound lane from the interior is filling with Catholics bound for the beach.

There was a time, Rosa has told me, when the twin main streets of Yamasá, northbound and southbound, were quiet and carefully swept. She had been a kind of pioneer, a graduate of the Miss Key Beauty Academy in Santo Domingo and proprietor of Yamasá's first beauty parlour. Her hair was straight and high-stacked then, in the style of Jacqueline Kennedy, or of the stewardesses on Pan American Airlines. Rosa goes to Yamasá now and hardly recognizes her hometown, with its roaring motoconchos and air the colour of dishwater. I step off the guagua into it all and Daniel Berroa appears like a pop-up cartoon, smiling and patting the seat of his scooter.

"Let's go!" he calls out.

"I'm only going to the police detachment," I reply.

"You need a ride!"

"No. It's right there." The detachment sits on a rise where the main streets join. The whole town is a matter of a few blocks long.

"But you need breakfast!" he cries. I laugh and give in. He rides a loop through town, earning his fare, and finally stops at a fry-house to order grilled cheese and orange juice for two.

"I'll wait for you outside the detachment," he says when I've paid for us both.

"I'll be fine," I reply.

"I'll wait."

It's the first time I've seen his face so sincere and so serious. And does his back seem to stiffen as we wheel up to the detachment? He rolls through the knots of people talking under the shade tree out front, and I have to admit that I'm glad he is with me.

Not that the Yamasá police station is intimidating, exactly. It's a wood-slat house in an odd bright green that is totally unlike the official gangrenous cast of every other detachment in the country. I'm on the front steps when I feel a presence at my back. Sergeant Wilson. He's younger than I expected and soft, with birthday-boy hands and a round face beneath tight, wavy hair. He directs me into a bare concrete room lined with benches facing a desk. I stand until he asks me to sit down.

"Tell me," he says.

"What?"

"Tell me." He leans against the desk, his eyes both suspicious and uneasy.

"What I'm doing here?"

He nods, closing his eyes for long enough to remind me of a Taíno carving of a frog in a Santo Domingo museum. I am starting to explain myself when two more policemen step into the room, one thick, with raised lumps on his face, and the other all bones, a scarecrow, like a teenager. Which, in fact, he might be. The three men form a wall of black slacks, grey shirts, dark baseball caps with PN—*Policía Na-cional*—in gold embroidery.

"Your passport," says the man with the lumps, his sergeant's chevrons like matte gold trinkets on his collar.

"What kind of work do you do?"

"Why are you looking for Odulio de los Santos?"

"Where do you live? What hotel?"

Without knowing why, I pretend confusion at this last question. It is a delayed realization—that this is not a conversation but an interrogation. Interrogation implies a threat, and so I am duty bound not to admit where I live, which would involve Rosa, Juan, the Scarboro priests.

"I have an apartment at Kilometre Ten," I say, which is both honest and hopelessly vague.

The men look at each other; none of them knows the Kilometre Ten barrios, and they are not surprised that I can't recall the address. A name and a barrio are usually enough: Santiago the Gringo, Kilometre Ten. The officer with the lumps is losing interest. He introduces himself as Sergeant Telleria.

"Odulio de los Santos is dead," he says with a shrug.

"For how long?"

"Four years," says Telleria.

"Two years," says the scarecrow. Telleria scowls, and the younger man adds, "More or less."

"He was a soldier," says Telleria. "He lived in La Jabon. I know his brother, and you can talk to him—"

"That's perfect," I say.

"—on Monday. Ah, but it is the Holy Week. You can talk to him on Tuesday."

"It is not possible to talk to him today? I've come here all the way from the capital."

He shakes his head; the scarecrow crosses his arms; Wilson averts his eyes.

"What's the name of the brother?"

"Ramón de los Santos." Telleria says the words tentatively, like a confession.

"And where does he live?"

"In La Mina," says Telleria.

"In Los Jovos," says the scarecrow.

And then the meeting is over. We shake hands all round and I step outside and ask Daniel to drop me at the guagua stop for Santo Domingo. He drives across the street and lets me off beside a man with a sack of dried beans on the ground beside him. Until the moment I step up on the bus, every eye in the shade of the police yard is hotter than the midmorning sun.

It's still early afternoon when I make it back to the barrio.

"How did it go?" says Rosa, looking over her glasses with worry. She had been reading the Bible.

"Well, Odulio de los Santos is dead."

"Ah."

"But his brother is alive."

"And did you talk to him?"

"No."

"No," she agrees. It's the answer she expected.

"I talked to the police. Really, three policemen talked to *me*."

"They're afraid," she says. "The people are afraid." Sergeant Wilson had called that morning, she says, just after I left for Yamasá. They had talked a few minutes, and he had told her that the people were wondering why the nephew of the dead priest would turn up now, after so many years.

"The people," I repeat. "The people of Yamasá?"

She nods, her expression granting me pardon for striking fear into her hometown.

I thought back to my search for Odulio de los Santos. I had spent a single day on the back of a motorbike in the campo. I had left my phone number with one person, perhaps two. I had told just one family, in the hill country of La Cuaba, that I was related to Padre Arturo. And now the people of Yamasá—*the people*—are anxious and preoccupied. They are considering my mission, discussing the case outside the church, weighing its merits in the bakery, debating the possibilities of revenge at the edges of fields at nightfall, when the tarantulas take to the roads.

WILL I MEET THE BROTHER of Odulio de los Santos the following Tuesday? It depends on three police sergeants, the sincerity of my lies, the good word of the motoconcho drivers of Yamasá, the phases of the moon. In the meantime, at least, there is the List of Fourteen. I sit in a night like hot breath and study the names, four military men and ten civilians condemned by forty years of suspicion in the streets of Monte Plata.

A single family dominates the list: the Contreras clan. Five men of the family are listed; only two of them, brothers named Rafael and Porfirio, are said to be alive. Of the remaining civilians, only one is sure to be among the living. He is Romeo Santana. His father, Fabio Santana, is at the top of the list of the four military men. Fabio Santana was the army lieutenant in Monte Plata in 1965, and it was he who had sent Odulio de los Santos into the campo on the day of the killings; it was Fabio Santana's wife who had broken down in the church when Arturo cancelled the Corpus Christi procession. Most suspicious to me is the fact that no one was sent running to investigate that night when gunfire killed three men only a few hundred metres from the military barracks. But Fabio Santana, the army lieutenant, is dead.

The other military men on the list include Evangelista Martínez and Ramón Restituyo, of course. Oddly, Odulio de los Santos is not the fourth name. The final figure is a long-dead officer remembered only as Sergeant Santana.

I look for the names of the few survivors in the telephone directory; there are twenty-six possibilities for Rafael Contreras, half a dozen for Romeo Santana and so on. It is the Holy Week long weekend now, the days of crucifixion and resurrection, but these men will be retired and, perhaps, won't be joining the crowds on the beaches. The pews are never emptier than during a Holy Week Mass, said Joe McGuckin. You could hold a dance in any cathedral in the country.

I start dialling; an hour later, I'm exhausted. Each time a person answers the phone, I have to explain exactly who I am looking for: so-and-so, who lived in Monte Plata in 1965. No one ever replies simply, "That person doesn't live here." Instead, a pause, and then, "What is this about?" After a dozen conversations with strangers, I have not found a single one of the men I am looking for.

There is one other possibility—a man I think of as the fifteenth on the List of Fourteen. His name is Julio Gil Reyes, and his place in the story is unique. Julio Gil Reyes was the police lieutenant who initially led the arrests in Monte Plata. After Arturo's protests in Santo Domingo and San Isidro, Julio Gil was abruptly transferred out of town and replaced by Evangelista Martínez. Why was he sent away? Maybe because Evangelista Martínez was the kind of person who did the dirty work. Maybe because Julio Gil Reyes refused to do it.

There is only one Julio Gil Reyes in the phone book, and the man himself answers the phone and listens patiently.

"No, no, no," he says gently. "I am not that Julio Gil. I was never in the police. I am a lawyer." He reads my silence as disbelief rather than disappointment. "I've met this other Julio Gil. Only once—I don't remember where. He was a captain with the police, I believe. I believe he has died."

Another one dead. The believers in Monte Plata would nod at the constancy of heavenly wrath. There is a problem with a faith in supernatural justice, however. It exonerates the survivors.

"You might check at the fortress," suggests Julio Gil, the lawyer.

He means the Palace of the National Police, a place I haven't returned to since the day Roberto Santana whisked me into the private chambers of the chief of police, that hour when it seemed the mystery of Arturo's murder might be solved with a wink and a smile, the way a magician pulls a coin from a child's ear. Since then, I have lost that belief. The secrets of the past are not neatly typewritten into documents for safekeeping into the future. From the outset they are blurred into evanescence, a tatter of deliberate concealments, imperfect recollections, idle speculations, suspicions, impunities, lies. The power to obscure may be the most fearful on earth. I have seen it in the way that men, women, even children avoid the police. The sudden cast of a figure in black and grey can turn a lively street corner into a place where people walk with brisk purpose, eyes ahead, allowing not the faintest opening into their private worlds.

Now, however, circumstances have changed. I am known to the police. They have written out the strange sounds of my name, letter by letter, in the Yamasá detachment. They will file the report to their superiors in Santo Domingo. I have lost the anonymity to criss-cross the landscape like a ghost among ghosts.

There is, perhaps, nothing more to lose.

19

ARTURO HAD DONE EXACTLY THIS, WALKED into this open mouth. I was right about the stairs to the Palace of the National Police: it is impossible not to feel watched. Like a reminder of history, a black Volkswagen Beetle is parked at the base of the steps. But it couldn't be. The SIM hasn't existed for more than forty years.

Inside, the vaulted reception area shimmers with light from an enormous chandelier that would not look out of place in a ballroom. Here, of course, it does. At a window marked INFORMATION, an indifferent constable waves me toward a door marked PUBLIC RELATIONS, where a receptionist asks me to wait beneath a huge oil painting. It's an almost life-sized portrait of a pale Jesus, who cradles in his arms, without effort, the corpse of a fallen policeman. It takes me a moment to recall where I have seen the painting before: on television, where it forms the backdrop for press conferences at the fortress. I'm still absorbing the power of this propaganda when an ancient woman appears. She embodies everything that public relations is not meant to be: she is small, silent rather than quiet, with an impenetrable face that is touched with cruelty, the face of a murderer's mother. I follow her into a parody of bureaucracy, all stifling air and blank doors, the stale moan of air conditioning. Finally we are in the anteroom of some nameless colonel, where I explain for the third time today that I am a journalist looking into the case of a priest who died in Monte Plata; forty years have passed, ancient history, everyone long since dead, only I am trying to contact the families of two policemen, Julio Gil Reyes and Evangelista Martínez. If I could even get a message to them—

The bullish woman who hears me out disappears into the colonel's office long enough for me to decide that this visit was a mistake. When she reappears, she seems to agree.

"We don't have that kind of information," she says curtly.

"But this Julio Gil Reyes, he must have died only a few years ago," I protest. "He was a policeman all his life. He would have had a pension—"

"I'm sorry," she interrupts, "we have nothing." Her underlings begin to flutter, waving manila envelopes, shouldering me out of her view. The silent crone appears at my elbow like a bailiff at a sentencing.

It is then that a man in the room makes a signalling motion so quick that I wonder for a moment if he is waving away a fly. His eyes meet mine an instant later, and I wander in his direction as though I've forgotten the way to get out of the room. He moves into an empty cubicle, and I pause at its door. "Hello welcome," he says in English, then shifts to an incredibly rapid, whispered Spanish. I strain to keep up, all my life energy focussed on his words. The information I need is available, he is saying, it is on a computer system. "But you need a password, you need a friend on the inside, someone with a sincere heart, you understand? The information is there but it must be *hurtado*." I shake my head on the final word, and he says, *"Hay que robarla."*

It must be stolen.

As I open my mouth, he makes a throat-slitting motion. I can feel a presence behind me even before the old woman slips past and perches on the edge of the cubicle desk. The man hands me my notebook with a beaming smile. I hadn't noticed that he'd taken it.

"We talk again," he says in English and reaches out to shake my hand.

The woman leads me back to the entrance hall. Her eyes burn my back all the way down those long stairs, all the way through the parking lot. The Plaza of Culture is only three blocks away. There's a niche I know, lost among the fountains and the mango trees. Four benches and four white statues of the classical Furies. I choose Fire and finally open my pad. On the inside back cover are a phone number and a name.

IT IS THIRTY DEGREES that night, and the air is an endless cobweb. It is almost too much effort to lift the phone receiver and dial the number. Which might not be a very good idea anyway.

He answers in that same whiplash Spanish, his voice like marbles in a leather pouch.

"Hey, what's happening, how are you?"

"I'm all right," I reply.

"Okay, we have a big problem." We; that is, he and I. "The police here are very secretive, yes? You know something about the police in my country, right? You have some idea about the police in this country?"

"Yes, yes, I understand."

"Okay, so you understand things have to be done with some discretion."

"Yes."

He begins to talk about a computer database. It takes some time, some stupid questions from me, before I begin to understand: the system covers every citizen in the Dominican Republic and includes even the most confidential telephone numbers and addresses.

"Anybody. Whatever person you want, you know? You understand that to get information from the police can be—can be very expensive, right? But if you have a friend, like the one you made today, you understand? You can count on me, I can get what you want. I can give you the information—you know, like the journalists say? Off the record."

I have almost found something to say when he starts in again. "Because you saw that person there, listening to everything? The woman who was sitting there. You saw her? She wouldn't move for anything. You saw her?"

"Yeah, the old woman."

"The old woman, the one who wouldn't move for anything. She's a person who collects information to pass up to the top. It's bad. It's a bad scene. You understand now, right?"

"You couldn't speak freely."

"Exactly, I couldn't speak freely. Here, every mode of communication is watched. Almost every mode of communication is tapped."

So why are we talking like this on the phone? But I don't say it.

"You understand, Santiago?"

"I think so."

"'I think so'—you doubt it! You have to be sure! You know what I'm saying?"

"Yes." But really: no.

And now he's laying out the plan. No one else can know his name. No one. I will call him next week. When he answers, I will give him a location, nothing more—the location of a computer centre. He'll come to meet me and we'll access the database and find all the necessary information about these policemen, Julio Gil Reyes and Evangelista Martínez. Then we will find their families together, he and I. "Understand?"

"Okay."

"Just give me your location. Maybe say something like, 'Hey, I'm doing that work for the university,' and give me your location. I've got a motorcycle—small, but it works just fine. What's the saying? 'Less luxury, less attention.'"

And then he hangs up.

I peel my sodden shirt off my chest and let the skin breathe. On a fresh page in my notebook, I write the first name that pops into my head. Charlie. My anonymous new friend will be Charlie. I will start forgetting his real name as of this instant.

I need to make one more phone call.

"Hello?"

She sounds sleepy. "Yanira. How are you?"

"I'm just about to have a bath."

"Do you have half an hour if I come into town right away?"

"Something exciting?"

"I have a recording of a phone call that I want you to hear."

20

YOU CAN FEEL THE SUN BEFORE IT RISES. It's still dark as I walk the eight short blocks from the apartment to Independence Avenue, where the guaguas roar toward the centre of the city, but already the air has a shimmering heat. With the first light, everyone at the downtown bus ranks is saying that there won't be rain for a week, maybe more. It will be good for the mangoes that hang green in the trees on the road to Yamasá.

I ride the guagua all the way to the foot of the police detachment, but Daniel Berroa putters up anyway. He casts me a wounded look, as though crossing Yamasá on the bus was a kind of betrayal. Flowers fall through the dry air from the great shade tree; today, all of daily life will be lived along the paths of shadows and the breeze. Even the sergeants are outside. Wilson and Telleria greet me warmly, and I overhear Telleria chuckling as he tells a passerby about the De los Santos family's fears of four-decade-old revenge. The mood in Yamasá has changed.

Wilson disappears for a few minutes, then returns with an unmarked white Chevy Nova and waves to me to jump in. "You know the joke, Wilson?" I say. "About the Chevy *no va?*" The words in Spanish mean, "It does not go." Wilson tries not to laugh but ends up giggling with his chin to his chest. It's too true. The car looks as if it will make it to the house of Odulio de los Santos's brother only if the route is a downhill run. Wilson picks a cassette off the floor and pops it into the stereo, a merengue loud enough to prickle the scalp.

Telleria and a woman jump into the rear seat, and we rattle out of town on a road worn down to a bed of stones, passing the usual kaleido-

scope of palmwood and plaster homes—pink, yellow, peach, blue—
with their baseboards muddied by the force of recent rains. Wilson stops
and the woman gets out. "Wilson has a lot of girlfriends around Yamasá," says Telleria, and Wilson flushes paprika red.

"It seems there are more women than men in the republic," I say,
and Telleria nods. "Each man can have two *dominicanas*," he says seriously, like a man with respect for the law.

In the campito of Los Jovos we stop at a pink breeze-block house
where a shirtless boy at the curb shouts without waiting to be asked
"He's not here!" And that will be that, I suppose. Ramón de los Santos,
brother to Odulio, does not feel like talking today. It will be back to
Santo Domingo, and another trip to Yamasá tomorrow, or maybe the
tomorrow after that.

But Wilson drives on, the car jostling in time to the merengue. We
come to a small sign demarking La Mina and roll to a stop at a shuttered
bohío the colour of straw—a slumping shack, really, and probably a
century old. It isn't possible to make these sorts of structures any more;
to do so would require the wood of the royal palm, which rises bottle-
shaped above every other tree in the subtropical forest but can no longer
be cut down, under penalty of law.

"Wait here," says Wilson in the serious tone I remember from our
first meeting. He goes around the high side of the hut and reappears almost immediately, signalling that I should come.

Ramón de los Santos is sitting on the root ball of a tree. "Welcome to
the *conuco*," he says.

"It's beautiful," I reply, and it is—shady, with tropical birds tootling
in a garden of unfamiliar plants. Of course he would choose this place
to meet.

The conuco, with all its mythic weight. Its history goes back to the
Taínos, who cleared and cultivated these long, raised mounds and
whose crops and methods were adopted by the early Spanish settlers before the island was parcelled out to land barons and slavers and the
Taínos were lost to extinction. By the start of the seventeenth century,
the conuco again began to dominate the human landscape of Hispaniola. After a hundred years as the first colonial power of the New World,
the nation of Santo Domingo became a backwater, its collapsing sugar

mills forgotten in the rush to conquer the Americas. Left behind were a few thousand Spaniards and an estimated twenty thousand Africans, all of them slaves, freed slaves or the runaways known as *cimarrones*. The Africans moved, unchained, to the *monte*, the wildland of forests, mountains and empty beaches. A vestigial colony remained in the city of Santo Domingo, receiving its edicts from Europe, but in the monte the people built their bohíos, lived according to their own laws and survived on the wealth of their shifting conucos, the land·and the sea. It is the monte that gave Hispaniola its Creole culture of indigenous, African, Spanish and French traditions. Not even Trujillo dared to strip away the heritage of land for subsistence farming. The conuco defined the nation. A visitor asks: How did Santo Domingo end up like a forest, so lush with great trees? And the Dominicans reply: The people brought the campo to the city.

The conuco is family ground. Ramón de los Santos is careful to explain that the land we stand on belonged to his father, Estanilado, and the bohío was kept by his mother, Géneros, and to introduce his two sisters, Ángela and Catalina, who stand nearby. Then the three of them acknowledge every member of the family who couldn't be with us today, including the dead. The list ends with their brother Odulio.

Ramón is a ropework of muscle and bone, even beneath an oversized camouflage jacket and a short but full salt-and-pepper beard. He's wearing black leather gauntlets on his ankles, above his sandals. He leads the conversation but can't control it; his sisters weigh in, as do passing neighbours and the sergeants. Words fold over words, disjointed, going nowhere.

"Is there a photo of Odulio?"

This brings a moment of quiet, and then Ángela moves toward the bohío. There is, she says, a Mass card. We wait, the stillness broken by the ringing laughter of a cuckoo.

Ángela returns with the card cradled in her fingers as if it were made of sugar glaze. It dates Odulio's death as October 17, 1998. The photo is the grainiest imprint, a shroud of Turin.

"He didn't like to talk about it," she says as she looks down into her brother's face. "He didn't like to talk about it, because they tried to blame him, and he had courage. Because when he arrived, he found the padre dead, and then they wanted to pin it on him. He said that's not the way it happened."

Ramón repeats the essential fact: "The padre was already dead."

"Yes," Ángela confirms. "When he arrived he said, 'Hands up!' But what happened then? The men who had killed the padre confronted him, they shot at him. He jumped, and then he fired his machine gun. He shot them—he didn't know who they were. He fired, and he killed the men who had killed the padre."

She pauses, giving Ramón a chance to nod his agreement. "They shot at him, and like a good soldier, he shot back."

It's not the story Odulio told Father Paul Ouellette.

"No," says Ramón. "He didn't talk about it for a long time."

It is a simple, believable explanation, and yet even this version is cinematic. There is Odulio de los Santos, twenty-six years old and returning at sunset from a solo patrol to investigate gunfire in the campo of Monte Plata. He hears shots up ahead. Taking cover in the muddy fields, he closes in on the sounds of an argument. In the falling light, two armed men stand over a body. Odulio shouts an order at the men, and they turn on him and fire. He leaps, and in the same moment he takes aim and pulls the trigger, killing his attackers with a perfectly placed round. A professional soldier.

He went to jail, says Ángela. Not to one of the ugly holes like La Victoria or La Cuarenta—he was held at the Transportation, the armed forces compound in the capital. He passed six months there before his day in military court, when his name was cleared. Odulio was declared innocent. He had fired in self-defence.

"Was he afraid afterward?" I ask.

"Of course," says Ángela, "because he thought the families of the two policemen could kill him. He didn't know the two men he had killed, he didn't know their families. It was safer far away."

The armed forces had transferred Odulio to Dajabón, a town on the border with Haiti, as far from Monte Plata as a person can go without leaving the country. Ángela recalls that Father Paul Ouellette had made arrangements to fly him to Canada, but Odulio decided to stay. He spent thirty years in Dajabón, returning to the family ground in Yamasá only in 1998, to live out the final two months of his life. He was sick, already dying, and thinking about that evening in Monte Plata.

"He used to ask, 'Why did they send me alone?' Because in military rules of engagement, you don't send someone alone on a case in the night," says Ángela.

"But in that era, was it strange to send out a soldier alone?"

"Yes. And in a case like this one. Why?"

We are a circle of bowed heads; Ramón is exploring the earth with a stick. There is no answer to her question.

Sergeant Telleria pulls up then in the Chevy Nova—I hadn't noticed that he'd gone. His face is sombre, but with a suppressed excitement. "I have a better photo," he says. Even Ramón stands up and raises his eyebrows. We gather around a sepia image of two soldiers. Ángela covers her mouth with a hand and points to the figure on the left. Odulio stands at attention in a helmet and combat uniform, one hand behind his back and the other on a rifle.

"A Mauser," says Wilson.

"Five shots only," says Telleria.

"A range of two kilometres," adds Wilson.

The two sergeants keep talking. It wasn't a Mauser that Odulio was carrying that night in Monte Plata. No, then he was armed with a Cristóbal carbine, a Dominican-made submachine gun. There were two ways to fire the Cristóbal. Pull the forward trigger and the weapon fired single shots. Hold the rear trigger and the gun was fully automatic; you could empty the magazine, up to thirty rounds. You had to define your situation.

I'm only half listening, looking into the face of Odulio himself. He is trying without success to appear stern. He seems gentle, decent, a little uncomfortable at having his picture taken, like a boy who's still surprised to be a soldier, like a man who hasn't yet lost his fear of the dark.

CHARLIE DOESN'T WAIT for me to call. The phone rings at the apartment in Santo Domingo just after nine o'clock the next morning, and he asks me for a location. I suggest a computer centre about a dozen blocks from the police fortress.

"Ten o'clock," he says, and hangs up.

I arrive at our meeting place just in time to watch Charlie's motorcycle drop out of the crush of traffic. He is shorter than I remembered, but more powerful, too, a tight black shirt pulling across his chest. His smile when he sees me is wide and sincere. "He's too interested," Yanira had said when I played her the recording of my first phone conversation with Charlie. "Watch for signs that he might be secret police." If he is, he isn't keeping it a secret. He's wearing police-issue pants and has a motorcycle helmet tucked under one arm. No one but the police wears a helmet in Santo Domingo.

Everyone stares as the cop and the gringo walk into the computer centre and sit down to share a carrel.

The information I need is on a password-protected web site, Charlie explains in his machine-gun Spanish. His fingers stab at the keyboard and—he can't find the system address. "Just a minute," he says. He gets up and calls his office and openly explains that he is trying to access the database but has forgotten the digital address. By the time he returns, I've found the site myself. He punches the air. "Yes!" he says in English.

He types in his password. It fails. Again he tries, and again, and then he's back on the phone, this time publicly trying to get his password for a confidential site so that he can, as everyone in the room now knows, give it to the waiting gringo. Is it all just an elaborate sting operation? Maybe every other person in the room is a cop.

Charlie looks deflated. "I can't get the password today," he admits.

Outside on the street, the roar of the traffic is a relief. Charlie lingers, so I ask him where he learned his smattering of English. There are *cocolos* in the family, he says. It's something that people are only beginning to say with pride. The original cocolos were former slaves from British colonies like St. Kitts and Nevis in the Leeward Islands; they came to the republic around the end of the nineteenth century, looking for paying work in the plantation economy that boomed after the cane fields of Cuba were abandoned during its war of independence, which began in 1868. The new sugar refineries were the nation's first engines of industrial capitalism, and the Dominican campesinos had no desire to be the blood on the gears: they had their conucos; they had the freedom of the monte. Instead, the cocolos—the origins of the word are still a mystery—were enticed to sail over in coffin ships to fill a system of indentured labour. Some of their grandchildren and great-grandchildren still speak English and attend the Protestant church, and the cocolos are finally being accepted as a part of the national culture. The cane fields, however, maintain their dubious inheritance. There is still nowhere more impoverished, more broken and forgotten, than the shanties of the bateys, and the people who live in them are still disdained as *negros*. The difference is that the cane-cutters are no longer cocolos. Today, they're Haitians.

"This guy you want to know about, this Julio Gil," says Charlie. "Did he kill somebody?"

I realize that I have explained almost nothing to Charlie, that it's my turn to tell my story. Almost immediately, I make a mistake: I say that Arturo was my uncle.

"Your uncle?" he cuts in.

"Yes."

"Never tell that to anyone," he says. "Never let anyone know you're a relative of the dead padre."

"Yes," I say. "The people are scared."

"Very scared." He moves to put on his helmet. "We'll talk next week."

I watch him pull into the demolition derby of Santo Domingo, then I return to the computer centre and dial Yanira's number on a pay phone. She picks up right away.

"I survived my meeting," I say. This had been her plan. I would call when the meeting was over; if I didn't call before sundown, she would go to the embassy with my tape recording of Charlie.

"And?" she says. "Do you think he's secret police?"

"I don't think he's secret police."

"No?"

"I think he's a fool."

That bright laugh. "Did you get the information you wanted?"

"No," I say, "he had forgotten his pass code." We're both laughing now. "I'll meet him again in a week."

"Well, be careful," she says, her voice regaining an edge. "Fools can also be killers."

21

I'M NOT SURE WHY I AM GOING TO Dajabón. How did it happen? I woke up before dawn and—I left. The air was thick, and there were neither street lights nor stars. Everyone had been wrong about the rain. It was back. It had come back like a grudge.

It rains the length of Duarte Highway, and the fields are quicksilver in the farms of the Cibao Valley. We turn west there, on the outskirts of Santiago de los Caballeros, the second-largest city in the republic and a place with the look and feel of some imagined principality of Creole cowboys. The arid savannah that leads west to Monte Cristi is a sodden plain. The final stretch of road, a straight southern run through thickening scrub, is a route that many people refuse to drive by night. Even in the mist, the bus driver stands on the gas until the sides of the bus shimmy and woof in the wind.

Finally we see the cockfighting club and know that the trip is almost over. The usual pharmacies, colmados, hole-in-the-wall restaurants and cheap hotels—a typical Dominican town, except that the streets are nearly empty. Almost miraculously, the rain has stopped. I've crossed the entire country, and it's still early afternoon.

I flag down a motoconcho and ask for the local military barracks.

The fortress turns out to be just east of the town, on a hill high enough to look out on a pattern of rooftops. It's the largest army camp I've seen outside those that surround the capital, and the front gate is well guarded. The sentries remember the name Odulio de los Santos, but as a distant memory. They're a breed of soldier I haven't seen before in the republic—hardened frontliners. They wave me through, and the motoconcho driver is glad to be free to leave.

The same kind of toughs, armed with submachine guns, stand outside the plaster archway of the fortress itself. They watch my approach, and I keep my hands in the open. The men nod a greeting.

"I want to speak with someone about a soldier who used to work here."

One of the soldiers shifts to a position more at ease. His manner is helpful, friendly even, as he hears me out. Then he turns to the others and says, "Odulio de los Santos."

They're taking an interest now, dropping their poses. They speak over top of one another.

"He was here—"

"—haven't seen him—"

"—a reservist—"

"—it's been years."

By the time he left Dajabón, Odulio was no longer on active duty. "It's a young man's army," says my friendly soldier with a shrug. "Even the lieutenant wouldn't know him."

"And what do the soldiers do in Dajabón?" I ask.

"The border," says the sentry. He draws a line across the western horizon with an upturned palm. Just then a metal door jerks open behind us, and out of it a man appears, blinking in the day's grey light, his clothes almost rags, his boots caked with dried mud. His hands are bound behind his back. The prisoner's face is stupefied, with the loose-hanging flesh of a person who has been too long without sleep. A guard gets him moving with a shove; the man staggers and the sentries laugh. "A Haitian," one says to me, as if to let me in on the joke. The man is almost certainly an illegal immigrant, the orange crust on his boots from the mud flats of the Massacre River, which marks the northwestern frontier between Haiti and the Dominican Republic. It is easy to assume the river takes its name from the slaughter in 1937, when Trujillo's soldiers murdered Haitians who were swimming and wading the river to escape the genocide. In fact, the blood in the water is older still; the name dates from a colonial-era battle between Spanish soldiers and French buccaneers.

I leave the soldiers to their work and walk the quiet suburban streets back to the heart of Dajabón. And then, a few blocks onward, I see the crowds. There are soldiers here, too, pacing the perimeter of the mob, their sleeves rolled up over popeye forearms and coils of siphon hose or wire in their hands. Beyond them, tarps are strung in mad designs through the streets, like the tattered sails of some eccentric schooner. The tribe beneath them is unfamiliar, men and women with skin like the smoothest dark chocolate who shout and leap and laugh with an explosive immediacy, and in the next instant are speaking in the roundest, most dignified tones about the quality of the legumes heaped in mountains in front of them. They speak in Creole or the most rudimentary Spanish. It's a Haitian market. Less than two months have passed since the president of Haiti, Jean-Bertrand Aristide, begged for international support against a coup by exiled soldiers; troops from the U.S., France and Canada arrived as soon as Aristide was deposed. Haiti is an occupied country, with a military instead of a government.

There are Dominicans in the marketplace too, of course—the whole of Dajabón, it seems. Some of them goad the foreign hawkers, but mostly they buy. The prices speak to life on the Haitian side of the border. For the price of a single pineapple from a street cart in Santo Domingo, I buy eleven peppers, three red onions, fifteen small tomatoes, a dozen cookies and a pineapple.

"Hey, white boy." A young woman leaning against the rolled-down hurricane shutters of a storefront. "You speak Spanish?"

"*Más o menos,*" I reply. More or less. She smirks at my accent and says, "Say *perro.*" I fail, as usual, to roll my *r*'s. "Say *vidrio.*" She runs me through *carro, terremoto, cristal, desafortunadamente.* I wait for *perejil,* the word for parsley, the word that decided the life or death of who knows exactly how many ethnic Haitians in this corner of the world in 1937. It's not an easy thing to say.

But now she is laughing. She's a small woman with sarcasm in her face, an expression dissonant with the tight, royal-blue T-shirt emblazoned with a leaping Winnie-the-Pooh. She's wearing jeans that can only have been bought in Santiago or Santo Domingo.

"Santo Domingo," she replies.

Her name is Aída, formerly of the capital city and now a volunteer with the Civil Defence. She saved her first life during Holy Week, pulling a man out of the path of a car. She had been assigned to the highway, a tough job in a week when drivers travelled at outlaw speeds and presidential campaign rallies lined the roadways, jamming traffic. More than forty people died. Political martyrs of a kind.

Aída asks me why I'm in Dajabón, and her face is serious as I explain the story of Odulio de los Santos. "We're not so different, you and I," she says. She, too, has followed the dead to Dajabón. Two friends were shot and killed here, she says; friends who were more like brothers. They had been soldiers. "One was hit here," she says, sinking a fingertip into the meat of her neck, "and one here." She touches her temple.

"But how?" I ask, puzzled. "Was there a battle?"

"It happened on the line," she says, and, like the soldier at the fortress, gestures to the border. Now she's following in her friends' footsteps. The Civil Defence is her stepping stone to the armed forces.

A question is forming in my mind, but I haven't yet found the words. Instead, I ask her if she knows the history of Dajabón.

"No, not much."

"About the massacre of the Haitians?"

A wraith passes over her face, a cloud shadow. "Not much."

"You don't know about Trujillo and—"

Yes, of course, she says impatiently, thousands of Haitians were killed here, even children, and women were raped and then butchered. But that is neither the beginning nor the end of the story. When did the French slave leaders first go to war against the Spanish on Hispaniola? In 1794. From whom did the Dominicans seize their independence in 1844? From the Haitians. Who can claim that the Haitians are not also capable of murder? In fact, they are more than capable. It was Haitians who killed her two friends as they patrolled the borderlands. Two more soldiers dead because not even the Haitians can live in their own godforsaken country.

"But the soldiers kill Haitians, too, no?"

"It's a bad thing," she says, dismissing the thought with a hand. "Let's talk about something else."

On the streets around us the number of soldiers has doubled, forming a line that presses slowly westward. The market day is ending, and the vendors grumble as they tie up their bundles, take down their tarps, move back toward the border and the bleakness of Haiti. It's a routine. The soldiers yell at some of the Haitians by name, and there are rituals of resistance and outrage, sometimes even laughter. But if the shouting and cajoling fails, there are the lengths of siphon hose, the lashes of wire.

"Why do you want to join the army?" I ask at last.

"Truthfully?" She searches my face with her eyes, drawing out a long pause. *"Venganza."*

"What?"

"Venganza."

I locate the word in my memory: revenge. "I want to work the line," she says, "to avenge my two friends."

For a moment I find myself speechless. She leans back against the shuttered gate, a young woman in a Winnie-the-Pooh shirt who is out for an eye for an eye, studying my reaction with the expression of a person who has asked herself all of the questions she knows I'm about to ask.

"Isn't it better to forgive?" That this is what finally comes out of my mouth is a surprise, it seems, to both of us.

"Give me your advice," she says.

I stare out into the market. The soldiers are pushing past us now with urgency, in part because the heavy cloud has abruptly turned the afternoon into early evening. The Haitians' faces are despairing, as though crossing the Massacre River is like falling from purgatory into a darker place. I find myself telling again the story of Padre Arturo, and I realize that it has changed; that there is, for me, no longer any question of a tragic accident. Rather, I am seeking the particulars of a crime, the guilt or innocence of faceless colonels and generals, of Evangelista Martínez and Ramón Restituyo and Odulio de los Santos, of fourteen men condemned in whispers and written into my notebook by a man who spoke in code. Somewhere in the midst of it all, I admit that Arturo was my uncle.

"Aha!" exclaims Aída. "We're not so different, you and I!"

"No, no!" I retort. "I'm only here to forgive." Am I? "My family, we have forgiven everyone." Have we? "We only want to understand. We only want to know the truth."

She is shaking a finger at me, grinning her sweet, malicious grin, believing and disbelieving, empathetic and dubious. Are you really so pure, white boy? Did you chase a ghost to Dajabón only to find the truth? Why do you need to know who killed your uncle? Why do you need their names? You say you have already forgiven them, so what more do you need from them now? I am sputtering against her accusations when suddenly she says, "You know they tried to kill me, too."

It was not so long ago. She had come home from a party on a Friday night and gone upstairs to her rented room in a Dajabón house. She was stripping for bed when she decided to turn on her computer and write a letter. I can see it exactly. The blue light on her dark teak skin, her bra seeming to glow. The light would be just enough that, when she sensed the presence in the room and turned, she could see the whites of the man's eyes and a stripe of reflection off the metal bar in his hands. He swung at her then. She cried out and fell from her chair, and was amazed to find she hadn't been hit. As she scrambled out the door of her room, her attacker seemed to be struggling, and in the next moment she realized he was caught in the mosquito net that hung over the bed, invisible in the dim light. On her run for the front door she registered, in glimpses and outlines, two other figures in the house, and then at last she was out, screaming, standing barefoot in the dirt of the street, the barrio coming alive around her, and she knew that the sons of bitches, the three fucking sons of Haitian whores, would already be running for their lives.

"The Haitians here are rebels, cheats, thieves," she says, locking eyes. "I want revenge. I want to work the line."

She has taken the high ground of raw experience, and I am, anyway, still reeling from her assault on my sense of my own mercy. In the next instant that feeling is transformed, and I am overwhelmed by a deep desire, almost a desperation, to draw her away from her oath. I have the image in my head of this woman in the moment of her vengeance; worse, I see her dying, murdered. I see the Winnie-the-Pooh shirt purple with blood.

"This country has a problem with revenge," I say, and she crosses her arms across her chest. I tell her more of the story, about Odulio de los Santos living in dread and exile for the rest of his adult life, able to return to his family, themselves still fearful despite the decades that have passed, only when he carried his own death within him in the form of some fatal illness. I speak about the hateful silence, the bitterness without end, the warnings that forty years is not long enough to wait to start asking questions.

"You might be right," she shrugs, "but I have a hard heart. It hurt me, it hurt me a lot, when my friends were killed." She reads my face. "Now you're afraid of me. Don't think badly of me, Santiago." I can see, though, that she is enjoying my discomfiture, showing off a little. She shows me the scar on her pinky finger from a fist fight. She says, defiantly, that she is not afraid to go into the fields outside the town at night, and when I seem unimpressed she tells me the rumours—that at night the frontier is stalked by Haitian zombies and the *bien-bienes*, the ghost-souls of escaped slaves. It isn't the bandits that keep people from driving the straight run to Monte Cristi by night. No, the bandits are the least of people's fears.

I can see the hardness in her face now, and by the time she has flexed a biceps I have already realized that she is muscular, her flat pectorals broadening from her breasts to her shoulders. I can imagine her as one of the soldiers who are fading now down the streets, their sleeves rolled up to draw the eye to the rolls of hose in their hands. The Haitians are moving to President Henríquez Street, named for one of the two consecutive presidents who resigned rather than wholly submit to the American occupation of the republic in 1916. From there, they are herded across the bridge between the two worlds of Hispaniola.

Aída takes me gently by the elbow and walks me through the empty streets to the plaza. "Don't think badly of me, Santiago," she says. "I have a hard heart, that's all."

I TAKE A LONG, long road back to Santo Domingo, rolling off the highway on the back of a motorcycle to ride across a near desert to the coast. My goal is Punta Rusia, one of the forgotten beach towns with not quite the right sand, not quite the jewelled reef to attract the all-inclusive resorts that have risen like some new empire from the palm forests of Punta Cana and Puerto Plata. It is a place where an old man on his mule might still raise a hand in silent greeting, not wanting to disturb the cheroot between his lips. The motoconcho driver drops me there, but he suggests I walk on to Playa La Enseñada, the beach where the June 14 rebels invaded against Trujillo in 1959 and were slaughtered. It was in many ways the beginning of the end for the dictatorship, a confluence of misfortune and hope.

"There were Cubans, yes?"

"Well," he replies, "the Cubans wore red, so the army killed everyone who wore red. The problem was, the Dominicans, they were also wearing red."

The trek to Playa La Enseñada follows a tidal flat the colour of weathered wood and dotted with brown pelicans and the hurrying shadows of shorebirds. The beach itself is at the edge of a shallow, soupbowl bay lined with empty stalls that during Holy Week would have dispensed crates of cold beer, platters of fried fish, basket upon basket of deep-fried johnnycakes and plantain chips. Even today, with only a few visitors wading in the Atlantic, two beach shacks boom, one bachata, one merengue. At the northern tip of the sand a faint trail leads into a jungle hung with blue orchids and starred with red flowers. It is a perfumed forest, spiced and floral, and the intense odour adds to the disorientation caused by the endless chittering, the constant tiny motions, of land crabs reeling toward their burrows.

I continue onward, by foot, by motorcycle over roads so rough they cause my stomach to cramp, and then by guagua, público, motoconcho again to a stream that I wade across. Walking once more, a dirt road between men digging yuca roots in a golden valley, until yet another motor scooter rolls to a stop and a man on his way to deliver a half-dozen eggs says, "Hello, let's go." We ride to a river, and it is only my new friend, Juan Carlos, who sees the boatmen asleep on the far bank. "Come on, move your asses!" he shouts, with a smile in his voice. The men rise with neither resentment nor hurry and pull their yola across the river on a line. We climb in, crouching on the seats to keep our feet out of the water that flows through the bottom of the boat, the boatmen somehow able to load even the motorcycle. The skiff is like a bank-side wreck, permeated with silt and the colour of mud, but it is lively in the current, and Juan Carlos says, "Columbus explored this river in little boats from the *Pinta*." I see no reason to disbelieve him. The Bajabonico River is only a few minutes' ride from the far shore to the ruins of

La Isabela, the second of Columbus's colonies in his New World, and on the point where the captain's home is believed to have stood we marvel instead at a *guayacán,* a gnarled, salt-pruned tree that is said to be 511 years old.

Onward again to the main roads, where we say goodbye as I realize Juan Carlos is now hours away from delivering his eggs. A guagua whisks me to Santiago, where men from the silvered valley of Cibao wear holstered pistols as they run their errands and where students and young lovers gather to debate democracy and contraception on a hill overlooking the city, a hill capped by a monument lit by a dozen coloured lights, the monument still capped by the figure of Trujillo in gold; and where I meet a street prophet named Manolo, who wears a panama hat and an aloha shirt and a large, grey, bohemian beard. He speaks a perfect, poetic English laced with words like "meandering" and "salutations," and he takes notes as I explain that I am looking for the truth about the murder of a priest by the Dominican armed forces in 1965.

"What you are doing," he says finally, "is using history as a weapon, no?" His expression makes, in a subtle way, the same accusation as Aída's wagging finger, only this time I don't deny it. "You are telling the story of our country, and you need to be careful. There are places where you would ask these kinds of questions and you would disappear. Colombia, Mexico, Guatemala—maybe you would disappear. I think you can ask these questions here, now. But be careful."

22

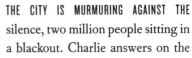

THE CITY IS MURMURING AGAINST THE silence, two million people sitting in a blackout. Charlie answers on the fourth ring and speaks for a minute or more without taking a breath. I can't keep up with a word that he says.

"Well, do you have any new information?" I interject, to bring him to a stop.

"You didn't hear me? You weren't listening? I have something on the one guy. Evangelista. No—the other one. I forget his name."

"Julio Gil. Julio Gil Reyes."

"Yeah. But he's dead."

"I know he's dead. The information you have, does it say where he used to live?"

Some banging and the sound of hands thrashing through paper. "Shit!" Something rolling off a desk. "There aren't any lights here. You going out tonight?"

"No."

"I'll call you when the lights come on."

The lights don't come on that night.

IN THE NEIGHBOURHOOD known as Little Haiti, men and women squat behind produce laid out on tarps and hiss *"Garçon!"* as if it were a crime to speak in French. Down alleyways I see the Haitian *taptaps,* like the Dominican guaguas but covered in carved and painted wood panels, voodoo symbols of protection, declarations in the name of the gods or God or the saints or the Virgin. Somehow these sagging caravans made it over the scarified mountains of Haiti and passed into the new world of Santo Domingo, and now to look at a taptap is to be standing once more in Port-au-Prince, breathing in the air that tastes like soot and sewage, hearing the endless arguments that pit the miserable against the desperate, retiring at the end of the day to a house like an anthill in a mountain of garbage. Yet everyone is waiting for the day when someone will appear and polish a spark plug or wiggle a wire and the engine of a taptap will wheeze back to life, a miracle, and it will finally and truly be time to go home.

"Garçon! Níspero!" whisper the vendors. Of all the rare fruits of Hispaniola, from the *guanábana* to the *ʒapote,* the níspero might be the most precious. It looks like a baked potato; it tastes like a pear soaked in rosewater syrup. No one can afford the níspero this year, the hawkers say, and so the presidential election is already decided. When the people can't afford the níspero, the government is bound to change.

EVENING AGAIN, hot and cloying. I dial Roberto Santana. He returns my call within half an hour.

"So, you are ready to talk to some generals," he says.

"Yes."

"General Imbert is on your list."

"Yes."

"You have an article that says he ordered an investigation into the case of the padre."

"Exactly."

"I will see what I can do. And then there is General José Cruz Brea."

"Yes."

"He was involved in the investigation?"

"Yes."

"He could be difficult, he could be very difficult. He is hiding. Was there another?"

"General Elías Wessin y Wessin."

"Ah, Wessin. He could also be a problem."

JUAN AYALA STEPS OUT onto the small patio at the bottom of the steps leading up to my apartment. He stretches his arms into the dawn and declares that it will be the kind of day when the heat makes you feel you're being pecked to death by birds. "I love the sun," he says.

"And what will you do all day?" I ask.

He chuckles. "All day I'll listen to politics on the radio." The election is less than a month away.

"Is it true that Wessin y Wessin has his own political party?"

"It's run by one of his sons now. One of the small parties—there are dozens of them. It's a good business. They sell themselves to the larger parties."

"How's that?"

"They sell their votes. A larger party will pay a smaller party a sum of money, and then the smaller party declares its support for the larger party. Any vote cast for the small party will be counted for its buyer."

"And that's what Wessin's party does."

He makes an indefinite movement with his head; it's impolite to speak with such precision.

"What's the name of his party?"

"It's the yellow party," Juan replies, trying to think of the name. "Ah! The Quisqueyan Christian Democratic Party."

I'VE BEGUN TO recognize the faces on El Conde. Not just the businessmen who stand outside their shops, but also the people who have turned the street itself into a livelihood. Unofficial tour guides who complain the world has become so afraid of itself that the tourists refuse to leave home; the portrait artist who draws every face the same, changing only the hair and the clothes that frame that mysterious, immutable visage; the man who calls himself Leave Me To Dance Alone and dresses like a Brooklyn bohemian and panhandles every gringo with the story of his deportation from New York. Then there is the man who is forever surrounded by garbage-eating dogs, the ones known as *viralatas*, spare cans, which look up and seem to understand him as he speaks. And of course there are the fruit sellers, the best-smelling men in the city and forever being followed by bees. The fruit sellers on El Conde were once notorious caliés, and perhaps they still are. The gossip of the city inevitably makes it way to the place with the sweetest pineapples, the most delicate mangoes.

In a telephone centre, I sit down with a phone book and the List of Fourteen. An hour later, still nothing.

JUAN WAS RIGHT about the heat, and Yanira refuses to meet until sundown. I wait on her landlord's patio until she emerges from the darkness behind the house. "I thought we might go to the book fair," she says.

We cross the university campus, where there was a riot a few weeks earlier to protest inflation. A few tígueres set fire to a car that was parked in the street; it turned out to belong to a man who was visiting his wife, a patient with cancer at the oncology institute that had once been the Marion hospital. But the campus is at ease tonight, with cheers sending up from the bleachers around the baseball field.

The book fair is on the grounds of a music academy. While the fair has officially opened, there is the sense that we have stumbled on a circus setting up in the night, strings of lights joggling into place, the walls of a false battlement—the police exhibit—rising through the palms. There are tables selling old Mexican comics, books on the healing powers of melon, pocket Bibles, tomes on the various defences against the evil eye, a collection of Haitian children's stories. The communists have a stall hung with tapestries of Castro and Che Guevara.

"Look there," says Yanira.

She's pointing to a stall done up in red and black, and then I see the banner: THE BALAGUER FOUNDATION. It's staffed by a young tough with acne scars and sunglasses. "It must be the moonlight that bothers his eyes," says Yanira with a sly smile. The waning moon is nothing more tonight than a sliver, a machete's edge catching the sun.

"Let's see that letter," she says, a little wearily, I think. It is a note to introduce myself to General Wessin y Wessin, and Yanira has promised to ensure that it bows and scrapes deeply enough without faltering over the language. *"Distinguished señor, I direct myself to you today in order to ask your generous cooperation with regard to the following matter . . ."* She makes a few pencil scratches and is almost finished when her mobile phone rings. She walks away and talks for a long while, returning with an apology and a face marked with distraction. We carry on, descending into a market of used books spread over tables and under tarps.

"We are friends, right?" she asks suddenly. "And as a friend you are interested in my life?"

"Of course."

Her voice is gentle enough, but the question has left me shaken. It's a reminder, softly stinging, that a world is going on outside my vanishing perspective, which now looks only backward, and that in that world a person, a young woman, for example, might simply be living in the here and now. Listening, I finally learn something of the private world of Yanira, her dreams and her wounds. The past is important, but the past is not where you find true love or a decent job; all the talk of history has yet to raise the dead or even turn the lights on every night. A decade of peace and democracy has passed. Was this the culmination of a century of sacrifice? Bankers and investors in Geneva and New York City who smiled on the increasingly unregulated markets that made the republic one of the world's fastest-growing economies? Now a full 50 per cent of Dominicans, more than four million people, share less than half the amount of income that flows to the richest 10 per cent. The world watches in awe and pity as boatloads of refugees risk their lives to flee chaos in Haiti or poverty in Cuba, but not much is said of the thousands of Dominicans who do the same. And those, like Yanira, who have a better chance—they wonder how to transcend the psychology of poverty without abandoning the poor; how to find love and family that is not a fetter to the rooms of some suburban apartment; how to sustain hope for the nation without fading into exile. She imagines life in Amsterdam or Madrid or in a travelling circus; she remembers standing on the empty shore of the Bahía de las Águilas, where she could convince herself that the story of Hispaniola had only begun to be written. "Places that are free," she says, "I love places that are free."

We have ended up on a bench in the shadows, our bodies crosshatched by pallid light through the leaves of a black canopy. We sit at the edge of a limestone sinkhole where, tomorrow, merengue and bachata will reverberate off rock walls flooded with strobes and a tangle of bodies will dance, drink, lose themselves. For tonight, the pit is only an oracle, breathing cool air from the earth. And when the night is growing long we walk back across the campus, almost empty now, to the bus ranks. We are wondering, I think, how two people say good-night when they have bared a glimpse of their souls.

Yanira says my name softly and I turn. She's pointing down the road, where a set of headlights is swinging from the curb. "Isn't that your guagua?" she says.

THE OFFICE OF THE Quisqueyan Christian Democratic Party is a calendula-yellow house on Bolívar Avenue, the boulevard of political dreams. It's clever, this use of *quisqueya*. The roots of the word are unclear, but it was probably the term used by the Taínos on the north of the island to describe their territory. Through the queer machinery of history, the Taínos have been granted a posthumous nobility, and "quisqueya" has come to mean the land itself, the most essential, most original nature of all things Dominican.

In the reception room, a kind-faced older woman sits at a desk beneath a black-and-white portrait of Elías Wessin y Wessin in his prime. In his suit and black-rimmed glasses, he could be a nuclear engineer from some 1960s newsreel.

"Is this the party founded by General Wessin y Wessin?" I ask, aware that the question is a stupid one.

The woman nods reverently. I show her the letter I have for the general and ask if she might be so kind as to tell me his mailing address. The question seems to startle her, and she confers with several different men in the room. Heated opinions are exchanged. A man appears on the walkway outside who has the power to decide the perplexing question. He turns to me and says, "Number Fifty-one, corner of Bolívar and Uruguay."

The address sounds oddly familiar. "It is very close to here?" I say, and the heads in the room bob supportively.

Well, then: my letter will be hand-delivered. I walk along Bolívar Avenue; it is a ghetto of political headquarters, white, green, red, blue, each of their walkways littered with pink flowers from the trees that line the road. At last I check my map—I seem to have passed the corner of Bolívar and Uruguay. I backtrack, finally spotting Uruguay Avenue and, in the same instant, realizing that I am once again in front of the offices of the Quisqueyan Christian Democratic Party. I scan the surrounding buildings for number 51. It is the yellow house itself.

The kind-faced woman is in her seat beneath the portrait. "I don't understand," I say. "The address for General Wessin y Wessin is the same address as this building?"

"Yes," she says, reaching out a hand without a trace of embarrassment. "We will bring the letter to him."

LATE AT NIGHT I reach Charlie.

"I have the information," he blurts. "It's all here. Just wait a minute. Wait. Shit." He says this last word in English, followed by fumbling sounds, the noises of his family in the background. "Shit. Shit!"

A long pause and he finds what he is looking for. Julio Gil Reyes isn't dead, Charlie says. He lives in Higüey, or possibly Santo Domingo. "There's a lot of information, a lot."

"Speak slowly," I beg him. "Slowly."

"I have the personal document, okay? When do you want to meet?"

"I think I'll be in Monte Plata for the weekend."

We settle on Monday at noon.

"I WAS TELLING HIM about the cannibal," says Fausto Moreno, the Monte Plata correspondent for the national newspaper *Listín Diario*. He's speaking to his friend Ydal, the three of us on a patio near the edge of town, where the houses fade into the fields. "What I didn't know was exactly when it happened."

"This took place in 1791," responds Ydal immediately. He's a young man, but he speaks with the professorial bearing of a committed autodidact. "That sadistic creature killed twenty-nine people in the single month of April. He attacked children, women and the elderly, and once he had perpetrated his crime, he would cut off the private parts of his victim, throw them into a suitcase and go out into the world. He ranged over two hundred square kilometres, attacking every community, every locality."

The two men take pleasure in Monte Plata's history. For them, it is not a living burden; the days of the 1965 revolution are not so different from the days of the cannibal—fascinating, grim, but also lost to time and distance. Monte Plata for them is a place with the right economic statistics, and Fausto can recite them exactly: so many gallons of palm oil each year; such-and-such bushels of citrus; the largest milk producer in the country; the greatest grower of passion fruit.

"Did they finally kill him?" I ask.

"In the end, a Spanish army garrison was commissioned to go out and hunt him down, finally trapping the killer in the immediate area of the town of Cotuí. They were to take him to Santo Domingo, but they arrived in Monte Plata and decided that the cannibal would 'die in a bid to escape.' They took him to what they called the Plains of Patience and hanged him in a tidy grove of orange trees, and then they went to Santo Domingo to make their report." Over time, and perhaps through the lies of those who had disobeyed orders to take vengeance on the murderer, a myth emerged. That one day a young man—thin, nearly bald, kind-eyed and with an astral whiteness—had appeared in Monte Plata and told the terrorized people that the cannibal was hanging in a mammee-apple tree in the campo. Troops were sent out, and they found the man-eater noosed with a knotted white cord, and when they returned the mysterious stranger was gone. Right away the patron saint of Monte Plata was changed from Saint Anthony the Abbot, protector of animals, gravediggers and swineherds, to Saint Anthony of Padua, who, like all the Franciscans, wore a white cord girdle with three knots to represent the vows of chastity, poverty and obedience.

The soil of the campo is rich with stories, says Ydal, gesturing across the road to the spreading pastures. Even the martyrdom of Padre Arturo has its place in the fields in front of us. In 1965, says Ydal, all the land was owned by the Contreras family. There were three clans of Contreras then, but the richest and most powerful was the family Contreras Alcántara and its patriarch, Quimo Contreras. Their properties surrounded the town. On the afternoon of the day that Arturo was killed, shots rang out across these fields and Odulio de los Santos would have passed—just there—as he went out to investigate.

"It was Porfirio, out hunting guinea fowl," says Fausto.

"That's right," says Ydal with a slow nod.

And it is suddenly clear why the people of Monte Plata had been so careful to tell Father Paul Ouellette about the gunfire in the campo on the day that Arturo died. The man who fired those shots, the shots that drew Odulio de los Santos into the field to be perfectly placed for the death of the padre and the two policemen, was Porfirio Contreras Alcántara. He is one of the survivors on the List of Fourteen.

"I'd like to meet this Porfirio," I say to Fausto as we walk into town.

"He lives right there," says Fausto, pointing to a narrow plaster condominium, "but he isn't in town today." He promises to see what he can do.

I CALL CHARLIE THAT NIGHT and tell him my trip to Monte Plata was cut short. I can meet him the next day, a Sunday.

"Where? What time?" he says.

"Anywhere, any time."

"Okay," he says, pausing to think. "Nine thirty in the morning. At the palace."

"At the palace?" I can't have heard him correctly.

"Yes," he says, as though there was nothing odd about the idea of exchanging stolen documents at the headquarters of the National Police. "Santiago—this call is confidential?"

"Yes, of course."

"This priest—he was your *uncle?*"

"Yes." Didn't I tell him that, weeks ago?

"When you come tomorrow, you'll be alone?"

"Alone, yes, of course."

"Okay, see you later."

Leaving me to stew on whatever all of that might mean.

IN THE BARRIO AT Kilometre Ten, a Dominican nun tells me that she remembers Padre Arturo. "You look like Art," she says in English. She laughs and squeezes my arm. "But all of you Canadians look the same to me."

THE BASE OF THE STAIRS at the Palace of the National Police. I'm wearing sunglasses and a baseball cap, my attempt at anonymity. At the top of the stairs, an officer directs me to remove my sunglasses. When I've obeyed, he tells me that I must not wait outside the fortress. I go to step inside. "Ah!" he says, making a gesture toward my head. I reluctantly remove the hat.

Beyond the bulletproof glass of the lobby, a crowd. It is a throng of policemen, filling rows of chairs or lining the walls, some in uniform, others in plain clothes, still others who appear to be accompanied by their wives and children. Then I see the priest, a faraway figure at the head of the great hall. It's a Mass. Sunday Mass at the fortress, the church of the National Police.

A guard motions that I should join the service, and I smile and nod and feel my heart falter in my chest. The padre has his flock singing, and every person in the room has time to take a hard look in my direction. There's no hostility, only a professional curiosity. A gringo at the fortress Mass? Why? Who is he? Who is he here to see? But I don't see Charlie until the service has ended, women still singing as the crowd breaks up in handshakes and God-be-with-yous. He's moving parallel to me through the crowd, catching my eye and indicating with his head that I should follow. I move toward him, shaking hands as I go. Now he is standing at a side door, and I see myself as I must look to the men in uniform all around me, this gringo idiot trying to look nonchalant with his plastered-on grin as he wades through the staring faces of traffic cops, secret policemen, street detectives, riot troops, investigators, thugs. I shake hands with Charlie as though he were just another partic-ipant in the Mass, and he pulls open the side door and leads me onto a second-storey walkway above an inner courtyard. There is no one in sight. He bumps my hand with a roll of paper and I take it, relay-style. "Put it in your bag," he orders me, but I wait until we've stepped into a closed stairwell, descending quickly into the darkness of the fortress. He points quickly at his eye as a sign that I should keep mine open to all that's around me. In a basement corridor we pass the barred gate of a cell, the dim hallway light revealing the moon faces of a crowd of young men sitting, some sprawling, across a bare concrete floor. I barely dare to glance at them, registering only tatters and grime, eyes that stare without emotion and wait for nothing in particular, another day, and then we are moving through a door and back onto the green streets of Santo Domingo.

"I did a deep search to get those documents," says Charlie.

"Thank you. Thank you very much."

"When do you go back to Canada?"

"I'm not sure. Not for several weeks."

"I want to go there, you understand? I have to get out of this country. I hope you can help me."

"It's difficult—"

"Not a miracle, Santiago. I don't expect a miracle. Just whatever help you can give me."

We have walked out to the front of the fortress, where the chain-link fence wraps around the parking lot. It is as though Charlie wants to position us perfectly within the scope of every surveillance camera on the block, and yet I'm certain that nothing he does is deliberate. They're the actions of a man so trapped within his world that he couldn't think of a better plan, a man who, perhaps, feels more anonymous and secure surrounded by the faces he knows than on a street corner among strangers or on a phone line with who-knows-who tapping in.

We shake hands. *Smile, Charlie! Smile for the cameras!*

"I'll see what I can do," I say.

"Before you leave the country, burn the documents," he replies.

Then my feet carry me once more to the Plaza of Culture, where trumpeters are practising scales in every hollow, where mangoes are falling and birds are singing—where there is life. I take a seat between the Furies of Fire and Earth. No one seems to have followed me from the fortress; there's no one watching from behind a tree trunk or a newspaper. I unroll the documents across the seat of my bench.

It is the personal history of Julio Gil Reyes, a living man. The same man that I had found in the ordinary phone book, a lawyer, a man who has never been a police officer, the man who told me that the other Julio Gil Reyes is dead.

The wrong guy. And I'm laughing out loud.

AT THE YELLOW HOUSE of the Quisqueyan Christian Democratic Party, they tell me that General Wessin is considering my request. I promise to return tomorrow, and they know that I will. It has become a daily ritual. I appear and they tell me that the general is busy, he appreciates my patience, he will make a decision *ahorita*, very soon, *mañana*, tomorrow, and then I retreat to wait for a bus. Today the guaguas are slow and a young man and woman approach—university students, perhaps. The boy is handsome in the fashion of a youthful Che Guevara; the girl is pretty, slim, pale, pony-tailed. They look as if they come from money. "Are you going somewhere important?" the girl asks in lightly accented English.

"Not really."

"We are," says the boy, also in English. "We're going somewhere *very* important."

"*Very* important," she confirms.

"We are intelligence agents," he says. "I know we don't look that way, but we're intelligence agents."

The words suggest a game in which I am to play the fool, but as I search their faces I fail to see sarcasm or mockery. There is something private going on, certainly, but it doesn't appear to be a joke that they share between them.

"Do we look tired?" asks the boy.

"Actually, yes, you do."

"We were drugged. We don't drink or do drugs, you understand, but we were tricked and drugged."

The girl, he says, is Agent Pepsimint; he cannot divulge his own name. They have been assigned to defuse a bomb in one of the skyscrapers of the Piantini business district. The bomb is set to explode on May Day, just a few short days from today.

"But it *won't*," says the girl, pressing her lips against my cheek.

"The bomb is nicknamed 'the May Day Sin,'" says the boy. "What does that sound like?"

"May Day Sin. Medicine," I reply.

"You get it? It's like a joke. The bomb is the medicine."

The weapon, they explain, was planted by American agents furious about the Dominican Republic's refusal to continue sending troops to support the United States in the Middle East. Until that act of defiance, the United States had been planning to make the republic a secret nuclear power, like Israel. The May Day Sin would have been the country's first bomb, powered by an element called "pontium." All of this rolls off their tongues, back and forth between them, without pause or hesitation or a hint of a smile. In fact, they appear exhausted and anxious, especially the girl, whose hand creeps up my arm to rest on my neck, the fingers slightly tight against my skin.

"This mission needs you," says the young man.

"Well, I can't join the mission. I'm waiting for a guagua. I need to go. I have an appointment."

"Don't go," says the girl, her nails digging into the nape of my neck.

"Is your meeting about a relative?" asks the boy, and I can see that they have noted the trace of surprise on my face.

"A Catholic?" he demands.

It is no miracle in a Catholic country to guess that a person might be a Catholic, and yet I still can't conceal a reaction.

"Don't go! They're going to kill you!"

I stand up, trying to respond, but my voice squeaks and cracks under the pressure of the girl's hand, and at last I see a guagua approaching and pry away her fingers, stepping into the street to stop the bus. The boy moves to block me, the girl beginning to weep, and I stand there gaping, baffled, uncertain how to escape. In the windows of the guagua I can see the curious, worried faces of the cobrador and passengers. The two are clinging to me now, and I calm myself and wave the bus onward. The couple relaxes as the guagua pulls away.

"I'm not going with you," I say with all the firmness I can muster. "You're not coming with me."

They stare at me with something like anger, something like pity. At last the girl says, "It's okay, he can go."

"You can go," says the boy. "You'll be safe. We'll make sure. We'll see you again. We need to hug." The three of us hug on the sidewalk, long and needful like friends at a funeral. The girl kisses my cheek, her own still wet with tears, and they step away, waving, finally turning and walking off. I listen for laughter as they move up the road. Nothing.

A second guagua is coming, and I climb aboard with an infinite relief. As the vehicle accelerates up Bolívar Avenue, I see the pair once more, their heads bent toward each other, speaking gravely, uneasy, at the brink of insanity.

SQUALLS ARE SPLITTING off a black wall on the southern horizon of the Caribbean Sea. In a small computer centre at Kilometre Ten, I receive a message from Roberto Santana. General Antonio Imbert Barreras, the man who was the provisional president on the day Padre Arturo died, the man better remembered as one of the assassins of Trujillo, has agreed to talk. There will be only one problem: the general doesn't remember a thing.

IN THE MIDDLE OF the night I throw up with such force that my feet come out from under me and I drop to my knees, hanging on the edge of the toilet bowl. It feels as if I'm vomiting splintered glass. It has been that kind of week.

My forehead rests on the cool tile floor. It's a reasonable place to think about the pattern of bullet wounds. I have begun to piece together in my mind those final few minutes of Arthur's life, and yet the bullet wounds perturb me, just as they perturbed Father Paul Ouellette and the criminologists with the Organization of American States. There remain only two possibilities that make sense. In the first, Odulio de los Santos shoots all three men dead, then uses Ramón Restituyo's pistol to finish off the priest. In the second, Odulio de los Santos kills the two policemen who have murdered Arturo, then shoots the padre's corpse to make it appear as though all three had died from a burst of submachine-gun fire. Either Odulio de los Santos is the matador, the killer, or he covered up the assassination.

Yet Father Ouellette had believed in the innocence of the young soldier, and there are no signs that De los Santos went on to be rewarded for his part in a bloodstained conspiracy. In fact, he endured a fearful life in a kind of exile, and his only later confession was that the story that he had killed all three men in an accident had never been the truth. The truth was that the padre had been dead by the time De los Santos arrived at the scene.

And there on the floor it comes to me. I need to take a closer look at the autopsy report, just as soon as I'm able to move.

23

JULY 1965. MORE THAN TWO MONTHS HAD passed since the first shot was fired in the Dominican revolution, and the Ambassador Hotel had begun to look less like a Marine Corps bunker and more, again, like a four-star facility. War is a social industry, and the rooms were filled with advisers, mediators, security consultants, aid workers, journalists, all sheltered from the mad reality of Santo Domingo by the same pleasant grounds that eased the eye in more ordinary times. There were still more M16s than mai tais, but a visitor could almost imagine that a return to a thousand peaceful cocktail hours was not so very far off. Since the end of Operation Mop-up it was even possible, at times, to hear the raucous screeching of the parakeets and not to be startled by the brilliant red flash of their wings.

No one envied the OAS criminologists. They had arrived on June 18 to carry out the first investigation into the atrocities of the revolution and its truncated civil war. There was human rights specialist Daniel Schweitzer of Chile, the leading Mexican criminologist Alfonso Quiroz Cuarón, and Jorge Avendaño Valdéz, an eminent jurist from Peru. The secretary general of the OAS himself, José Mora, had explained to them the allegations that prisoners of the Government of National Reconstruction were being executed along the banks of the Yuca River, just north of Santo Domingo. The rumours that as many as thirty-nine men and women had been put to death were among the worst the secretary general had heard since he had arrived in the republic to witness the repercussions of this new chapter in the history of American intervention.

The criminologists uncovered four bodies under a bridge on their first day of work, transferring what was left of the corpses to Santo Domingo for autopsy. The dead were ordinary men in button-up shirts and slacks, who even in death carried with them the traces of lives that had been storied and full: a broken red comb; an envelope containing two blurred photographs; a tattoo with the word for "darling" misspelled; a medallion of St. Joseph on a gold chain around one ankle. The men had been bound with rope so tightly that it cut furrows in their flesh. Two had been shot in the chest and left, with fragments of broken ribs drifting into their lungs, to drown in their own blood. A third had been riddled with bullets through the chest, arms and face. The fourth had been savagely beaten; the bones of each leg were broken beneath the knees, the left arm shattered at the point where it had been bound with rope, the skull split by radiating fractures. The eye sockets were empty.

By June 29, the team had found fourteen bodies, all of them along the roads to or from the notorious La Victoria prison. That day, however, they received a new directive: to investigate the killing of a young Canadian priest and the two men who had died alongside him on the outskirts of a town called Monte Plata. It was a remarkable day all round, and the Ambassador Hotel was abuzz. The rebel leadership was predicting that peace talks would lead to an acceptable compromise government within two weeks, and as if on cue that devilish old trujillista, Joaquín Balaguer, had returned from exile. The Americans were promising a free election.

At least this time there were no trenches to dig, no bloated bodies to be fished out of back eddies after being washed from their shallow graves by heavy rains. The priest and the two policemen had received proper burials. The criminologists ordered the bodies exhumed and transported, as usual, to Salvador Gautier Hospital, a somnolent medical campus just north of the bloodstained battleground at the western gate of the Duarte Bridge.

On July 1, the team received a parcel from Paul Creighton, a Canadian diplomat. The label read, CLOTHING OF FATHER JOSÉ (ARTURO), MONTE PLATA, though the package contained only a pair of black cotton trousers that appeared to have been cut off a body. They were dirty, spotted with blood and yellow mud, and the pockets were empty. There was also a series of ragged holes, one each on the inside faces of the left and right thighs, two more at the height of the right-hand crest of the hip and four in the seat of the pants. Three Dominican ballistics experts were assigned to the pants, and a file was opened for cadaver number 15.

The body arrived the next morning in a simple wooden coffin. Working in the hospital amphitheatre, the team started with an inventory of garments and adornments.

A white undershirt.

Trunks-style underpants, bloodstained, with bullet holes to match the trousers.

Black-striped cotton socks and a pair of black dress moccasins.

A braided Santa Lucía rosary.

Wrapped in a white sheet, a set of priestly vestments: amice, sash, alb, cassock, cincture, stole, maniple, chasuble.

The body had begun to decay, but compared with the putrefied remains from the banks of the Yuca River, the autopsy was straightforward. The man on the table was five feet, eight inches tall and muscular, with some muscles that actually bulged. His skin was taut and white. The bullet holes stood out black and perfect.

The three men worked from the top down. A small orifice beneath and behind the jawbone on the left side—an entrance wound, but of a particular nature. A bullet fired into the brain cavity is like a cork forced down into a bottle, and in the split second before the projectile exits the skull the pressurized blood and fluid will erupt toward the entry, devastating bone and tissue. The clean, round hole with the powder burns told a different story. The gun had been pressed against the priest's skin, impeding the blow-back. Instead, the bullet shattered bone along its course and then blasted through the back of the head, high on the right-hand side. The exit wound was a gaping hole.

The neck: bruised on both sides, as if someone had attempted to strangle him. Bruising on the chest, too, this time profound enough to affect even the tissue beneath the breastbone, the kind of damage done by a boot or a rifle butt.

A tear in the flesh over the ribs of the right underarm.

At the crest of the right hip, what appeared initially to be the entrance wound of a bullet, but which proved, from separate nicks in the bone, to be the point of entry for two separate bullets, one exiting the body through the right buttock, the other through the back of the thigh. Just below the right hip, another entry, with the bullet having taken a downward course, destroying the head of the femur before blowing out the left buttock. Then a strange one: a bullet hole high on the inside face of the left thigh, roughly the same diameter as the others, but with the path of the wound travelling downward, backward and inward, exiting deep under the crotch. As though the shot had been fired from directly overhead.

But an autopsy report is not a place for speculation. It demands statements of clinical fact.

There was a second body to examine that day. Cadaver number 16 was the body of Evangelista Martínez Rodríguez, second lieutenant of the National Police. The corpse housed only a single wound—a hole the size of a fist in the left side of the head. The bullet had struck just below the left eye, destroying the socket as it angled outward to the temple; together, the entry and exit wounds created an open pit. The bones of the skull and face were, as expected, split and splintered in every direction.

The following morning the team began work at eleven o'clock in the General Cemetery of Bonao, where officials representing the provisional government of President Antonio Imbert Barreras were doing their best to appear co-operative. The body of Ramón Restituyo Santiago, constable of the National Police, was removed from its grave and transported to the capital. Restituyo was four inches shorter than the priest, but built like a side of beef. Cadaver number 17 had been torn apart by at least a half-dozen bullets that had punctured the lungs, shattered the ribs and collarbone, fractured the left hip and the ball of the femur, perforated the buttocks, seared through the abdomen. No single shot was necessarily lethal, but the sum of the damage was extreme.

That same Saturday, July 3, the ballistics investigators turned in their report on the trousers worn by James Arthur MacKinnon on the night he died. They found that the holes at hip level were glazed with so much gunpowder that the shots must have been fired from between twenty-five and thirty-two centimetres away—not even the distance of a footstep. The holes in the seat of the pants were tiny coronas of fibres pulled outward: bullets exiting the body. The single hole on the inside of the thigh, corresponding to the peculiar wound that seemed to have been inflicted on the priest from above—that hole was different. There was almost no gunpowder around it, and the experts agreed it had been fired from a distance of at least one metre, possibly much farther away than that.

The file on cadaver number 15 could be closed. The cause of death was obvious enough: "Multiple lesions caused by a firearm." The priest had been young, healthy and strong, and none of the shots to his abdomen or thighs would have immediately killed him or even rendered him unconscious. It was the shot beneath the jaw that had ended his life.

But there was more that the criminologists wanted to say about the case. It hardly surprised them that they had been given only a single shell from the scene of the crime, and that shell only because Father Paul Ouellette of the Scarboro missionaries had found it. The site had been sanitized, of course, by the same military and police officials who had obstructed, with smiles and promises of goodwill, every step of the OAS investigation. Requests—even for information as simple as which officer was identified by a particular police badge—disappeared into the office of Commodore Francisco Rivera Caminero, the secretary of state of the armed forces in the Government of National Reconstruction and an ally of convenience to General Wessin y Wessin, who remained untouchable in his fiefdom of San Isidro. Interviews with individual soldiers proved laughable. Their testimony was as unlikely as it was reticent—the soldiers had so plainly been coached that each repeated stock terms and phrases. The people who lived along the Yuca River would not speak freely, either, even behind closed doors. Prudence had always assured them of their lives, and they preferred to remain in the world of the living.

No matter: the material facts spoke plainly enough. Had the Government of National Reconstruction taken care to investigate the Yuca River killings? It had. A judicial tribunal decided that the murders had perhaps been carried out by a group of armed civilians. The criminologists declared the finding an absurdity, the investigative equivalent of a show trial. What happened along the road to La Victoria was common knowledge, and that knowledge was supported at every level by the evidence. By night, Dantesque convoys of jeeps would pass through military checkpoints and stop somewhere in the curfewed darkness of the La Victoria road, where gunshots rang out with an executioner's rhythm. The headlights, the ringing gunfire, the cries and weeping—none of it was missed by the families who lived in the scattering of shacks spilling outward from Santo Domingo. Indeed, it was not the killers who rolled their murdered victims into their graves; that was the work of unnamed and silent figures, risking their lives to bring this small dignity to the dead. Anyone could tell you who controlled the roadways along the Yuca River—it was the Government of National Reconstruction, backed by the White House and led by President Antonio Imbert. Anyone could say what crest was stamped on the doors of the jeeps that drove those roads—it was the crest of San Isidro.

The case of the dead priest in Monte Plata had been "investigated" as well, by the same men who swept clean the scene of the crime and refused to show the OAS team Restituyo's revolver, or Martínez's rifle, or the submachine gun fired by Odulio de los Santos. The little military men, the chest-puffing police—they had made it impossible to solve the crime. And so, perhaps, there was room for speculation in the criminological report after all. They might say, for example, that the killing had "the appearance of a hurried execution." They might point out that the body of the priest had "wounds from at least two different weapons." It was an invitation to the reader to probe more deeply, to pay attention to the slightest detail.

Odulio de los Santos had walked into Monte Plata on the night of the killings carrying three guns, including his own Cristóbal carbine. What might a person learn about the Cristóbal? He might learn, for example, that it was the first infantry weapon produced under Trujillo's domestic arms-manufacturing project. Named after Trujillo's hometown of San Cristóbal, the weapon was based on a Hungarian design, with semi-automatic and automatic settings. It had a calibre of 7.62 millimetres.

De los Santos also carried a pistol, the .38 well known to belong to Ramón Restituyo, as well as a gun that was remembered as a *fusil*, a rifle. But Odulio de los Santos had been more specific than that when he had spoken to Father Paul Ouellette. "An FAL rifle," he had said—the kind of detail that matters to a soldier. It is the kind of detail that could lead a person to the Fusil Automatique Léger, Belgian-made, developed in the 1940s and eventually deployed in the armies of more than fifty countries; it was first imported into the Dominican Republic in 1958. Not a "rifle," then, but an assault rifle. With a calibre of 7.62 millimetres. On the night of June 22, 1965, Odulio de los Santos and Evangelista Martínez were both carrying automatic weapons, both of which fired the same calibre of ammunition.

THE FINAL WORD of the OAS criminologists on the death of Padre James Arthur "Arturo" MacKinnon:

"It was not possible for us to complete the investigation of this case, which is entrusted to the police and military authorities now continuing it."

A masterpiece of irony.

24

IF THE MAN WHO SHOT TRUJILLO LOOKS tiny in his corner of the room, it is only because everything that surrounds him is oversized. The stone tiles are too large, the framed paintings too tall, the ceiling too high. The space between each monumental object—say, the huge darkwood chest covered with gigantic flowers, and the chairs with their rocketing backs—is a vastness. General Antonio Imbert looks like a child, his feet barely touching the floor from his seat on an enormous green sofa. It seems to be the room of a man who has tried to contain the freedom of the outside world within walls.

Even here, Imbert can never feel totally safe. The descendants of Trujillo still walk the earth, after all. In the weeks following the murder of the Generalissimo, the army and police captured all but two of the assassins and conspirators. To describe the suffering that those men endured before they died, people will talk about the dwarf. In the final years of the Era of Trujillo, there was a rumour that among the torturers at La Cuarenta prison was a dwarf; it was his job to bite off the testicles of the worst of the Chief's antagonists. Whether the story is true or not is immaterial. What they say about the torture of Trujillo's assassins is this: it was worse than the dwarf.

No, that kind of hatred doesn't fade easily. The trujillistas could take their revenge at any time; in fact, tonight would be a better night than most. Tonight, even the weather is out of proportion. It's the kind of rain that comes down so hard that to stand in it and breathe, you have to bow your head as if in prayer. You need to stuff rags in every crack and crevice in the house or you'll wake up to find the storm has come in through the keyhole. Thunder is howling. Even the cadre of soldiers and police paid to guard Imbert are cowering in the garage tonight, rubbing their hands on their guns to stay warm. It could happen on a night like this one.

We cluster into the corner, the general, Roberto Santana and myself. It's a testament to Imbert's importance that Santana arrived only ten minutes late to bring me to this meeting. The general takes my hands in his without rising. He wears a perfectly ironed uniform, encrusted with medals and tailored to fit his low hips and pot-belly. His bright, pale eyes search mine with the skill of a fortune teller. His face is jowly, his mouth made small by overbite, and his ready smile makes his eyes crowd with wrinkles. People say he is never without his .45-calibre revolver, but he appears to be unarmed and his hands are soft.

"Is it true that you never eat pasta?" I ask.

"What? Who in the devil said that? Is that in that book?" he says, playing at outrage.

"Yes, Mario Vargas Llosa." The Peruvian master's novel *The Feast of the Goat* recounts the assassination of Trujillo and the days that followed, including Imbert's six months in hiding with an Italian diplomat and his wife. Imbert could never again bring himself to eat pasta, writes Vargas Llosa. The general dismisses the suggestion with the groan of a man who has been wronged by gossip, at the same time pleased by this reminder of immortalization.

But the general is waiting. He is impatient to discover the precise nature of our business. Then, perhaps, there will be time to talk in pleasantries. Santana begins to explain that we have brought a copy of an article about the death of Padre Arturo, and Imbert reaches for it immediately. He reads aloud.

> A military tribunal will judge the policemen and soldiers involved in the death of Padre Arturo of Monte Plata. Order Number Seventy of the provisional Government of Reconstruction announced yesterday the establishment of the tribunal. The soldiers to be judged are Corporal Odulio de los Santos Castillo, Second Lieutenant Evangelista Martínez Rodríguez and Constable Ramón Restituyo Santiago.

"I don't remember any of this," says Imbert, slumping back and seeming almost to disappear into the cushions.

Roberto Santana takes the sheet of paper and reads on. "The first article of the order states that those named as judges are Lieutenant Colonel Angel Urbano Matos—"

"Dead," says Imbert.

"—Major José Ernesto Cruz Brea and Captain Narciso Elio Bautista."

"Ah! Cruz Brea," says Imbert, wagging a finger at Santana. "An old friend of yours," he says, and then turns to me, "A brother of his."

It's a joke, but a thin one, and Santana's laughter is strained. "I told him," says Santana to Imbert while pointing a finger at me. "I told him Cruz Brea was a hard man."

"Oh, completely," says Imbert. "A criminal. But he's alive."

"And Elio Bautista?" I ask.

"I don't know. Dead, I think," says Imbert, taking back the article. He reads the next line in silence.

> The order was signed by General Antonio Imbert, president of the
> provisional government.

"And the Canadian embassy didn't follow up on this?" he asks.

"In reality, the embassy did nothing," I reply. "The consulate didn't have the resources to do anything. They waited for the report from the OAS." I'm fumbling with my copy of the criminologists' report on the autopsy of the fourteen dead found along the Yuca River, as well as the bodies of Arturo, Martínez and Restituyo. "The title is *On Atrocities Committed in Santo Domingo.*"

Imbert is unnaturally quiet again. This report he cannot have forgotten. It splashed his name across the front pages of newspapers worldwide, under headlines like REPORT OF IMBERT ATROCITIES and CANADIAN PRIEST A MODERN MARTYR. He was the head of the provisional government only by the grace of the White House, and the report had helped to cement the view of several of Lyndon Johnson's personal advisers that Imbert had outlasted his usefulness. But the general had some American friends, too, and Antonio Imbert is nothing if not a survivor.

"The investigators said they didn't get much co-operation from the Government of National Reconstruction—"

"That means Wessin," says Imbert, giving a snort. "But Wessin was a different question, something else altogether. Almost a separate government." Imbert had, on the second full day of his presidency, cashiered and deported eight generals and other senior officers as a step toward a peace agreement with the rebels who were then still divided between Ciudad Nueva and the barrios altos. The next to go should have been Wessin. The hated face of San Isidro had given U.S. ambassador Tap Bennett a letter in which he promised he would go into exile provided he was not deported like the others, like some kind of common criminal. But then Wessin refused to leave. Imbert remembers driving to the San Isidro air base, just across the little two-lane highway from Wessin's tank brigade command, and inviting Wessin to come for a meal and talk. "He wouldn't cross the road," says Imbert. "I tell you, he didn't have the personal courage."

The rebel leadership's response to the deportations is still famous: *They've killed the flies but left the beetles.*

"Did you talk to Wessin much while you were president?" I ask.

"No, no, no. He was a world apart, with the most powerful brigade in the country. He had the barracks, he transferred the troops."

He looks again at the newspaper article, ignoring the OAS report. His finger taps the various names. "Dead, dead, dead," he says. Almost everyone is dead. Except Cruz Brea. And himself.

"I spoke to the family of the soldier, De los Santos," I say.

"And what did the family say? What the hell could they know? Did they tell you something?"

"That there definitely was a tribunal, and that the judges found De los Santos innocent, and that then he was transferred to Dajabón."

"The investigators on the tribunal—who did they report to?"

It's a good question, and Santana and I are silent. Imbert: a survivor.

"I tell you the only person who could know is Cruz Brea. Why haven't you talked to Cruz Brea?"

He has addressed the question to Roberto Santana, who stares at his hands and appears, for once, not to have an answer. "Well, I don't know, I don't have any connections," says Santana. His voice is dropping. "I know some names, but . . . but . . ."

"Yes?"

"They were the ones who were looking to kill me."

"No!" says Imbert, as if shocked that such a dark plot could exist.

"Yes, yes."

"Well—I don't know," says Imbert.

"That whole group, when there was the feud between the group of Nivar Seijas and the group of Pérez y Pérez during the Twelve Years of Balaguer—back then that whole group was out to kill me. I was saved several times."

Imbert rapidly makes the connections in his mind; his memory of the time has a startling clarity. As for so many others, the revolution was a turning point for Enrique Pérez y Pérez, whose perspective on the rebellion had been shaped by the fact that he was the first envoy sent from San Isidro to negotiate with the rebels in Santo Domingo. He was forced to flee when his car was set on fire by the crowds at the Duarte Bridge. Trained in counter-insurgency at the U.S.-operated Caribbean School in 1962, Pérez y Pérez would go on to become secretary of state for the armed forces, rising from colonel to general as the old guard of trujillistas were deported or demoted. He would go on, in fact, to become one of the most notorious military figures during the murderous first years of Balaguer's rule. But it was not to Pérez y Pérez that Cruz Brea would have gone with the tribunal's report. Pérez y Pérez didn't rise in the new regime until 1966; the investigation into Padre Arturo's death was ordered on July 13, 1965. The chief of the army at that time was Jacinto Martínez Arana, a man remembered as the protege of Wessin, and now dead in any case.

"General Imbert has buried everyone on earth," says Santana with a smile that conceals the teeth in the compliment. Then he draws Imbert back to the question of the tribunal. Perhaps there is an archive?

"There's nothing," says Imbert. The general's few lonely months as president, the months when he imagined he might continue as leader of the republic—they have vanished, been carelessly lost and wilfully forgotten. There's no mistaking his bitterness. "And what do they say in Monte Plata?" he asks me, changing the subject.

"There are people in Monte Plata who believe it was an act of San Isidro and of powerful families in Monte Plata, as well."

"Ah, powerful families," says Imbert. He pauses, thinking. "But you know that Wessin was from there."

"Yes," says Santana, clearly remembering now. "Yes, from Bayaguana."

"Well . . . ?" Imbert is spreading his hands.

"Yes . . . ," muses Santana.

"Wessin was born in Bayaguana?" I confirm.

"Yes," say the two of them together.

Santana: "It's next door to Monte Plata."

Imbert: "He has a property there."

Santana: "He had properties, family, everything."

Even a month ago, I would not have understood. Native ground is a lifelong, intimate connection. The strongman of San Isidro would have been a friend to the most influential men and women in Bayaguana and Monte Plata; he would have heard, like a neighbour talking over a fence, every rumour of communism to come out of the campo.

Santana: "It's an important fact, yes?"

We're all nodding, laughing like conspirators.

"There's a saying," says Imbert. "'What time leaves behind remains to be forgotten.'"

And so goes the conversation, proceeding cryptically, inscrutably. Imbert speaks in a grandfatherly cadence, crinkling the corners of his eyes with patience and humour as I fumble away in Spanish. I have read that he speaks some English, but he never slips in a single word of the language. He's enjoying the fact that I'm no match for him. His mind is quick, finely tuned to see the way out of every accusation, every difficult situation. A survivor. The man who shot Hot Balls dead.

So this Canadian priest died in Monte Plata—well, says Imbert, he had no control over Monte Plata. He was the president, really, of the besieged city of Santo Domingo, and that only because the Americans found him useful. Not even the OAS understood that he had no power to control the "loyal" military, let alone that rogue general Wessin y Wessin. If, forty years later, I bring him evidence that he signed an order to investigate the death of Padre Arturo—well, then he must have done so. The question is, why would he sign the order? The only explanation is that he was pressured to do so by the United States or the OAS. He signed the order, and then the armed forces took charge. They assigned the "investigation" to this criminal Cruz Brea, who would turn in his tribunal's report to an army chief of staff who considered Elías Wessin y Wessin a national hero. As for the rest of these atrocities uncovered by the OAS, it was an error for the criminologists to suggest that the Government of National Reconstruction controlled the road along the Yuca River. The government did not; the military did. And the military was still listening to the generals in San Isidro.

"What we had was a difficult situation," says Imbert. "Too many chiefs, each one doing what he thought he ought to do."

"A serpent with seven heads," says Santana, and again I admire the sting concealed within his words.

After almost precisely one hour, Roberto Santana rises from his seat. "Well, Tony, we have taken so much of your time." He has waited for these closing moments to speak as friends and call the general "Tony." I offer the warmest thanks I can muster, realizing at the same time that my words are sincere. I like this general; I like his sly laughter, his loneliness. He comes with us to the door and apologizes that he can't remember this case of the Canadian priest.

"Cruz Brea knows," he says.

He takes my hand once more, without letting his figure appear in the frame of the door as it opens. "Come by any time," he says with dancing eyes. "I'm an easy man to find."

Yes, I like Antonio Imbert. That doesn't mean I believe him.

ROSA IS RELIEVED to see me return. It is late, but she heats some sancocho and we eat the stew in the trembling light of a candle. She is trying to understand why I would lead myself into the same dark circle as men like Imbert, Cruz Brea, Wessin y Wessin. They are people to stay away from, for both practical and spiritual reasons. To understand through men like these why Arturo was killed, and how—it is impossible. She has always preferred the path, no less difficult, of finding revelation through faith. Then it is not a question of accumulation, of piecing together facts and motives and events that resolve themselves into bullets that tear through a living body on the side of a road. What kind of understanding is that? As if the raising of a soul to heaven could be explained by the same laws that govern interest rates or a coconut falling from a palm to the beach. More important is to examine the nature of the sacrifice. Why was it necessary? What does it teach? What is its message? And then, once more, she is telling me about that day.

"I had been cooking in my house but was just going to see my father, who was ill," she begins. She was in the street when her friend, a young man and good Catholic, came running toward her. He had just come from the church. "They've killed Padre Arturo! They've killed Padre Arturo!" he shouted. Then his legs buckled and he collapsed, pressing his fists to his eyes in despair. She remembers turning for home, stunned. "I was running through the plaza and suddenly I had to sit down. I had to," she says, looking up from that point in the middle of the table where her eyes always rest as she remembers some moment of suffering. "I think now that it was the first time I ever felt the flutter in my heart. I felt it then. I don't recall ever feeling it before." It was in that moment, she says, that she realized they were capable of anything, that the whispered horrors of her lifetime seemed suddenly, terrifyingly real. She took in in that moment a glimpse of original sin, the potential for evil in humankind. It struck her hard enough to throw the rhythm of her heart.

"It was a day like this one," she says, dabbing an eye. "So much rain, so much rain." For the first time in my memory, the whole city seems silent.

25

MORNING AGAIN, THAT MERCIFUL HOUR before the sun lurches into the sky.

Juan is spreading crumbs for the birds that nest in the eaves, chasing back the pigeons so the sparrows get their share.

How will I pass the day? Well: At the yellow house of the Quisqueyan Christian Democratic Party a functionary will inform me that General Wessin y Wessin is considering my request. Then I'll walk into the Zona Colonial and the man who calls himself Leave Me To Dance Alone will, for the twentieth time, tell me that he was deported from the United States and needs just a few pesos for his daily bread. Maybe I'll end up at the K-ramba Bar, sitting at the edge of a pocket park named for a Dominican poet who signed his works "Byron" and where, if I'm prepared to wait, there will eventually be a fight between the garbage-eating dogs. I'll sit there and wonder what miracle is going to lead me to the door of General José Ernesto Cruz Brea.

"There are so many generals—too many," says Juan. "Every one of them has to be maintained with their houses, guards, wages, pensions, nice cars. All of this, in this poor country." Most have fought in no war and some have never commanded a soldier, earning their rank through government patronage or a military sinecure. "This kind of general we call 'General Toshiba,'" he says. "You understand?"

"No."

"You know this brand name, Toshiba, yes? But what do we know about it? It comes out of nowhere and suddenly it's powerful and everyone has heard of it. It's not like General Electric. General Electric, it's been around a long time, seen a lot of battles and survived. Now you understand?"

I'm already laughing.

"And what can a poor man do about all these generals?" Juan continues, his own smile fading. He isn't a young man any more. Even now, with the election rallies and protests, he has to live like a snail. Every day there's another report of street battles and even gunfights between the purple party and the white. He can stick his head out to look around, but if there is trouble he vanishes into his barrio, his home. What if, as the pundits endlessly despair, the government tries to hang on to power through fraud and the nation slides once again toward rebellion or a military coup? A person need only look across the border to Haiti, where U.S. and French troops have been marching in the streets for two months. If it comes to a revolution or a coup, Juan would prefer a corrupted government and a General Toshiba army. Suppose a boa constrictor has moved into your house. Which is wiser: to feed the snake, or to try to starve it out?

THIS IS HOW I COME to believe that I have found José Ernesto Cruz Brea.

Yanira, I realize, has shown me a first step: the Balaguer Foundation. The book fair by day is crowded with the blue-and-beige uniforms of students, and the chatter of voices beneath the trees' canopy is like the inside of a madman's head. The *balaguerista* booth appears unpopular; the young man who wears his sunglasses at night is bored. He slips the glasses down his nose to inspect me as I step up into the stall and introduce myself.

"So I'm trying to find someone who knows how to contact General Cruz Brea," I say.

"Cruz Brea?"

"He was one of the top men in the army when Doctor Balaguer was the president. I thought someone with the foundation would know how I can contact him."

The tough with the sunglasses waves to another man of about the same age, perhaps early twenties, who is standing in a tide of passing high-school girls. The second man responds reluctantly, but he nods as the two confer for a moment, then writes a phone number on a slip of paper.

"A very good friend of General Cruz Brea," he says. "General Hernández Fernández."

"General Hernández Fernández?"

"That's right, Fernández Hernández."

"Fernández Hernández?"

"Hernández Fernández, yes."

We shake hands all round, and I am about to leave when I spot the book: *Memories of a Courtesan in the Era of Trujillo,* by Joaquín Balaguer. It takes a minute to thumb through, but then the page is there in front of me, exactly as Yanira had said. To be precise, it is not exactly "blank." There is a photo of the assassinated journalist Orlando Martínez, wearing the owly, polarized eyeglasses of a 1970s radical. Below his face, these words:

THE CASE OF ORLANDO MARTÍNEZ HOWLEY, JOURNALIST

This page is inserted blank. For many years it will remain mute, but one day it will speak so that its voice may be recognized by history. Silent, it is like a grave whose secret will rise, accusing, when time finally permits the tombstone to be lifted under which the truth remains asleep. Its contents are in the hands of a friend who, for reasons of age, can be supposed to outlive me, and who has been charged with the responsibility of making this missing page public some years after my death.

It seems unimaginable to me, this idea that a president could admit to intimate knowledge of the murder of a popular journalist and yet never be brought to a court of law, never compelled to speak. Thirty years have passed since Orlando Martínez was killed, and his death has become a grail to contain so many other assassinations that have never found resolution. The case itself is a symbol. On August 4, 2000, three former military officers and one civilian were convicted of the killing; late in 2002, their sentences were annulled. It was an outrage, but so, too, would have been the imprisonment of the men who pulled the trigger on Martínez while those accused of planning and ordering his death were never brought to trial. The court did hear, for example, that in the weeks before his death, Orlando Martínez's fear of José Ernesto Cruz Brea descended into a fixation. The general was, ultimately, called to testify. He said only this: that he knew nothing of the case.

I try the phone number of General Hernández Fernández. It is no longer in service.

Back at the Balaguer Foundation booth, the two young men suggest that I go to see General Hernández Fernández at the foundation office on Mahatma Gandhi Avenue—the rear door to Balaguer's former home—at ten o'clock in the morning the following day. "He will be there. He is always there at ten o'clock on Tuesday." Next I pay a visit to Wessin's yellow house, where a woman tells me she will check on the status of my request for an interview. Ten minutes later, still sitting in my chair in the waiting room, I see her slip out a side door and into a waiting car.

Black sheets of rain come over the town. In the house at Kilometre Ten, Rosa asks me if I know Ecclesiastes 3. *To every thing there is a season, and a time to every purpose under heaven.*

The following morning, General Hernández Fernández is not at the Balaguer Foundation at ten o'clock.

"He comes and goes, he comes and goes," says a man who appears from a back room when I call out from the empty reception desk.

"Is there a day that he is normally here?" We cough lightly between each exchange; the room is choking with dust from renovations to the former president's home.

"No, but he's here every day."

"Maybe I should wait?"

"No. No, I don't think that would be a good idea."

He is correct, of course. It would not be a good idea. I write a long note, and the man promises to deliver it into the hands of General Hernández Fernández. Not at all optimistic, I step out the door and into an avalanche of plaster chips from the scaffolding overhead.

A time to weep. A time to laugh.

The following morning there is no one at the Balaguer Foundation, and when I have walked Bolívar Avenue to Wessin's headquarters, tired even of the flower trumpets that continue to fall from the trees, a woman tells me that the general is considering my request for a meeting.

"Listen. Is there no one here who can help me? I can't stay in this country much longer," I say.

"You've never spoken to Josefina?" she asks, as though somehow this is my fault. She leads me out the door of the headquarters and around the building to a side door that leads into a series of offices. The first of them belongs to Josefina Pichardo, a woman in late middle age who has the face of a person whose job it is to deliver bad news.

Josefina picks up the phone and makes a call. Then another. And another. In each case she speaks with the quiet intimacy of access and authority, and finally I realize that she is speaking, if not to Wessin y Wessin himself, than at least to someone in the same room as the general. "Yes, I understand," she says and sets the phone back on its receiver.

"He has read your letter, and he remembers nothing of the case," she says.

I am prepared for this response. "Ah, but I have articles and documents about the case, and perhaps if he sees them it will help his memory."

"He doesn't remember the case and it is the election, you understand. He does not have a space available to see you."

"I'll stay until after the election."

Her lips tighten, and she says nothing.

"Please, would you check with him again? I can leave another letter that explains more clearly my work."

She nods with what appears to be relief, and we shake hands. In this moment I recognize a change. My hand is dry—as dry, at least, as could be expected on a thirty-three-degree day in air that ripples with humidity. My shirt is dry. Something within me has heaved, some anxiety or anticipation. The sweating has finally stopped.

Then it's back to Kilometre Ten. The days have become half days, really. In the morning the city moves freely, life continuing at its regular pace, but by midafternoon the sky sags toward the ground like wet paper, then ruptures and closes the streets behind a grey curtain. There is nothing to do but stare out at the warm rain until nightfall, and then to watch it tracing orange past the street lights until the blackout, and then only to listen. In the blackness, above the thrumming, a telephone rings.

"Santiago!" It's Rosa calling up to me, reluctant to step into the midnight downpour.

"I'm here!" I call into the storm.

"It's General Fernández Hernández!"

"General Hernández Fernández?"

"Yes!"

Three minutes later I have a phone number for José Ernesto Cruz Brea, the very good friend of General Hernández Fernández. Five minutes later, the phone rings again. This time I answer it myself.

"Hello, Santiago. It's Fausto Moreno in Monte Plata. You can meet with Porfirio Contreras tomorrow at eleven o'clock."

A time to cast away stones.

A time to gather stones together.

PORFIRIO CONTRERAS ALCÁNTARA, surviving member of the List of Fourteen, doesn't seem to trust me. On the other hand, it might only be his lips. They are thin and bloodless, which make him appear suspicious despite the fact that he is certainly polite, almost gracious. Besides, I am accompanied by Fausto Moreno, whom everyone seems to trust.

Not much over five feet tall, the man better known as Little Porfirio lives where the Monte Plata road bends out of town toward the cemetery. He doesn't invite us in, and we climb an outside stairway to a second-storey balcony. Vehicles accelerate out of the corner below us, and the howls of motorcycles and groans of trucks are interminable.

The story of what he was doing on the afternoon before Padre Arturo was killed has been all mixed up, says Little Porfirio. It isn't true that he was hunting guinea fowl. No, but he did leave town about two in the afternoon to walk out to his father's property, a distance of perhaps a kilometre or more. "I had a rifle," he says, "but we used to have a lot of bullets that were defective. I went out to the pasture and put up a target for practice." He was a soldier in those days. "What happened? Well." He shot down the target, set it up again, shot it down again. The ammunition was good.

He was coming back into town around four o'clock when he passed the army checkpoint and was confronted by the guards, among them Fausto Moreno's father, Juan Moreno Fabiano.

"Who was shooting out there?" they demanded.

"It was me," Porfirio said to them. "I was checking to see if I had a set of bad bullets." The sentries grumbled—what kind of fool goes shooting in the campo not two months after an armed revolution? The army lieutenant, Fabio Santana, had wanted to send a couple of men to track down the shooter, but in the end it was Odulio de los Santos who went out alone. He still hadn't returned.

They waved Porfirio through the checkpoint and he wound out the day in the centre of town. Just as darkness was falling, he heard the gunfire. Everyone heard it. It was sounding off the foothills and the belfry of the church, as his own shots must have, and it was hard to tell what direction the noise was coming from, but anyway from the campo.

"So they came looking for me," he says, spreading his hands. "They arrested me, and I said, 'For what?' And they said to me, 'Because they've killed the priest.' And I said, 'Well, I had nothing to do with that. Nothing, nothing!'"

He was in a cell at the barracks when they brought in another man. The face was familiar enough—it was Odulio de los Santos, and he was telling anyone who would listen that he fired his gun to protect a man in uniform from what he thought was a pair of rebels. Somehow he had killed them all. Porfirio knew the padre, of course, and he knew Constable Ramón Restituyo, the type who likes a little trouble. He had never met the new lieutenant, Evangelista Martínez. The men at the barracks said Martínez had come to town from San Isidro.

"You're to blame that I killed those three," De los Santos said to Little Porfirio after his story was finished.

"And why?" Porfirio replied.

"Because you fired those shots and I had to go and investigate. If you hadn't fired those shots, I wouldn't have ended up shooting those three."

"Well . . . ," said Porfirio, but he could see that De los Santos would need some time to see things clearly.

The investigations started that night and continued the next day. They took Porfirio to an army camp in Santo Domingo and kept him under arrest for a month, but in the end he was free to go. His superiors were more interested in Odulio de los Santos.

The conversation is winding down, and I still have not asked the impolite question. I have had no opportunity. Nothing about Little Porfirio makes me suspect he was an accomplice to murder. He speaks without hesitation, does not shy from the details of the killing, is curious to learn that Odulio de los Santos had passed his life in Dajabón. "I never heard what happened," he says. The accusation that hangs over him seems more an answer than a question.

With the killing of Padre Arturo, every person in Monte Plata knew there would be no justice. No tireless inquiry, no evidence weighed and tested. Instead, each person would be left with his or her own experiences, overheard details, third-hand stories. To some people, the fact that Little Porfirio fired his gun in the campo might be instantly forgotten—the Contreras Alcántara family had always been a good one. To others, the suggestion that the gunfire was coincidental would be outrageous and naive. Does it make sense, under such circumstances, to believe in innocence until there is proof of guilt? Or is it fairer to name every possible suspect and stand them forever accused? A shadow is often larger than the object that stands in the light.

I put the question.

Porfirio Contreras Alcántara, your family was wealthy and influential. They had friends at the highest levels in an era of secrecy and brutality. Your mother and father, your brothers and uncles, your grandparents—what did they think about the young rebels who rose up in April 1965? What did they make of the foreign priests who saw in the suffering of the poor an offence against the divine? Which side, in the end, was the Contreras Alcántara family on?

I have asked the question in half a dozen ways before I realize that Little Porfirio does not feel it is a question he has to answer.

THE AFTERNOON SUN has found a hole in the clouds and its rays come down like a confetti of pins. The bus for Santo Domingo will leave its muddy pullout in a few minutes, but I am feeling, today, the provocations of time. Behind the church, across the plaza, and I slip into a telephone centre. I have the number in my pocket.

After three rings, a woman's voice. "Hello?"

"Hello, I am looking for General Cruz Brea."

"Who?"

"General Cruz Brea."

"General Brea?"

"Yes."

"And what do you want?"

As usual, I do my best to explain.

"Just a moment." I can hear her calling out through the halls and rooms of a house, and at last a hand rattles the receiver. The voice is a surprise. It is deep, lucid, friendly, even jovial. It's not at all the voice of a man in hiding, with so much to hide.

"Well, sincerely, I don't remember anything about the case. A priest, you say?"

But he agrees to meet in two days. I put down the phone and realize that I am starting to tremble, beginning at my head, like a marionette dropped onto twisted strings. I'm sweating all over. Even my ears are sweating.

· · ·

Yanira is covering her closed-lip smile with a hand. We're sitting in the colmado, the one whose flagstones were laid by conquistadors. It's late afternoon; in other words, it's raining.

"I'm sorry, but it's funny."

"I suppose."

"The wrong general!"

She tucks into a ball on her chair and laughs lightly, peering out at me over her knees. Yes, the wrong general. I have just come from the meeting. My one satisfaction is this: that I did not blink when the general leaned back in his chair and said, "There has been some mistake." There had been no mistake. What had happened was this: I had been misled. General Hernández Fernández–Fernández Hernández had not given me the phone number of his very dear friend, the notorious General Cruz Brea, as promised. Instead, he gave me the phone number of a man with a similar name, General Brea Garó. In his mind, I imagine, Hernández Fernández had told a perverse kind of truth. I had left a message for him, to try to find out, but I already knew I had heard the last of Hernández Fernández.

"It couldn't have been an accident?" says Yanira.

"Everyone at the Balaguer Foundation knew I was looking for Cruz Brea. I said the name a thousand times. It was written clearly in the note . . ."

"You're right. It's too perfect to be a mistake."

I had sat for a while with the wrong General Brea. Why not? I had no idea what to do next, and General Robinson Brea Garó had a genial face and a patio spun with ivy and vines. When the revolution broke out on April 24, 1965, he said, he had been a lieutenant colonel and second-in-command of the cascos blancos, the shock troops of the police. The following day, he told me, his forces had arrested five thousand people, but they released most of them because there was nowhere to lock up so many. The prisoners flowed out into the ragtag rebel army, which began, after San Isidro's strafing of the capital, to attack the police. The cascos blancos were stationed in the Fortress Ozama, where they were surrounded by insurgents. For the next four days they fought to hold the fortress, firing .50-calibre machine guns from the Tower of Homage that had once housed the son of Christopher Columbus. On the fifth day, a helicopter dropped rations to the starving and sleepless men, a moment that the general compared without hesitation to manna from the heavens. Within an hour, however, the rebels launched a sustained grenade and mortar attack, and the order was given for covering fire. It was every man for himself in retreat. Some died, some surrendered, some joined the revolution and some went over the walls and into the Ozama River, swimming for the eastern shore while around them men drowned or were torn apart by sharks. Brea Garó, a marine in the Era of Trujillo, knew the dangers of the river. He found a hiding spot in bales of newspaper covered by a tarp in the customs house of the port, then slipped out at midnight for a terrifying journey through enemy territory to his mother's house, just north of the Duarte Bridge. Two days later, he presented himself for duty at the Palace of the National Police.

"Crimes of war happen in difficult times," said Brea Garó. "It is not only the soldiers and the armies. People act in unexpected ways."

Brea Garó could come up with only one way for me to get a phone number or address for General José Ernesto Cruz Brea. A particular military office, he said, would have the information. On the other hand, they would be very unlikely to reveal that information, and if they did, perhaps for a price, it would only get me as far as Cruz Brea's front door. "It's not everyone in the world who will be open to talking to you," he said. His face made it clear this was an understatement of epic proportions.

"Did you go to the office?" says Yanira.

"Yes."

"And?"

"And they told me to come back tomorrow."

Again, she tries to hide her smile. "There is something you need to learn from this city," she says. "You need to learn to relax."

She's right. I need to relax.

In the next moment, Yanira suggests that it might be time to put my documents, my notes and my tapes, into hiding.

26

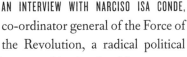

AN INTERVIEW WITH NARCISO ISA CONDE, co-ordinator general of the Force of the Revolution, a radical political party. Our conversation takes place at a table. A pair of doors opens onto the second-storey patio of the building in which the Communist Party of the Dominican Republic was founded in 1944. Isa Conde sits beneath a poster of "Carlos Marx."

I have tried to find General José Ernesto Cruz Brea through his friends, and now I will try his enemies.

Q: Have there been discussions here about the possibility of a commission of "truth and reconciliation"?

A: Like in El Salvador?

Q: Yes, or in Chile or South Africa. I think there is also talk of a truth and reconciliation commission in Guatemala.

A: No, here we continue to struggle against impunity for state crimes. There is, for example, a lawsuit that is still going forward, the only one that has been kept alive—the case against the assassins of Orlando Martínez, our *compañero* who was killed in 1975 by the military high command, which was then made up of figures from the counter-revolution of 1965. Some of them still hold official positions, even today. And although the material perpetrators of the assassination, who were soldiers in that era, have been found guilty, the intellectual authors of the crime have not been brought to justice—men who were the perpetrators of a chain of similar crimes.

Isa Conde is a middle-aged man in jeans, clean-shaven, built like a hatchet. His black eyes seem to simmer with anger.

Q: The fact that these killers are walking free, these people who played such a dangerous part in the history of the country—how does that affect Dominican society today?

A: Well, look, the fact is that the political forces that once played a role in the struggle against the regime of terror, against state terrorism, and that also participated in the revolution of 1965—these political forces have themselves been revolutionized, in a negative sense. They now serve to reinforce the culture of impunity.

The Dominican Revolutionary Party, for example, made alliances with some of these military men when they were still in active positions of command—with Wessin y Wessin, for example, during the Twelve Years of Balaguer. The same forces that were a part of the democratic movement of this country evolved toward the right, they played at the politics of reconciliation with these generals, they protected them. There is an element of society that has sympathy with our demands—the ongoing case of Orlando is highly admired and much appreciated in society at large. But those who hold the positions of permanent power—the high hierarchies in the Catholic church, big business, the traditional political parties— are mixed up in and reinforce the culture of impunity. The result is frustration, a sense that there has been so much struggle and still there is no justice. There were so many crimes. So many criminals.

Q: It must be difficult to establish any idea of justice.

A: Of course. Everything has turned to a politics of corruption. Impunity rules in this country. We might say there is a power like a mafia, with its frauds, its influence peddling, its corruption, its underworld, its criminal police, its perversity, its kleptocracy. The most rotten institution in the country is the National Police. It has given form to every kind of criminality. Of course, all of this is covered up by the mass media. Yes, there are breaches—I have a column in a newspaper, we have a program on radio and on television where we can say all of these things. But in the face of the total volume of opinion, it's minimal. It is no challenge to the culture of impunity. It is difficult to imagine a person as he was forty years ago. Who was Narciso Isa Conde in April 1965? He was at the heart of the revolution in Santo Domingo, a rising youth leader with the Popular Socialist Party, a typically fractious group of the left. He was also number 3 on a list of fifty-four alleged communists and extreme leftists that was released by the U.S. Embassy as belated evidence that the American invasion had been a legitimate response to the threat of a "second Cuba." The list was hardly impressive: visiting journalists found that many more of the April revolutionaries were fiercely anticommunist; in fact, an investigation later revealed that twenty-six rebel officers had actually received training from the U.S. Army.

I had pictured Isa Conde as taller than he turned out to be, if only because there was a time when he made the world's most powerful nation nervous.

Q: You have said that the revolution was followed by thirty-nine years of counter-revolution. Could you explain what you mean?

A: The April revolution was a triumph up until the moment that the Americans landed their troops. The counter-revolution, then, was imperialist—a counter-revolution imposed by American troops, who rebuilt the old military apparatus that had been almost totally dismantled by the popular revolution. So it was re-established, this time with a brain trust of the American intervention, from military consultants to intelligence organizations like the CIA. They created a situation that was then imposed through the fraud of Balaguer. Balaguer returned to power in the context of the American intervention, which he supported, and then began a program to exterminate the popular leaders, the revolutionary leaders and combatants, and this affected the movement a great deal. Then came the neo-liberal era through the policies of the International Monetary Fund and the initiatives of globalization, and so, well, we speak of thirty-nine years of revolution—because the ideals of the April revolution were never achieved. That job is still to come.

Q: Are there ways in which Dominican society today is actually worse off than before the April revolution?

A: In many ways it is worse. In economic and social terms, it's worse. I would say the country has more poverty, more marginality, more unemployment, more crime. The natural environment is noticeably worse off; the rivers and forests have been devastated. Transnational capital has ultimately appropriated the principal national resources, practically all of the public services, the better part of the natural commonwealth. But in the realm of liberties—we can say that we enjoy more liberties today. They are liberties constrained by the powers of big business, by the dictatorship of the mass media, by economic interests. They are constrained by the political and electoral systems. But we are not living under a military regime, a regime that was despotic in every way, like the one that led to the April revolution, much less under the absolute dictatorship of Trujillo.

The headquarters of the Force of the Revolution is on Independence Avenue, magnificently shaded by the avenue's laurel trees. Across the street, taxis slow to a stop beneath the peach facade of the Casona Dorada Hotel. The people who step out are pale. They have dropped out of the sky from northern climates and now they make the first adjustments to their beach hats and sunglasses. Facing them are two billboards. The first is the unmistakable portrait of Che Guevara, staring fiercely into a red-and-black future. The second is unfamiliar to them—a guerrilla soldier. The concierge will perhaps explain that this is Francisco Caamaño Deñó, who emerged as the leader of the 1965 revolution after the rebel victory against Wessin y Wessin's tank brigade at the Duarte Bridge. A placard between the hoardings reads, POPULAR, CAAMAÑISTA, COMUNISTA!

Q: Does the American intervention continue to affect the Dominican mentality?
A: Yes, yes, it affects us. It affects us.
Q: In what way?
A: Well, it wasn't only an invasion—the entire ideological machinery came under American supremacy. The North American dream of a consumer society is, for a country poor in resources, a nightmare. It

creates a consumer illusion that only a tiny minority can achieve, while for the rest of society it is an ideological order: to consume, to consume, to consume. People are ranked by the brand names of the products that they use, and most of those products are American. And since the economy doesn't generate enough wealth to give everyone access to all of this, a segment of society falls into crime in order to make themselves a part of the economic accumulation, to be a part of the consumer society. Every day, new pockets of crime emerge—reflections, really, of a criminal state, a criminal government. It is the culture of impunity reproducing itself.

Isa Conde is comfortable here, on the bridge between the present and the past. He is one of those who reject, utterly, the desire to live outside time. Father Joe McGuckin speaks of keeping the martyrs' blood from drying, and Isa Conde has found his own way to honour that promise. It has become a life's work. He refuses the erasure of history, refuses to allow guilt to pale into innocence. But it is more than that. When he sees the poverty in the bateys, when he considers the zonas francas—the factories that came to be famous as "sweatshops"—he sees the heritage of Trujillo and Balaguer. When he reads that fully 50 per cent of the national income this year will be paid in service of the external debt, he recalls the American occupations. He has witnessed glories, too, and each of them emerged, sometimes slow-burning and sometimes explosive, from the most pessimistic of circumstances. The future, then, is hopeful. The only certain dystopia is the here and now.

Q: I wanted to talk to you, too, about this case of Padre Arturo in the era of the revolution. You are familiar with the case, yes?
A: *(He nods.)*
Q: In your opinion, is there any doubt that the death of the padre was planned?
A: It was a treacherous, deliberate crime.
Q: Without a doubt?
A: Without a doubt.

Q: Do you know what part of the armed forces would have had control of the area around Monte Plata after the revolution? Would it have been San Isidro?

A: San Isidro, yes. And San Isidro played a powerful part in the crimes of that time. San Isidro came from a tradition of officials who were tainted by crimes of the highest order. It was a centre of torture. Look at this case of Orlando Martínez—the man who put together the group that committed the crime was the chief of investigations in San Isidro at that time. The base had a lot of that kind of criminality, and traditionally San Isidro controlled the part of the country east of the capital.

Q: General Imbert told me there was a total division between San Isidro and his Government of National Reconstruction.

A: A total division?

Q: A total division, yes. That General Wessin y Wessin had his world of San Isidro and the Government of Reconstruction controlled what was left.

A: No. Imbert supported the military that were holed up in San Isidro. An example that stands out is Operation Mop-up, in the northern part of the capital—the Government of Reconstruction spoke for that operation and protected it. The Government of Reconstruction was an administrative structure and the United States used Imbert, who had killed Trujillo and was a national hero, to give it legitimacy. Imbert never really had direct military command. You understand?

Q: He said he was a bureaucrat for the United States and the OAS.

A: Exactly. He was designated by the United States, though naturally he has to take political responsibility—everything fell back onto the Government of Reconstruction, and it was that government that represented the counter-revolution. But it is fair to say that Imbert didn't have military command, and he didn't use it.

Q: What more can you tell me about José Ernesto Cruz Brea?

A: Cruz Brea was one of those officials who came out of the military intelligence of Trujillo—from the same school of thought, with a certain intellectual air, okay? His heroes would have been Franco, Hitler and later Pinochet. Cruz Brea is a man totally tainted by crime, above all in the intelligence work necessary to carry out assassinations. He was cold, very cold. He was in the army, and later he was chief of police when they killed Gregorio García Castro, another journalist. Orlando Martínez accused Cruz Brea in an article, and it was Cruz Brea who put together Orlando's articles and put him under surveillance, and it was he who presented Balaguer with Orlando's final article, WHY NOT, DR. BALAGUER? He said, "This cannot be permitted to continue, Mr. President." And Balaguer gave him the green light.

Despite his allegations, Isa Conde's voice has softened. It is a strange thing to be a survivor. The days of killing seem to be over, and here he is among the living. Why? He had the same beliefs as the ones who were killed. He spoke out, marched in the streets. His article in the *World Marxist Review* was brandished by American politicians and intellectuals as proof of a communist insurrection. By what calculus was he left to live? Was he too obvious a rallying point? Was it luck? On the day of his planned murder did he walk down an unexpected street, stand behind a telephone pole that blocked the rifle sight?

Q: You haven't seen any signal of regret or reconciliation in these men?
A: There's no self-criticism. They supported and joined with the American intervention, and the consequences have been swallowed up by history. The same can be said of their crimes. You see ex-generals or majors who were in the highest positions during the Twelve Years of Balaguer, and who put into practice the genocide and all the repression, and through all the effort that Dominican society has made to liberalize itself, to open itself, all that has happened is that some of these men have lost their official positions. Some are still a part of the apparatus of the state. So we don't accept the politics of reconciliation—or what we call conciliation—because there has not been a single signal that would allow us to renounce our principles and accede to some process of understanding with these people. The few who enter the debate at all continue to defend their same positions.
Q: And what kind of signal do you want? What kind of signal are you looking for?

A: Eh?

Q: What kind of signal is possible?

A: No, look, what we are trying to resist is the idea that "the past is the past," that "we can't understand now what was happening then," that "we are all Dominicans together," that it was "a war of brother against brother." That these were historical acts, forgivable from that point of view. That's what we want to resist. We don't have the least illusion that we are waiting for some signal that will change our minds.

I thank Narciso Isa Conde as I rise to leave. He does not know how I might contact General José Ernesto Cruz Brea.

. . .

The next morning, shortly after nine, Josefina Pichardo, assistant to General Elías Wessin y Wessin, greets me in her calm and friendly manner with a total, immutable refusal. "He has received your letters and he says it is impossible to meet."

I stand there stammering, searching my mind for a way forward.

"I'm sorry," she says, "it is a difficult time." It seems she is referring as much to 1965 as to the general's schedule for the coming weeks. I watch her face close down, and there is nothing more to say.

I find myself walking, ignoring the cobradors as they tout their routes. From the churning belly of the old city I climb the hill to the lawns of the National Palace, the pink dome washed with sunlight like a shell thrown into the sky. Within a few blocks the city slumps back toward decay, its sidewalks jumbled and broken, the gutters piled with plastic and paper, funerary mounds of lime heaped over the road-killed dogs. At the edge of a plaza of dying trees, encoiled in an inner-city freeway, I stand once again in front of the offices recommended to me by General Brea Garó. Somewhere inside, someone knows exactly where and how to find José Ernesto Cruz Brea, but the building is a monument to hopelessness. It's like a discarded cardboard box in an underpass, and just as poorly lit. People stand around wearing pointless expressions. I pull open a door and find a lone bureaucrat surrounded by banks of filing cabinets and huge accounts books the colour of bruises. He is dialling phone numbers from a list, but now he pauses, his eyebrows raised in surprise.

"You told me to come back tomorrow," I say, "and tomorrow is now today."

He has forgotten how to smile. "The major is here, but he is not here. You'll need to wait."

The light in the room comes from a single, yellowed window. Above it sits an unusually bleak portrait of the president. I am wasting my time, and my greatest wish is that the officer in charge will finally appear and assure me that I never again need to come to this place with a withered sprig of anticipation in my heart.

A man enters the room. He is largely bald, and his slacks, his sweater, even his skin are such a perfect grey-brown match for the walls that he seems to vanish the moment he stops moving. Yet he smiles. After announcing himself as the major, he listens carefully as I explain what I am looking for. Then, in a rasping voice, he calls to a figure whom I had not even noticed was standing in the room. This secret presence indicates that I should follow him, and we walk the sombre hallways to a sunlit parking lot and onward to an office building that is as brisk and radiant as its neighbour is deadened and pallid. Inside, a clean-shaven man in a razor-creased suit asks me to explain what I am looking for. Then he tells me I will need to speak to the major.

"It's the major who sent me here," I say.

He shrugs and says to my companion, "He will need to talk to the major."

As we recross the parking lot I accept that I am now in limbo. The major will say, "I need permission from headquarters." And headquarters will say, "You need to talk to the major." Forever and ever, amen.

But the major is waiting for us; he is already standing when we walk into the room. I begin to explain, but he silences me with an unintelligible squawk and steps to a filing cabinet. He opens the top drawer, flicks through a row of yellow cards and pulls one up. I see the name: José Ernesto Cruz Brea. There is a headshot of a light-skinned man with a bushy moustache, straight hair and aviator glasses—a Dominican playboy, circa 1986. The major reads out a phone number, slips the card back into the cabinet and closes the drawer. His eyes sparkle, and I realize that the man is a master of the system he lives within. He had known immediately there was only one way he could give me the information. First, he had to send me to a higher authority. That higher authority, in turn, would send me back to him. Through the magic of that transaction, he would be free to make his own decision, but any blame would rest with his superior.

"Thank you," I say. "Thank you very much."

"Godspeed," he replies, beaming, his eyes squinting, a soul somehow never destroyed.

27

A LOW VOICE, HEAVY WITH MISTRUST: "YES?"

"Is this General Cruz Brea?"

"Yes." The word is barely audible.

"Excuse me, but my Spanish isn't very good."

"No, you speak well. I understand you perfectly." A trace, a scintilla of warmth. He listens silently as I make my usual explanations.

"I have absolutely no recollection. I don't remember anything."

"Ah, you don't remember anything." There are never any questions—a Canadian, you say? A young man? He was a Catholic? And how did you say he died? With the generals there is only an automatic response: "I know nothing."

"Well, I have some articles and a report about the case, if we might be able to meet, I can show them—"

"We will meet on Monday. Call me Monday."

"Monday. Okay. Okay. Perfect."

"Perfect."

BUT WE DON'T MEET on Monday. On Monday, the general says he would like to meet on Tuesday. At the appointed hour, I cross the city to Piantini, one of the better neighbourhoods that spread across Santo Domingo's west side. It's a barrio of luxury car dealerships, French bakeries and street advertisements entirely in English.

On an avenue of stately villas, the general's house is a sandwich duplex squeezed between shops. Where there should be a garage and entranceway, there is instead a white-painted wall of iron plate capped with a crown of blossoming vines. One panel can roll back to let a car in or out, and the only other access is a locked gate so narrow that you would have to turn sideways to enter. From the gloom within, a security guard appears with a pump-action shotgun loose in one hand. He has none of the lethal professionalism of the brigade that watches over General Imbert.

The guard lets me in as far as the front door, where an elegant doña introduces herself as the general's wife. "Was it busy in the streets?" she asks.

"Well, yes. The streets are crazy with the campaigns for the candidates. A day or two ago, Independence Avenue was completely blocked by the white campaign, everyone drinking and dancing."

"Even Independence Avenue!"

It's like speaking to someone who doesn't live in the city, or a new visitor to the country. "I never vote," she says, "and I will not vote this time. This politics—it is dirty." She says the word as though she were speaking of a floor that needs to be mopped. "Well, José is not here," she says then.

I keep smiling.

"He enjoys the politics. Perhaps you could try us again at seven o'clock?"

But there is no one home at seven o'clock.

WHEN I CALL THE next morning, the doña picks up. "He is here now," she whispers. It takes an hour to reach Piantini. The guard opens the gate, and I empty my lungs to step through.

Keeping one hand on his gun, the guard drags a chair into the garage, making it clear I will not be entering the family home. I take a seat. There are two parked vehicles here, a sedan and a luxury four-by-four, both in teal green. A pocket-sized Bible is open on the dash of the sedan, as though to cast the holy words outward in a protective shield. The oil paintings and antiques that I can see through the open front door spill out into this caged garage. A stained-glass image of Mary and the baby Jesus hangs above the doorway.

I spot the general then. He's far back in the dim of the house, his eyes on me. He turns away and vanishes from view, but I can hear the low murmur of his voice addressing the lieutenant. When I see General

Cruz Brea again, he is buttoning the sleeves of a French-blue, long-sleeved shirt tucked into new jeans and a brown leather belt. His only military adornment is a camouflage cap. As he enters the garage, he carries a heavy wooden chair with his name, José, carved into the back-board in a mediaeval font.

The moustache is the one from the bureaucrat's file card. The face, though, is fleshier, with a budding sad-dog jowliness. He has skin like a Spaniard's, burnished by the sun. Perhaps he is a man who enjoys the beach. His handshake is like taking an oyster in the palm of my hand.

"What do you want to talk to me about?" His voice seems to come from some point behind his back or in the ground below his chair.

And the story is retold.

"This was during the time of the revolution."

"Yes, in the summer of 1965."

"I wasn't here during the revolution." A pursed smile. When the rebels took Santo Domingo, he says, he was living in Washington, D.C., as an auxiliary to the military attaché to the United States. To have been living overseas, to have missed those first bloody days of conflict—it gives him an unusual innocence. He rests his hands on his knees as though the conversation were over.

"But you returned that year, no?"

He makes a noncommittal noise.

"I have here an article," I continue, and pull the carefully placed copy of *La Hoja* out of my shoulder bag. It's the same article that General Imbert had read aloud, the article that names José Ernesto Cruz Brea to a three-person military tribunal that would judge the case of Padre Arturo MacKinnon, shot dead in Monte Plata. He takes the article in his hands but doesn't read it.

"So you returned that year?"

He says nothing.

"And what did the tribunal do?"

"We went to Monte Plata," he says at last. "Talking to people, getting information." He leans toward me and meets my eyes. "Like you're doing."

He is perfectly at ease, his face the mask of a man who feels no discomfort in telling as little of a story as he pleases. He watches me with small eyes. All of his features have a smallness: his gathered lips, his unremarkable nose.

"What did your report say? What did the tribunal decide?"

"Who can say?" he replies. The hazel in his eyes is alight. Is it mischief? Irony? "It was very difficult to know reality at that time."

I have learned to watch for these statements, these slivers of the coded language that make it possible to talk about the past. *It was difficult to know reality.* There were obstructions, obfuscation. It's not as though Cruz Brea and the tribunal were crusaders. They were military investigators in the business of denial.

"In the opinion of the tribunal, was Art's death an action that was planned?"

"No one can say."

"But in your opinion."

He shrugs with a slight smile, still with that light in the eyes. He's amused, but there is no cruelty in it. It's as though he is laughing inwardly at himself, at the total impossibility of sharing the truth. Instead, he begins to describe Monte Plata in that era, a wonderful town where everyone was in bed by nine o'clock, a place without discos or colmadóns, a place without vice. The death of the priest, he says, created an indignation in the people.

"But how did your investigation go in Monte Plata? Did you learn a lot?"

The corners of his eyes tighten. "I couldn't really say. I don't remember." And now the message seems to be: What is your goddamn problem, gringo? Have you failed to grasp that this will be a conversation in which truth might only be revealed through triangulation, if any truth is revealed at all?

When he returned from the United States, Cruz Brea says, Santo Domingo was still divided by the American troops, but bands of insurgents roamed the city. He stayed in his home, then on Wenceslao Álvares Avenue only a block from the rebellious university, because he was a known right-winger and a military man. At night he could hear the shots and confrontations. He was young then, rising through the ranks, and it was not his generation's moment of truth. That would come later, during the Twelve Years of Balaguer—for him, a bitter memory. He had served his country, he says, perhaps not always in ways that gave him sweet rest at night, and in the end he was thrown aside. Cruz Brea was chief of staff of the national army when Balaguer won back the presidency in 1986 and purged the military of the men who had been his loyal soldiers during his first dozen years in power.

Military life is dirty, says Cruz Brea. A life of bad wages, few freedoms—a life of obedience, he says, screwing up his face and snapping a tin-pot soldier salute. His laughter is shallow and acidic. "I would serve this country without remuneration if it was a position that actually *served* the country," he says. For the moment he's an ally of the Dominican Revolutionary Party, the party whose supporters, in 1965, roamed the streets of Santo Domingo looking for men like Cruz Brea to kill. It's an irony so plain that he says nothing to explain it.

His face has grown lively in subtle ways. His smile is still restrained, but now his lips part; I can see that even his teeth are small. He seems frustrated by the need to carefully consider every word before it falls from his mouth, seems pained by every noise on the street. The noise, of course, is a constant assault: motors, car alarms, people shouting, campaign processions blasting merengue, workers unloading planks, the background drone of traffic. "The most cacophonous streets in the world," he says.

I can feel him slipping away.

"I'm curious," I say. "You're a military man, and you also have had the experience of an invasion by the United States. What do you think about this war in Iraq?" The Dominican Republic's troops have just returned from the war zone, but the American occupation continues. Two weeks have passed since the world first saw the images of U.S. soldiers abusing and degrading inmates in Abu Ghraib prison near Baghdad; the video that shows the beheading of American hostage Nicholas Berg has been on the Internet for fewer than twenty-four hours. There is killing every day.

Cruz Brea's gaze slides back to me, roaming my face. His expression has dissembled, and now there is a hint of pleasure in it. Even his posture is changing. He leans forward on his hard chair until I can see his name in script, once again, over his shoulder. "I believe—and this is only my opinion, you understand, and my truth is different from your truth, and your truth is different than mine—but I think the world is worse for the war in Iraq." This is not, then, to be the conversation I had expected. "When a powerful country tries to impose itself on another, it damages the likelihood of peace."

He begins to weigh aloud the psychological costs of war. It is Cruz Brea the soldier speaking, the alleged intelligence operations specialist, the man trained in tank warfare in France. A human being who has made and lived with the decision to unleash deadly force. He slides to the edge of his seat, seeming to hold toward me some fragile, invisible object. "There are thousands that die, you understand?" he says. "Children, women, old people—dead." He points to Israel, armed and funded for decades by the Americans in its war with the Palestinians. He lists General Augusto Pinochet, whose *coup d'état* in Chile was aided by the American Secret Service and who went on to hold tyrannical power for sixteen years, during which his agents executed some three thousand men and women. Then Cruz Brea recalls the 1980s, when Saddam Hussein, the dictator of Iraq, was a favoured White House ally against the Islamic theocracy in Tehran. In a pause I realize Cruz Brea has spoken not a word of Trujillo, embraced for decades by the most powerful nations of the world, nor of Balaguer, who rode into power after the American occupation of Santo Domingo. We are still speaking in tangents.

"There is no way out of these situations," he concludes. "These things unfold for centuries."

Cruz Brea is aloft now, while I am dumbfounded. The cold, closed warrior has disappeared, to be replaced by a character of passions and erudition. He has become a student of history, he explains, and it leads him again and again to travel to France. He loves to stand where the Armistice was signed to end the Great War, to walk in the footsteps of Gustave Flaubert's *flâneur*, to marvel at the endless graveyards filled with the war dead. It was France that had inspired the young Juan Pablo Duarte to return to Hispaniola and fight for his nation's independence. It was France in that same era that gave the world Victor Hugo and his masterpiece *Les Misérables*, the manifesto of a new humanism. "There may be no greater book save the Bible," Cruz Brea says.

The general misses France. The economic crisis has sunk the value of the peso, and he can no longer make the trip once a year as he used to.

"I stay home, I stay inside," he says, casting a theatrical glance over his shoulder toward the street. "It doesn't matter to me what happens out there."

I am still lost in his devotion to *Les Misérables*. What character would strike so deep a chord with General José Ernesto Cruz Brea? The hero of the book is Jean Valjean, a thief and thug who reforms himself into a symbol of—the word is *caritas*, an active, out-reaching love. But it wouldn't be Valjean. It would be Inspector Javert, surely, the gendarme for whom the police force is religion, the chilling figure whose face twitches whenever someone thinks him capable of making a concession. Javert, relentlessly hunting Valjean until the tables are turned in the heat of insurrection and it is Javert who is captured. His life, though, is spared—by his nemesis, Valjean. Later, when the rebellion has failed and Valjean crawls out of the Paris sewers and into Javert's hands, the gendarme collapses into crisis. His sense of duty is, for the first time, impaired by his sense of forgiveness. *He could no longer live by his lifelong principles; he had entered a new, strange world of humanity, mercy, gratitude and justice other than that of the law.* How do such words sound in the ears of a man like Cruz Brea? *Authority was dead within him.* What does the general feel as he reads that Javert has given Valjean his freedom and then, unable to live with his moral chaos, hurls himself into the rapids of the Seine? *Did anarchy itself descend from heaven?*

"Would you like to see the work-in-progress?"

I'm only dimly aware that the general has begun to talk about model boats.

"Of course," I reply.

He steps inside, his feet quick across the flagstones. When he returns, he is cradling a carefully lathed block of wood in his arms. The hull of Sir Francis Drake's *Golden Hind* awaits its three masts, gunwales, bowsprit and sails, but Cruz Brea seems already to see every detail in the rough shape he turns over in his hands, proud with the kind of pride that is also a loneliness.

At last I rise to go. "Is there anything more, anything at all, that you remember about the case of Padre Arturo?"

He pauses, then looks at me and away. His face has lost its restraint, and he waves aside the question with an anguished expression. Then he meets my eyes, certain now that I will understand. "I do not remember the unfortunate things. I prefer to remember the good."

The world is darkened, he says then, by a creeping inhumanity. We have a hunger to live ever faster, to live more and more through the lenses of technology, to commercialize every aspect of life, to reduce experience to a series of trivialities—and yet we cannot escape our violence. The violence continues, some of it inevitable and some of it avoidable. The great horror is this: we seem to bear that violence with less and less pain.

"And what if," he continues, "what if in this high-tech world, someone came and said simply, 'I am love. I am the way, the truth and the light'?" He pauses, but he's not waiting for an answer. "He would be ignored. He would be ignored."

General José Ernesto Cruz Brea, agent of repression in a lethal regime, accused author of assassination, architect of concealment, turns his model tall ship in his hands as we say farewell. Purple flowers tumble from their vines above the iron walls, and I think of Narciso Isa Conde saying there have been no signs of repentance among these old soldiers.

ROBERTO SANTANA has asked me to lunch. At the foot of the tower that houses his apartment, I realize that my two bottles of table wine are too poor an offering. It's a neighbourhood of embassies and wedding-cake apartments that climb a ridge to overlook the Caribbean Sea, no longer jewel-blue but a green like the North Atlantic, the whole coast coloured by the silt spilling from the mouth of the Ozama River.

So much rain.

Santana is standing in the open door of his apartment, and he wraps an arm around me like a brother. The home is a study in good taste: where there is wood, it is dark; where fabric, rich and textured; where there is artwork, it is bold. From the kitchen, the sound of a daughter repeating French verbs to a tutor. There are bottles of fine wine placed carefully on display.

We take lunch in the kitchen: meatballs, avocado, sweet green tayota squash, the stewed rice and beans known as *moro* and so essential a foodstuff that meal time is sometimes called *la hora de moro*. It's the comfortable food of the country. "I come from the campo," says Santana. "My family was campesino, poor but always politically active." He seems to find the past fatiguing, but he's not prepared to change the subject. He knows that I've spoken to General Cruz Brea.

It was 1969, he tells me, when he entered the Autonomous University of Santo Domingo, the oldest university in the western hemisphere and a campus with such total independence that the police were not permitted to enter the grounds. The United States was losing in Vietnam but had won the race to the moon. The British army was installing martial law in Ulster, and Latin America hung between socialism and fascism. President Joaquín Balaguer was nearing the end of his first term and heeling down on his opponents in preparation for the following year's election. People said: Life isn't better, but less bad. Roberto Santana was elected president of the student union.

They came for him.

Over the next nine years, Santana grew to understand intimately the quiet police state of the Balaguer regime: the riot police, the Banda Colorá, the Pérez y Pérez group, the chilling machinations of José Ernesto Cruz Brea. The CIA, of course. At times, he moved through a network of safe houses, even hiding for two weeks with a Spanish priest in the casa curial in Monte Plata. At other times he was in prison. A few days at first, then weeks, and eventually a stay of fully two years.

"What were conditions like in the jails?" I ask, immediately wishing I could take back the question.

"Conditions were bad," he says flatly. "There was solitary confinement, with only the floor to sleep on. But others had it worse, Santiago. There were others who had it much worse."

Santana leans back in his chair. The soft cheese and figs in syrup have arrived at the table.

"Has anyone from that time admitted regret? Is there a chance for reconciliation?"

It is as though he has been waiting for this question. He looks at me gently, his voice soft when he says, "I don't think so. They justify their actions, they justify." A hush falls again, and when he speaks it is directly to the part of me that wants so badly to give pardon, to believe that men like Wessin y Wessin and Cruz Brea and Lyndon Johnson and even Hot Balls himself have their moments of doubt and pain, their hour when conscience or their god calls them to account and repent. Roberto's eyes, far more than his words, ask me to guard against forgiveness given too easily. There is a hesitation within him, as though he's afraid that the price of understanding is the ruination of something pure.

He leans closer.

"They killed a lot of people, Santiago. A lot of people. A lot of widows. A lot of orphans. A lot of lives cut short, forever." He sinks back in his seat and looks out to the sea. "It's a shame. It's a shame."

28

THE PHONE RINGS IN THE APARTMENT AT Kilometre Ten.

"Hello?"

"Hello, Santiago, my brother."

"Charlie?"

How long has it been? Two weeks? A month?

"Santiago, my friend, I've got something. It's this lieutenant, Evangelista Gil Reyes."

"No, Charlie, there's no Evangelista Gil Reyes. There is a Julio Gil Reyes and an Evangelista Martínez Rodríguez."

"Yes, yes, Evangelista Martínez. Can we meet?"

There is absolutely no possibility that he has found Second Lieutenant Evangelista Martínez. The lieutenant is not on Charlie's database for the same reason that we could not find the former police captain Julio Gil Reyes—because he is dead. The database contains only the names of the living.

"Yes, Charlie, we can meet."

IT'S THE EVE OF THE ELECTION. Juan Ayala sits in the glow of morning and leans into the radio. All week he has kept company with the radio or the television, or both, and all week there has been electricity in Santo Domingo, because the president wants to show that he is still able to make miracles. This morning's news report says twenty-four thousand *dominicanyorks*, expatriates living in New York City, have registered to vote. For the first time, the Dominican diaspora, not only in Manhattan but in Miami, Boston, Montreal, Madrid, will have a chance to cast their ballots. "Little by little, we progress," says Juan. "But still there are men with money, with properties, with resources, and men who have nothing but these," and here he sticks out his wiry arms, turning them in the sun as though they were goods for sale at market. "If all you have in the world to earn a living is your arms, the problem is very clear. If you get sick, you die."

The guagua into town can only creep through the seething streets. Every few blocks, another patch of pavement has been claimed by this or that political party, a street-side concert for a throng in red, a caravan of white, a chanting crush of purple, or in a places a swirl of them all, each competing for the attention of every passerby. "Stay the course!" shout the white, "Out they go!" shout the purple, and their voices are hoarse against the horns and the stereos and the speakers mounted on flatbed trucks where men and women shake and sway. The schools have been let out and children are everywhere. A motorcycle roars through the crowds, dragging sheet metal on the end of a rope, and everyone cheers. It's the biggest party since the Carnivals of February, and then, too, the celebrants were divided, dedicated to the Slave King in his tall top hat; to King Monkey; to the Paper Demons; to the Cocorícamos, almost naked and covered in black greasepaint, their faces hidden in long knots of hair as they crack their whips into the crowds; to the famous *diablos cojuelos*, the Lame Devils of La Vega with their popping eyes, fangs and shining horns, each one lashing the unwary with bladders full of cow manure.

But the politics have faded by the time we reach Máximo Gómez, and it is early enough that there are patches of shade. Charlie's motorcycle turns out of the traffic and pulls to a stop. He's like a shadow in the sun: black pants and a midnight T-shirt, skin like scorched wood. He nods a greeting, something irrepressible warming his eyes. Already he is fishing in his pocket, removing a document folded in four. At a glance I can see that it is some kind of form, and that the rings of paper mould have photocopied in dark grey. There are two photos on the page, one face-on and one in profile, along with a set of fingerprints. Now I can read the heading: NATIONAL POLICE PERSONNEL CARD. The first line, marked "Rank," reads "2do Tte." A second lieutenant.

It is Evangelista Martínez Rodríguez.

"It's good, no?"

"It's good, Charlie."

I can't tear myself from the page, afraid that this opening into time might somehow slam shut.

"It's a dangerous week in this country—very conflicted," Charlie says. "People will kill for a word. Don't say a word about the political situation, you understand? This week you are mute." When I look up, he is grinning. We are standing there beaming, making small talk, sharing the wordless knowledge that we will not meet again, that Charlie has risked enough, too much; that already somewhere in the crumbling panopticon we might hear the creaking of gears, see the beam of a spotlight turning. Charlie pulls his road helmet over his big smile, and we shake hands. I watch my peculiar friend fade into the heat-struck city.

There's a policeman walking down the street toward me.

I'm on the move instantly, embarrassed at my own paranoia, the folded document still tight in my hand. Where else? I could put it in my pocket—but pickpockets stream through the election-campaign crowds. In my shoulder bag—but today will be the day that the tígueres pick me out, snatch the bag and roar off on a motorcycle. I glance over my shoulder: the constable seems disinterested, I admit, but he is keeping my pace. I would be safer surrounded by people, lost in the buzz and the howl. At the last possible moment, I step up into a passing guagua. The cobrador's arm is like a mothering wing.

Back at Kilometre Ten, I lock the door. There, in the dead air, I spread the double-sided page on a table. Evangelista Martínez Rodríguez, the ghost. I had given up on him. Worse, I had begun to let his mystery shoulder the burden of guilt. He had become the assassin from San Isidro, the cold-blooded killer with a hit in Monte Plata, the man without a past who didn't leave behind so much as a death certificate. And yet here he is. Handsome, really. His uniform is crisply pressed, with its sashes and pins; it might have bothered him to see that his tie was not perfectly straight. His face is serious, calm, dignified without seeming proud. He is listed as five feet, six inches tall, an inch taller than he measured on the autopsy slab. Brown eyes, curly hair, good teeth and the dark-honey skin the document describes as *indio*. His fingerprints have a thickness that suggests he used to work with his hands. He's not a new recruit, and yet there's an innocence in his expression. The face is strikingly similar to that of the dead officer being carried to heaven by Jesus in the propaganda painting I saw hanging in the palace of the police.

There is the bare outline of a life story. Evangelista Martínez was born on September 21, 1935, in the cordillera town of Padre Las Casas. At the age of twenty-one, he gave up working as a plumber and signed with the armed forces. Six years later—and two years after the death of Generalissimo Trujillo—he moved overnight from the army into the National Police. His career took him from Santo Domingo to the pilgrim's city of Higüey, the agricultural centre of El Seibo, the pretty rivermouth town of La Romana and finally back to the capital. Forty-six days before the April revolution, he was named the detachment commander in Villa Agrícolas, a sprawling barrio of rural migrants in the restive barrios altos. On June 6, 1965, he failed to appear at the Palace of the National Police, and as a result was imprisoned without loss of wages.

Something familiar about that.

It is months since I began my search for Evangelista Martínez, when I sat in the General Archive of the Nation with the crackling copies of *Patria*, the rebel newspaper. An article marvelled that the wife of General Wessin y Wessin could stand to sleep with "a monster of genocide and evil"; another proposed a simple solution to the problem of communists in the insurgency: "Kill them." Every issue denounced traitors or heralded victories, and on September 26, 1965, an unnamed writer reported on the "presumed assassin" of Padre Arturo MacKinnon. Just ten days before the killing, the article stated, Evangelista Martínez was languishing in La Victoria prison as an accused supporter of the revolution. A week later he was the chief of police for Monte Plata. And then he was dead, the priest alongside him.

The cause of death, according to the personnel card on the table in front of me: "Bullet wounds received while travelling in a jeep on the highway outside of Monte Plata." There's more. Evangelista Martínez had a pension. It would go to the lieutenant's two little girls, Celeste and

Teresa, and to his widow, Elba Altagracia Quezada. The woman from the tattoo. *Remember Quezada.*

It takes only a minute to discover that one of the three, Celeste Altagracia Martínez Quezada, is listed in the phone book.

I dial the number.

"Hello?"

"Hello. With Celeste Altagracia, please."

"One moment."

The usual pause.

"Hello?"

"Ah, hello. Is this Celeste Altagracia?"

"No. I am her grandmother."

The guardian of the household. She is polite and direct, but also exacting. Celeste is in New York City, she says, and Elba Quezada lives in Santiago de los Caballeros. She will give me Elba's phone number, but only if I will explain myself. As I do so, a heavy silence builds on the other end of the line.

"Why don't you call the Martínez family?" she demands.

"Señora, I don't know the names of anyone in his family, and there are a lot of people with the last name Martínez in Santo Domingo. They fill pages and pages of the phone book. Do you know how I might contact them?"

"Oh no. I know nothing of those people." Has a bitterness crept into her voice? "How did you get this phone number?"

I have to lie, of course, something about a soldier in Monte Plata who remembered the names of Evangelista's wife and children. The grandmother weighs each word in quietude, and then she gives me a number for Elba Quezada. I don't let myself pause, not even to think.

"Hello?"

"Hello. With Elba Quezada, please."

The voice on the line sounds like an older woman, one who is used to receiving bad news on the phone. She wants to know my name, my location, the reason for my halting Spanish and my interest in this woman Elba Quezada. At the mention of the name Evangelista Martínez, the questioning becomes an interrogation.

"Where did you get this number?" the woman says fiercely.

"From a woman who said she was the grandmother of Elba's daughter Celeste."

"What was her name?"

"What? I don't know."

"But you spoke to her!"

"She told me she was Celeste's grandmother. I don't know her name."

"This woman—what was her phone number?"

I read the numbers one by one. I can hear her taking deep breaths.

"How did you contact this family?"

I tell my lie, and then I just keep talking, about forty unanswered years for the families of Padre Arturo and Evangelista Martínez and Ramón Restituyo and Odulio de los Santos, about remembrance and the fact that everything is forgiven, really, almost totally forgiven except that we need the truth, don't we, the whole truth, and then the dead can rest. And when I run out of words and arguments I ask her: "Are you Señora Quezada?"

"No!" she cries out. "No! No!" She begins a fresh attack, but then she stops herself. When she speaks again, her voice glows a little and she is thoughtful. No, she says, Elba Quezada and her daughters are all in New York, and she doesn't know how long they'll be there. She doesn't know of any way to reach them.

"Who are you?" I ask. It feels good to put her back on her heels.

Just an old woman keeping house, she says, staying in the apartment until Elba comes home.

"So she must call you sometimes."

"Yes," she says with hesitation.

"So I could leave a message with you."

"Yes." Her voice now is barely a squeak.

When I have left my name and number, I put down the phone, think for a few moments, then pick it up and dial. Too late—the line is busy. A minute later, the call rings through. The grandmother answers, and she is testy and impatient. All I want to know, I say, is whether she can tell me how to contact her granddaughter in New York City.

"I don't have any number in New York," she says.

"Any address?"

"No address."

"And you don't remember the names of anyone in the Martínez family?"

"I don't know those people." This time, she almost spits it.

IN THE BLACKNESS before dawn, the whole city is awake. The odours of frying eggs and salami, the sounds of ablutions and radios picking up the morning news. Outside, there are figures in the dark; I hear the warmth of their greetings as they recognize each other beneath the street lights.

It is election day. Downstairs, a single lamp lights the kitchen. Rosa is preparing sandwiches, the light shining off her arms and the lines of her face. Juan has left his radio turned off for the first time in two weeks, as though the day were sacred. He doesn't even talk about politics. He talks about love at age sixteen.

We walk out together at six o'clock, when the sun comes with its sudden alchemy and turns the barrio to gold. As we follow the crowds to the polling station at a local school, friends of Juan and Rosa join us. Everyone is carefully dressed as if for Mass, and they join the ballot line-ups, one for men and another for women, with the patience of pilgrims. A few people carry radios, which report quiet and order all over the city. From the long cast of the lineups it is hard to imagine that anyone has stayed home today, but then I remember the doña in the house of Cruz Brea.

Independence Avenue has the feel of a general strike. The traffic is a trickle, and in place of the mad bustle there is a delicate respect. It's as if democracy depended on this decency, as if a *coup d'état* would erupt the moment someone failed to say "good morning" as they stepped up onto a guagua. People walk the streets, pausing to listen to the news reports that play from every colmado. But there is no news, really, only a reverence for a day of voting more peaceful than any in the nation's history. Turnout has been spectacular. It is an election that would make any nation proud.

I'm making my way into the barrios altos. It's a connect-the-dots journey; seek shelter with every cloudburst and move on only with the return of that rising razor-blade sun. When I find the street I'm looking for, I almost turn around. It's that kind of barrio. The plaster homes are too small for the families who fill them, so everyone spills into the street to share beer from the tiny colmado. Everyone knows everyone, and strangers there should have good reasons. It's the kind of neighbour-hood where pariah dogs play outfield for a game of stickball, where the manholes have lost their covers, where every rainstorm washes away another few feet of the sidewalk, where the garbage service is apoc-ryphal. Two radios sit in the middle of the roadway, one tuned to the news and the other to bachata.

"Hey, gringo!" shouts a young man. He beckons me closer. "What do you want?" The question is blunt, but not unfriendly.

I am looking for the Martínez family home. According to the "next of kin" entry on the police personnel card, Braudilio Martínez, father of Evangelista, lived at number 74 on this street in 1963. It's the definition of a long shot.

"Martínez!" the young man calls out. A pair of eyes lifts from a cir-cle of men whose heads are bent together in discussion. The grey, crew-cut head makes a jerking motion, an invitation. The street watches my approach. The man's name is Ramón Ramírez Martínez and he lives in the pink box marked as number 74. He has never heard of any Braudilio Martínez. "It's strange," Ramón says thoughtfully, "because I've lived here since I was like this," and he flattens his hand at the height of a little boy.

"Maybe you remember a person named Evangelista," I say. "He was the son of Braudilio Martínez."

"A military man? A soldier? He was guilty of killing the padre?"

In an instant the world has shrunk to just the two of us, these words between us, our eager faces. "Yes! That's him! Exactly!"

"Mother!" yells Ramón.

From the open door of number 74 I hear the croak of an old woman, then her brisk shuffle. She appears, a matron in a meadow-flower purple housedress, her hair naturally straight and drawn back into a loose grey bun. Her skin is the colour of almond, and she walks with her head tilted regally upward, which seems to help her see. She takes hold of my hand and elbow and stares into me as her son floods her with questions about Evangelista Martínez.

"Oh," she says, widening her eyes dramatically. "He killed the padre! He killed the padre in—San Isidro?"

"Monte Plata," I say.

"Ah! Yes."

Evangelista and Elba—those two she remembers. The children, especially—she remembers the children. They all lived here at number 74. She remembers the shock of the news. Not the news that Evangelista was dead; it was the time of the revolution, and everyone in Santo Domingo seemed to have lost a son or an uncle or a cousin or a mother. The shock was that Evangelista had killed the priest.

"So they say that he was guilty?" I ask, trying to sound doubtful.

"Oh, his mother died of it," she says.

The old woman goes quiet for a moment, then she rests a hand on my shoulder and leans in to speak. "Tell me, what about those three children? How's the little one? I am the godmother of that little one."

"Well, I have heard that Celeste and Teresa live in New York," I say. Ramón's mother nods, but she is waiting. "I didn't know there was one more," I admit.

"Oh yes, oh yes. The wife, she was like this when he died." She smoothes her hand outward from the ribs and cups an imaginary belly.

"Oh, no."

"Yes, yes. I am the godmother."

Ramón asks if I want to see where the couple lived. His mother looks at me with a long-ago sadness and shuffles back toward her door. I turn and follow Ramón, who seems almost too large for the narrow passage as he leads me off the street and into a pocket courtyard. Number 74 is not the single home that it appears to be from the street; this inner sanctum is surrounded by white slatwood doors, most of them hanging open to reveal the tiny, butter-yellow tenements within. "There are eighteen in total," says Ramón. "Evangelista lived in that one." He points to the final door in one corner of the complex. Somehow it seems the most desolate of them all. It is the kind of place where nothing could be hidden; where the houses are too small to contain even the smallest, darkest truth, which would spill into the courtyard to hang with the lines of washing, or, worse, would be something seen only in glimpses, an object of speculation, a piece of gossip moving from every neighbour to the street, from the street to the barrio, from the barrio to the city, the country, the world. I imagine the young mother, pregnant with her third, and there is not a moment of privacy, not even that moment when the policeman arrives and asks to speak with her in her home, and even his quiet voice isn't quiet enough, and even her first stifled sob is overheard and remembered. She is, anyway, the last to know. *Haven't you heard? The lieutenant killed a priest in Monte Plata! A priest!* The voice of the people is the voice of God.

I know then that I am ready to leave Elba Quezada alone.

29

IT'S TWILIGHT, THE RAIN ON THE ROOF LIKE the voices of the dead. I'm stretched out on my U.S. Army wool blanket in the falling light.

It was a night like this one.

The scene is the high plateau that rolls to the rise of the Cordillera Oriental, the landscape drenched with June showers. Lakes spread over the fields with a shine like dull metal, and every furrow is a quicksilver vein. The half-moon has set ahead of the sun, and on the southern horizon the lights of the capital city warm the bellies of black clouds. The streets of Monte Plata are a dim hatch-work; only the hard strip through the centre of town is lit, with new lamps, from the cathedral toward the water tower. The air smells of earth and rotting mangoes.

A man walks along that bright-lit strip, almost alone as the nighttime curfew approaches. He is a stout figure, the sort who looks more comfortable in a uniform than in these stiff civilian clothes. A .38-calibre pistol is holstered to his belt. He stops in front of a green clapboard house with a jeep parked in the street—the casa curial, the parish house. Does he falter at the gate? Doesn't he seem to pause? Now he enters, calling out.

A woman appears. A housekeeper. She is apologetic as she speaks with the man at the door, but he is insistent. With hesitation in every movement, the woman leads him through to the dining room, where a man is eating. He's young, with the skin of a foreigner. He wears dark-rimmed glasses and simple clothes. The priest. His face is unnaturally calm, as though this was a visit he had been expecting, as though some sinister rumour had finally taken shape. It's a complex expression; there is sadness in it, and fear, and anger, and resignation. He speaks and gestures at his plate, but the visitor remains hard-mouthed. There is some business that urgently demands a priest. Of course: someone is dying, a soul crying out for last rites.

The priest rises and speaks briefly to the woman. He leaves the building with the man with the holstered gun, and the two of them walk to the jeep. The priest doesn't take a cassock or other vestments; he doesn't carry a Bible, holy water, blessed oil. He's in a checked grey shirt, white undershirt, black trousers, black shoes. He steps up into the driver's seat, and the visitor climbs in beside him.

The headlights pool on the hardtack road as the vehicle begins to move north.

After the bend onto the road out of town the jeep passes a bar, almost empty now, though a man is waiting up ahead on a street corner. He's in a uniform, the grey slacks and shirt of a policeman, with the chevrons of a second lieutenant on his collar. His face, too, is resigned, but there's no peace in the expression. More like a kind of self-annihilation. An assault rifle, the Belgian make known as the FAL, is at ease at his side.

The priest steers the jeep to where the lieutenant is standing, and the man with the holstered pistol steps out and salutes. Now it is clear: he's a policeman in plain clothes. He climbs into the rear seat, behind the priest, and the lieutenant takes the front passenger seat. The jeep bobs back out onto the road, but now the attitude inside the vehicle has shifted. The men have begun to argue.

This, really, is the end of Monte Plata; there is the army checkpoint in front of the barracks, but the sentry on duty plainly recognizes the men in the jeep and waves them on. There are only a few more houses now, then the cemetery walls, then nothing but the blueblack fields, lit here and there by a candle or a charcoal fire glowing inside some campo shack. The argument in the jeep has become heated. Has a blow been struck? Is the figure behind the priest leaning forward, as though to threaten him?

But the vehicle is stopping. They have reached the last house at the edge of town. A man, tall and proud, his face a long oval, steps toward the jeep from a bohío set back from the road. His children huddle in behind him. This man recognizes the priest warmly, though he glances with concern toward the two policemen. He exchanges a few words with the padre—two friends making small talk. And now the priest does a strange thing: he leans forward to rest his head against his hands on the steering wheel. There is no mistaking this expression of total despair. In an instant, however, he is resolved. He speaks again to the man, puts him at ease. They exchange a farewell.

The jeep rolls forward.

It has barely entered the long S bend into the fields when it is clear that the argument inside the jeep is now a fight. The priest has become demanding; he no longer believes, if indeed he ever did, that this journey is for some sacramental purpose. He has lost whatever fear he might have had, or it has been transformed. Suddenly the man in the back seat lunges forward, his hands on the priest's neck, squeezing, squeezing hard.

The jeep lurches and zigzags; it is nearly at the point where a final cluster of houses marks the crossroads to Yamasá or Sabana Grande de Boyá. But the priest can't wait. The air is dying in his lungs. He slams on the brakes and throws open his door, sliding out of his seat, turning, breaking the grip on his neck. But he doesn't run. It's true he must be out of wind, and that the fields of yuca on either side of the road are thick with mud, even patches of wild mangrove, but there is more to it than that. It's as though running is not in his nature, as if he is waiting for his enemies to climb out of the jeep.

They do.

Everyone is shouting: the priest at his two assailants, and the assailants at one another. They are three tiny figures in the cupped palms of the campo, men raging into the silence of a nation under martial law.

The lieutenant slams his rifle butt into the priest's chest.

A hanging moment. The priest is reeling backward, buckling, the lieutenant bellowing, the plainclothesman standing mute. The priest is a knot of rage. His fists clench. He is willing himself to rise. Now the muzzle flash, one-two-three. The succession of shots is impossibly swift, the priest twisting away to the right, instinct taking over. He drops onto his side, his face stunned. The lieutenant shot him, actually shot him; he has been shot. It isn't pain, exactly; in fact, he is surprised at his own strength. He could stand up, though the feeling in his gut might make him sick. And why stand? To be shot again? He would sooner turn his mind to other things. He knows now that he is about to die.

It is clear that things have not gone according to plan. The two policemen are arguing—neither has the appetite to kill a priest. He was not supposed to resist; it wasn't supposed to happen here, within earshot of Monte Plata, not half a kilometre from the police and army barracks. Now it has to happen here. The lieutenant is making threats to the plainclothes officer. What does he have to hold over the man's head? Imputations of cowardice? The threat of a court martial, a ruined career? An end to the paycheques and perquisites of a life in uniform, everything that earns a police officer his keep and allows him to send money home to his mother, that feeling as big as the world? And then there is the fact that the priest has already been shot; he is dying already. Isn't it better to end his misery? Isn't there something almost holy in that final act of mercy?

The plainclothesman draws the pistol. The priest sees him approach. He is within himself, preparing and acquitting his mind for death, thinking of his family, surely, of friends here and away in his northern homeland, of his priestly brothers, of his God and the sweet Son of God.

The gunman crouches and places the muzzle against the priest's jaw. In the instant of the muzzle flash, a queer sight. The killer has the face of a doomed man, and his victim's eyes are unafraid. In their last light—what? Is it anguish? Fury? Love? Is it forgiveness?

There's a new figure in the darkness. He is hurrying from the crossroads toward the sound of the shots and the voices. He's in the drabs of a soldier, both hands steadying a Cristóbal carbine submachine gun. He circles away from the far-cast light from the jeep, slipping off the road and over the sheen of a ditch into the ebony stalks of a field. The smell of the yuca in the soil is enough to remind him he is hungry; he has been on foot all afternoon in the campo.

Closing in, he can smell the gunpowder.

In the headlights, the two men are silhouettes. The one with the rifle is in uniform—the soldier can tell by the cut of the clothes. The other man, the heavy one, appears to be in civilian dress. The two are arguing again. There is something else, too—a person on the ground, his head pointed toward the soldier. But not a person—a body. It has that stillness.

Now the soldier can see that the other man also has a gun. A pistol in his hand. He takes in all of this in a moment.

He shouts out.

The two men start with surprise. The one in the uniform shouts, and then the man in the civvies, and then both of them are moving. The soldier pulls the trigger.

The shots start low. The corpse on the ground shudders from a hit, but the soldier pulls up toward the big man and sees him spin in a whirl of shells and then—the man in the uniform drops, his arms and legs falling out uselessly beneath him.

Three bodies in the lights of the jeep. As the soldier's ears stop ringing, the mourning of cicadas and crickets. It's a cold night. June is a cold, wet month.

The soldier steps out of the field. The night hasn't yet taken all of the day; it's as though he's looking at the world through the blue of dark glass before it is blown, the blue of deep water on the windward side of a reef. He places his footsteps carefully, his gun still ready though he is sure that he emptied its chamber. He calls out, but there is no sign of life.

He goes from one to the next to the next.

The face of the man in the grey uniform is staved in and spattered with brains and blood. It takes a moment to come to recognition. *The new lieutenant.* The soldier turns to the man in plain clothes. *Ramón Restituyo.* He knows now that he has killed two policemen; his panic is rising. And now the final figure. *It is the padre.*

The soldier moves automatically, collecting the weapons, then stands. He is, as they say, between the point of the sword and the wall. He can explain the dead policemen. He heard gunfire, he came running, he saw a man in civilian dress with a pistol in his hand, fighting in the road with a man in uniform. He took aim to defend the lieutenant, but the lieutenant moved, or a shot went wild. But the priest. To say there was a body on the ground when he arrived at the scene would be to accuse the police of murder, the assassination of a foreign priest, and what would happen then? He'd be lucky to see tomorrow. Yet he has to explain how three men came to die, how bullets from his own gun found their way into the bodies. He looks again at the priest. He's not in his cassock, not even his collar. Well. So. Two men in civilian dress and one in uniform. Shots ringing out, and shouting. All in the blackness of night. He turns and begins to walk the road into Monte Plata.

It must have happened something like that.

JUST BEFORE MIDNIGHT I get up to meet the footsteps on the stairs. Juan appears in the light of the apartment doorway and does a little jig, his guayabera wet across the shoulders from the storm. He is holding a bottle of Presidente beer in one hand and two drinking glasses in the other. He sets the glasses down on the table, pours out the beer and holds up the empty bottle.

"*El Presidente* has conceded," he says with a chuckle.

I snap on the television, and we watch as the picture winks onto the screen. It's the news clip of the moment: the president, shrugging too often as he tells a scrum of reporters that he accepts his defeat. The country has traded the white party for the purple. "Tomorrow, nothing will change," says Juan. "Onions will still be expensive, chicken will still be expensive. But the price of hope is going down." I hear his hiccupping giggle as he steps back into the rain.

Part
THREE

30

IN SAN JOSÉ DE OCOA ONLY THE CACTUSES
are green. The silver-leafed trees
are spangled with papery flowers.
It's a season of butterflies, some as bright as the sun and others a brilliant
morning-star blue, but in Ocoa everyone is hoping for rain. For weeks
they've watched the afternoon clouds pile against the mountains only to
slip off the eastern slopes toward the capital. But rain will come. After a
spell like this, it'll come hard.

"Hello, Frank. I've almost finished my goodbyes."

Frank Sinatra jumps in his seat—he had been lost in the music filling
his courtyard office from a pair of speakers. Now he smiles and wags a
finger as if it had been only hours, not months, since he'd last seen
my face.

"Guess who this is?" he asks, tilting an ear to the rising baritone. It's
music from another time, that much is clear, maybe old mountain songs,
campesino songs. I shrug. "It's Father Lou," he says. He can see that I
don't believe it. Father Lou's voice today is a shallow rumble, and this
singer is ringing and unrestrained. The recording is decades old, Frank
explains, probably from the years after the revolution—hard-times
music; hunger music. Frank's expression is melancholic. He's worried
about Lou, who has just returned from a Miami hospital where they
catheterized his heart, releasing him two days later to fly home and cast
his ballot for a new government. They're not going to last forever, these
old rebels.

Frank listens for a few moments longer and then spreads his hands
toward me, inviting me to begin.

"I think I understand now what happened with those firearms," I say. His eyebrows rise. He eases himself back in his chair, and I tell him the story: the final minutes in the life of Padre Arturo MacKinnon.

When I have finished, a stillness.

"There was a pistol and a—what kind of rifle?" he asks at last.

"An FAL. It's an automatic, not like a rifle for hunting."

He stares at the flies standing upside down on the ceiling. "I think," he says, cautiously disagreeing, "that they must have shot him with the pistol first, and then the rifle to make sure he was dead."

"That's possible."

"It was a common method of assassination."

"They had to shoot him from very close," I say, coaxing him to think further.

Frank Sinatra rocks his chair forward onto all four legs. With his index finger and thumb in the shape of a gun, he presses the barrel into his jaw. "It wouldn't have been easy to shoot him like that. The padre was tough," he says. He mimics a man rolling up his sleeves, his grin widening at the memory. "No, they would have to have shot him first with the rifle."

I nod. "I think he resisted."

"I think you are right," he says. His gestures are grand in his bright yellow button-up, the pleats not yet softened in the dry heat of the day. "And what about the higher levels?" he says.

"There are people who believe that not only the military was involved, but also some civilians, some powerful people in Monte Plata."

"And what do you believe?"

The question had been decided when, the day after the election, I found one more living member of the List of Fourteen. Romeo Santana was a civilian in the summer of 1965, a teenager. His father was Fabio Santana, the army lieutenant in Monte Plata; his mother was the woman who collapsed in the church when Arturo cancelled the Corpus Christi procession. I reached Romeo in San Cristóbal, the birthplace of Trujillo, and he asked to meet on the patio of the Hotel Constitución. It was a careful choice, the most public place in the city. In any case he brought muscle, two young men who leaned with crossed arms against the wall behind him. Romeo Santana seemed older than his years, his pallid, nearly translucent skin touched with liver spots. He remembered the story of Padre Arturo, but many of the details had flown from him. He was surprised—disbelieving even—when I reminded him that two policemen had died with the padre. Then he remembered that, yes, his father had been called to Santo Domingo to answer to an investigation, and later the officials showed up in Monte Plata. After that: nothing. His father stayed on as lieutenant, and he never spoke of the case. Never. I asked Romeo, "What kind of man was your father?" He slipped off his sunglasses to deliver an incredulous glare. "Don't ask *me* that question," he said, his lips hard. "Talk to the people in Monte Plata." That, really, was the end of the conversation.

"Sometimes in this country the sons don't want to know about the lives of their fathers," says Frank Sinatra. "And can you imagine a father telling a son?"

So many secrets. So much ordinary evil that it is difficult not to imagine the worst. What was Monte Plata in 1965? A place of calm and familiarity, of concealment and ancient hatreds. There is little reason not to believe that there were men who spoke ill of the foreign padres, women who wrote letters to complain that Cuban radio had been heard in the parish hall. A narrow band of families stood to lose a heritage of wealth, land and influence to a popular rebellion. It is easy to forget that this was once what democracy could mean: not a minuscule chit in the administration of a system, the rules of which have already been decided by the International Monetary Fund and the World Bank or the Paris Club, but a handover of power from a privileged few to the majority, a smouldering, impoverished majority with a fearsome appetite for change. The priests of Monte Plata had made themselves clear: they were on the side of the revolution. Who can doubt that the tutumpotes, the powerful ones, whispered their condemnations? Their words found ears among the generals, among military men who feared that their time in history was nearing the stroke of midnight, men who had been spinning lies into truth for so long that they could no longer see themselves as they had become: tyrants, torturers, killers. "I don't remember," say the old soldiers. General Cruz Brea looking pained in his iron cage, speaking a kind of confession: *I do not remember the unfortunate things.*

"To forget is a voluntary act," says Frank.

But the whisperers are not murderers. I do not believe that Porfirio Contreras Alcántara fired his gun in the fields outside Monte Plata on the afternoon of June 22, 1965, to fulfill his role in a conspiracy, or that Romeo Santana sat with his father to help plan the death of Padre Arturo. I do not believe that, on the night Arturo was killed, there was celebration in the houses that had spoken against him, nor among those in a position to have known he was about to die. Only a shock that it had *come to this,* a creeping sense of culpability like a poison in the blood. It would have been impossible, in 1965, in a town crowded under the shadow of its cathedral, to put together a list of fourteen people who were willing to have the blood of a priest on their hands. In the end it took a stranger, a lieutenant who had been jailed for insubordination; who was suspected of harbouring sympathies for the revolution; a man who stood to lose everything he'd gained in his eight years in the armed forces, with a wife and two children and a baby on the way, and who, on the day of the killing, tried to drink away the horror. That's the kind of person it took. It took a much different kind of man to give Evangelista Martínez his orders.

"I left a letter for General Wessin y Wessin," I say to Frank, fumbling in my bag for a copy. "I have tried to be clear with him."

> Sir, I have spoken with many people about this case, including the families of the soldier and of one of the two policemen. A significant number of these witnesses believe that the orders to kill Padre Arturo came from the base in San Isidro. These people maintain that the majority of prisoners were in San Isidro, and that Padre Arturo made his protests in San Isidro, and that the lieutenant who killed the padre came from San Isidro, and that the forces of San Isidro controlled in that time the area and the access to the area of Monte Plata.
>
> Sir, I have limited myself to a single question: How do you respond?

Frank lets a silence settle between us. "Nothing?" he says.

"So far, nothing," I reply. I don't add: only this urge to escape, the feeling that my sojourn in the republic is coming to a close. The two of us drift into small talk and laughter, neither willing to say farewell.

Frank asks me to stay another night in Ocoa, and we shake hands and promise nothing.

I know that I'm going to keep moving.

There might just be enough time.

THE GUAGUA OUT OF the town of Barahona is late. The driver won't leave until it's full, but he can't keep track of how many are waiting. None of the passengers is willing to sit in an apparently immovable bus. For one thing, the air has been crackling since dawn, and for another, the seats are like a heap of loose bones covered with a light blanket. Three hours have passed, and then suddenly the driver is shouting that he has had enough, he is leaving this instant. Now he has too many fares. We press in, heaped against each other like animals through a stockade. On top of us the driver stacks baskets of beans, a new television, two roosters with burlap hoods over their heads, an enormous ball of fabric.

All of this, and the guagua cannot take me as far as I hope to go. I have decided to try for paradise, but there isn't a bus that goes there.

I have only this one day, and then I need to be back in Santo Domingo for a flight to Miami, Denver, Vancouver. If I hadn't stopped in Barahona—but the people had convinced me. The men and women on the guagua from Ocoa had an excitement I hadn't seen in any other part of the country. They were *going home*. And I did love Barahona when I saw it. The town sits at a crook in the Pedernales Peninsula, a jut of land that swings south from the border with Haiti. Below Barahona the landscape is green, and above it is arid and brown, but Barahona has decided it will be a desert town. The air is desert air, clear of everything but this moment in time. The streets are uncrowded and idle, the plaster splits on the colonial buildings, there are wood-slat colmados so gapped and crooked that the old men inside them hang onto their hats when a dust devil blows from the plaza. On the shore, where some towns might have a line of resorts, there is a mine instead. A twelve-year-old boot-black named Wilkin showed me the way beyond it to the little local beach tucked in behind the mangroves, then refused even a bottle of soda as payment. He'd become a bootblack, Wilkin said, so he wouldn't have to be a thief.

"Hey, gringo, you want to run?"

The challenge came from a boy of perhaps sixteen. He really did want to run; it would be a joy to be running. His name was Carlos, and every day he ran a lap of the beach with anyone he could persuade to accompany him. He did it to keep his lungs healthy, he said, because in between running, he smokes.

"Should I?" I asked. Wilkin nodded his approval, and we tore off down the sand. We were barefoot, and Carlos laughed as I faltered over a patch of broken shells. As we turned at the tip of a headland, I could see that Carlos wasn't even winded. He let me catch up for a final sprint to the finish, a decrepit yola where a group of kids had gathered for the race. Searching out old muscle memory, I found myself gaining, coming abreast at the line, both of us slapping the yola in rhythm, me turning to collapse into the ocean, Carlos climbing calmly onto the skiff to retake his place as the prince of beach urchins. It was these *muchachos,* these boys with nothing better to do than throw rocks in the park, who decided that I must not worry if the bus south from Barahona cannot take me where I hope to go. If I go in the right direction, perhaps I will make it. If I don't, I can be sure that I won't.

Now the claptrap guagua is rising, rolling, falling, like a cutter on pitched seas. Already the desert is a distant memory. The highway threads the mountains that stand against the shore, their slopes lush and misted, their crowns heavy with cloud forests. It's an ecstasy, spare and wild, the road a lone intrusion between villages stacked in ravines or at the mouths of rivers. Finally the blacktop spears across a coastal plain and the cactuses and thorn trees return. This, for me, is the end of the line: Oviedo Lagoon in Jaragua National Park. The guagua wheezes to a stop among a clutter of concrete bohíos, and an army of children appears out of nowhere to lead me to the entrance post. Each of them wants a few pesos, but there are too many hands, and I walk on toward the shimmering lagoon, giving in to the fact that is impossible to be alone with your thoughts in this country. Only at night, in your dreams. I can see the brown water through its silver reflection, and the tufts of mangrove, some of them far from the shore, like skeletons on the salt flat. A dozen flamingos stilt-walk through the shallows.

In an instant the crowd of children has vanished. I hear their feet slapping the ground and turn to see them streaming toward a white four-by-four. It rolls slowly onto the flat and turns to creep toward me. The windows are tinted black.

Finally it stops. On the white earth beneath a one o'clock sun the vehicle is impossibly bright, as though it were composed of light itself. The children stand open-mouthed, waiting for the door that will open into another world. When it does, the man who steps out is ordinary enough, tall and bony with a gulping Adam's apple. A gringo, I guess a European, and I think: They would say he looks a lot like Padre Arturo. He makes his way toward me, handing out biscuits to the children and cigarettes to the oldest boys.

"You speak English?" he says to me in Spanish.

"*Sí.*"

"I am René."

René is on a holiday from Haiti, where he lives in Port-au-Prince. When Haiti overwhelms him, he drives all day to the Dominican Republic. It's just different enough, he says. There are trees, for example. So many more trees.

The children stare into the shining leather interior of the four-by-four.

"Shall we drive out to see more flamingos?"

I step up into the passenger seat; it feels strange to be the one who is allowed inside. I look down at the faces of the children. It is impossible to read their expressions, but in any case they are not surprised. "If I let them in, they'll get into every pocket," says René as though in apology. Every pocket, I notice, is filled with packs of cigarettes.

We pull slowly down a track along the edge of the lagoon, René searching the trail in front of us. "On this island there are two kinds of places," he says. "There are places where you need luck, and there are places where you need more luck." Far along the eastern shore of the lake, the rough road disappears into the mangroves. René stops to let a group of children catch up; they have followed us on bikes and on foot. He waves to the oldest. "I can go much more?" he asks in Spanish.

"There's a river," says the boy. "You can't cross it."

"A lot of mud?" I ask.

"A lot."

René turns off the engine, and we get out. The landscape is covered everywhere with dazzling white powder; only the lagoon is a soothing silty brown. We walk toward it, the ground spongy underfoot. It isn't until a boy disappears up to his knees, and René up to one ankle, that we realize we're standing on a skin of mud and algae above a bottomless, viscous murk. Flamingos and spoonbills, ibises and stilts, strut across the illusion of solid ground.

"Well, we have been to the moon," says René, taking in the scene one final time. He points to the sky, and I see that clouds have begun to blacken the horizon. They have a seething, latent presence. "How do you think this mud will be in the rain?" he asks. I don't need to reply. We make our way back to the vehicle, where the kids race to claim spots on the bikes. One small boy is left standing.

"He must be quite a runner," I say. "He came out on foot, as well."

René looks at him, a tiny boy in rags, his head shaved perfectly bald. "Okay," he says, and pulls open the back door. The boy looks fearfully at the two of us before he climbs in, touching the perfect seat with as little of himself as he can. Back at the guard post he is relieved to be set free. We hand out biscuits and pesos, and then we roll up the windows and vanish. "Where do you want to go?" says René. "Back to Barahona? Or keep going west?"

We go west.

The road is empty—there isn't even traffic, and there is always traffic; there isn't even garbage, and there is always garbage. Here and there a few houses line the strip, places to buy a warm beer or a corked bottle of gasoline. Because the road leads to Haiti, there are military checkpoints. At each one, René stops without waiting to be asked and pulls a packet of cigarettes from the map pocket, from the glove compartment, from behind the sun visor, and passes it out to the sentry on duty. In Haiti, he says, cigarettes are his currency, smoothing every transaction, every introduction, every encounter with soldiers or the police. Wherever he goes he leaves behind a small and fleeting cigarette economy—every person who receives a pack will smoke only a few, saving the rest for sale or trade. René still isn't sure how he ended up in Haiti. He is Swiss, and when he finished his compulsory military service, he travelled to Colombia. When he returned to Switzerland, he found himself hungry to see more of the world. He saw a television advertisement for aid workers in Haiti. His housing and food would be free, and he needed only to buy the airfare. He didn't know a thing about Haiti, not even where to find it on a map, but he was confident of one thing: it couldn't be more desperate than Colombia.

He was wrong. He ended up as a concierge in a hospital in Port-au-Prince.

The highway has entered a long stretch of thorn forest clinging to a karst. To either side of the road the surface of the earth is a nightmare of sinkholes and razorback ridges, every hollow filled with the root of some spiny plant. It is uninhabitable and impassable; a person trying to cross through this country on foot would end the day bloodied by a thousand nicks turning septic, with shoes cut apart as if by knives, with eyes driven mad by the endless movements of lizards. There would be no soft earth to sleep on at night, nowhere to hang a hammock when the spiders and scorpions came. It is perhaps the only landscape on Hispaniola that is just as Columbus would have found it, and just as he would have left it.

"You become hard," says René. "Haiti is heavy. Working in the hospital was heavy. But the heaviest thing I ever did was make coffins for children. By hand I made little coffins." He stayed, though. When his aid work was done, he found a job with a cigarette company.

We're silent for the first time since we pulled onto the roadway. The wheels hum westward, the air conditioner whistles. I'm thinking to myself: The heaviest thing. I'm remembering an afternoon when I rode west out of Santo Domingo to visit a trio of Canadian nuns in the former sugar refinery town of Ingenio Consuelo. There was a time, the nuns told me, when the whole town was black with soot from the factory. Those were its twin products: purest-white sugar and purest-black ash. The refinery had been shut down years ago, but the town is still surrounded by endless cane fields, and the cane-cutters still live in the bateys. The nuns had set up a rest home for men too old or broken to keep working, and one of their patients had recently died. A bed was available.

I rode out with Sister Catherine O'Shea, a lively Irish Canadian, to bring in the next man on the list.

The batey was nothing much. A clearing with shanties of tin and breeze-block and scavenged wood. Young men playing stickball and young women putting up their hair in rollers. We came to the house of Jackie Pies. That was the old man's name, though no one seemed certain how it was spelled. The neighbours were pleased at his good fortune, but it was not at all clear how Jackie Pies himself felt about leaving behind his one-room breeze-block home. The only hint was in his clothes: jeans, a button-up, a canvas cap, all of them spotlessly clean, his best. He could not fully extend his legs, which were permanently bent in a cane-cutter's stoop. "This leg is *floja*," he said, favouring his left. The word can mean weak or loose, and in this case the meaning was literal. Jackie Pies's hips were so worn that he had to hold his joints in their sockets with his hands as he walked. The distance to the nuns' truck wasn't far, but he stopped more than once and seemed to wonder if the journey was worth it. I carried his bag. It was the kind of backpack a child might use to bring books for his first day at school, and it carried everything that Jackie Pies had to show from a lifetime of labour. A few shirts, a pair of pants. As we drove out past men swinging machetes in the fields, the whole world smelling sickly and sweet, Sister O'Shea said to Jackie Pies, "That was your work?"

"Many years, many years," he replied, and laughed with, I think, a mixture of astonishment and relief. "I'm hungry," he said. "I'm hungry all these days."

René wheels off the pavement onto a red dirt strip. "How about Cabo Rojo?" he says, and I nod absentmindedly. We each open a large beer. We don't even have time to finish before another checkpoint appears, this time the entrance to a declining bauxite mine. "Is this the road to Cabo Rojo?" asks René, handing out cigarettes. We've missed a turnoff, the guard says, but it isn't far to go.

What is this place, Cabo Rojo? Nothing but the tiniest village wedged between a limestone crag and the sea. We've barely stopped when a face appears at my window. "You want to take a boat to the *bahía*," the man says, as though there isn't any question. It's a moment before I realize: I have made it. I had given up on getting here, not even allowing myself to say the words out loud, but I had gone in the right direction and ended up where I wanted to be. Sometimes in this country that is all the magic you need.

"Bahía de las Águilas?"

"Of course," he says.

"How long does it take?"

"In my boat, fifteen minutes."

René is already gathering his snorkel and flippers.

We load warm beer and a bag of provisions I brought from Barahona into the captain's yellow yola. The engine makes a dubious sound, but it keeps us on the green behind the swells that bound into and off the sea cliffs. Brown pelicans pass overhead with a sound like blades cutting air. As we round a headland, I see it: a crescent of white sand, too long to measure in a glance. The fierce clouds still shroud the horizon, but at a distance too far to fear.

René and I are swimming even before the yola is settled on the beach. The water is from a dream. Right away I spot a huge starfish, every dapple on its ochre flesh as crisp as if I held it in my hand, and I dive down toward it. It's only when the pressure sings in my ears that I realize I was looking down through twenty feet or more of ocean. The quiet swell, the light off the white sand, the perfect clarity—everything seems just an arm's reach away. In its coolness, its brilliance, the sea seems clearer even than the air. I submerge again and sit, tucked in a ball between the sky and the earth, all around me the flash of silver. I pull the names from my memory: tuna, tarpon, mullet, mackerel, scad, jack, wahoo. An enormous porcupine fish passes lazily beneath me, its spines flat against its body even as I dive down to swim beside it. When I finally raise my head and look to shore, I can see the thin strip of beach, the thorn forest beyond, a band of bare stone rising out of the bramble. Our boat, our boatman, are small against the sand, somehow too far away.

There's a riptide.

René is nearby, and his face registers a mild alarm. The alcohol is taking the edge off our fear. "Do you feel a current?" René shouts.

"It's not too powerful," I reply.

We begin to swim shoreward, angling to one side to break out of the rip. It is slow going, but we gain ground, ploughing steadily. It's meditative, really. It would be a beautiful place to drown.

On the beach, I open two more large beers and break out my stash of salt cheeses, crackers and olives. René rolls some Haitian marijuana. We stay too long to make it back to Barahona ahead of the sunset.

By the time we are back in the four-by-four, nightjars are hunting over the cactus fields of Cabo Rojo. René takes us east at a tear. The soldiers at the checkpoints smile, wave us through and raise their cigarettes in salute. We find ourselves talking again of the heaviness; of the bateys, of the girls who sell themselves in the resorts, of the bootblacks, of men and women born with nothing but muscle and bone, of the hanging revolution. There are theories that explain and justify, but for the moment, racing through the blackening mist of the cloud forest, we only want to resist, to dwell in the impulse that tells us it is wrong; wrong that a man should reach the end of his life with nothing to show but a body he holds together with his hands, wrong that his sacrifice has helped to make others rich, wrong that our wars are in endless repetition; wrong that we name the dead while their killers go nameless. It is wrong to be building so many children's coffins.

We want to reject impunity.

The two of us against the night in our air-conditioned bubble.

WITH THE MORNING comes the rain. Clouds boil in the sky and press down like an avenging hand. Water falls with a force that wakes a terror in the animal mind. It is a storm that warns: you are not in control.

I have a bus to catch for Santo Domingo. It will take all day on highways running with mud and spume, but in the end I'll make my way to Kilometre Ten, amazed to find myself shivering. I'll wrap myself in dry clothes and call Yanira and say, "Guess where I spent the past day?"

And she will say, "Where?"

"Bahía de las Águilas."

"No!"

"Yes."

"But this rain!"

Yes, this rain, this rain that will not stop and will blow under the door, weep through the shutters, stream from the tiniest seams in the plaster. The streets will bob with ten thousand plastic bottles, and the green sea will turn brown, and the television news will announce that an unknown number of people have been killed in a flash flood near the town of Jimaní, people who died because they had nowhere to build but the flood plain of a river. But Yanira and I will defy the rain. We will arrange to meet at the K-ramba Bar, where she will arrive two hours late and glittering with raindrops in her hair, over her shoulders, her legs. She will sit, kick off her wet sandals and say, "Do you consider that rude?" And late at night we'll hear a hush. The city outside will be washed of every human scent, and instead there will be the breath of great leaves, the perfume of tree sap, the ancient odour of soil. Yanira will find two stars in the sky and we will know that the rain is done. We will realize once again that we've never known how to say goodbye, and my bus will be leaving, there will be a scramble, kissed cheeks, the driver revving the engine. She will shout out and I'll call back to her and she'll laugh and say, "You've taken my umbrella!"

In the morning the radio will report that the flooding near Jimaní has killed at least two hundred people. That afternoon, I will go with Rosa to the church. She will pray, and I will talk to my uncle. Like the children in Ocoa, I have a better sense of Arthur than I do of his God. I am too late for his church, but I have, at least, come closer to his faith.

And when the service is over we will learn that the officials have revised their estimates. Two thousand men, women and children have died under the water and the mud of Hispaniola. Two thousand endpoints in history. Two thousand more martyrs, the blood still wet.

BRIEF HISTORY OF THE DOMINICAN REPUBLIC

EARLY HISTORY

circa 4000 BCE   Greater Antilles settled by indigenous explorers, most likely from Middle America.

circa 250 BCE   Ancestors of the Taíno people occupy the island they call Haiti, replacing earlier cultures that likewise had risen through the Antilles archipelago from South America.

1492   Christopher Columbus visits Haiti, establishes first European settlement in the New World; names the island Isla Española (Hispaniola). Indigenous population estimated at 500,000 to 750,000.

1496   Spanish establish first permanent European colony in western hemisphere, at Santo Domingo.

1520   Licenced trade in African slaves to Hispaniola. Sugar industry booms over next eighty years.

1550   Taínos considered virtually eradicated by disease, genocide, slave labour, suicide.

1600   Spanish colonies on Hispaniola decline; lengthy era of peasant autarky begins; Creole culture develops.

1697   Hispaniola divided into Saint-Domingue (present-day Haiti) under France, and Santo Domingo (present-day Dominican Republic) under Spain.

1795   Santo Domingo ceded to France.

1804   Haiti declares independence from France, becomes first independent black republic in the New World.

1809   Spanish Creole uprising returns Santo Domingo to Spanish rule.

1821   Insurrection against "Foolish Spain" administration results in brief independence for Santo Domingo, then known as Spanish Haiti.

1822   Haiti invades, conquers Spanish territories on Hispaniola.

1844   Bloodless coup in Santo Domingo; Dominican Republic declares independence.

1861   Dominican General Pedro Santana agrees to annex the republic to Spain.

1865   War of Restoration secures Dominican independence.

ERA OF TRUJILLO

1905   United States take control of Dominican customs to secure debt repayment.

1916   U.S. invades Dominican Republic to secure debt repayment, quell political instability.

1924   U.S. occupation ends; constitutional government established.

1930   General Rafael Leonidas Trujillo Molina forces resignation of government, establishes personal dictatorship.

1937   Dominican army massacres 12,000–20,000 ethnic Haitians in the republic.

1960   Joaquín Balaguer named president under authority of Trujillo.

1961   Trujillo assassinated on May 30.

REVOLUTION AND OCCUPATION

December 20, 1962   Social democrat Juan Bosch and his Dominican Revolutionary Party elected.

September 25, 1963   *Coup d'état* deposes Bosch; military junta established.

April 24, 1965   Armed forces factions revolt against junta government.

April 25, 1965   Popular revolution in Santo Domingo; junta government falls. Rebels call for return of Bosch and constitution of 1963.

April 27, 1965   Loyalist armed forces fail to recapture Santo Domingo from rebels.

April 28, 1965	U.S. president Lyndon Johnson announces military intervention to protect American citizens in the Dominican Republic.
May 2, 1965	Johnson announces broader U.S. military objective of preventing communist takeover of the republic.
May 5, 1965	Organization of American States approves International Peace Force intervention in Dominican crisis.
May 7, 1965	Provisional Government of National Reconstruction formed with Brigadier General Antonio Imbert Barreras as president.
May 14, 1965	Provisional government and loyalist military launch assault against mainly civilian rebels in northern part of Santo Domingo, with some support from U.S.
September 3, 1965	New provisional government installed following OAS negotiations.
June 1, 1966	Joaquín Balaguer, a senior figure during Era of Trujillo, elected president.

RECENT HISTORY

1966–1978	"Soft dictatorship" of Balaguer; opposition suppressed, elections strongly affected by fraud.
1978	Balaguer loses power; improvements in democratic rights and freedoms.
1979	Hurricane David devastates Dominican economy.
1985	International Monetary Fund austerity measures lead to widespread rioting.
1986–1996	Balaguer re-elected; later driven from office by fraud allegations.
1996	Leonel Fernández elected president in free and fair election.
2000	Hipólito Mejía elected president.
2004	Fernández re-elected.

SELECTED SOURCES

THE TAÍNOS

Deagan, Kathleen, and José María Cruxent. *Columbus's Outpost Among the Taínos: Spain and America at La Isabela, 1493–1498.* New Haven, Connecticut: Yale University Press, 2002.

De Jesús Galván, Manuel. *Enriquillo.* Santo Domingo, Dominican Republic: Biblioteca Taller No. 97, 2000. First complete edition published 1882 by Imprenta García Hnos. Fiction.

Rouse, Irving. *The Tainos: Rise and Decline of the People Who Greeted Columbus.* New Haven, Connecticut: Yale University Press, 1992.

Wilson, Samuel M. *Hispaniola: Caribbean Chiefdoms in the Age of Columbus.* Tuscaloosa, Alabama: The University of Alabama Press, 1990.

EARLY HISTORY AND GENERAL INTEREST

Bell, Ian. *The Dominican Republic.* Boulder, Colorado: Westview Press, 1981.

Bosch, Juan. *La Mañosa.* Santo Domingo, D.R.: Editora Alfa & Omega, 2003. First published 1936. Fiction.

Columbus, Christopher. *The Journal of the First Voyage—Diario del Primer Viaje, 1492.* Trans. and ed. B.W. Ife. Warminster, England: Aris & Phillips, 1990.

Connolly, Joyce, and Scott Doggett. *Lonely Planet: Dominican Republic & Haiti.* 2nd ed. Victoria, Australia: Lonely Planet, 2002.

Dominican Studies Library. CUNY Dominican Studies Institute, The City College of New York. New York.

Eme Eme: Estudios Dominicanos. Santiago, D.R.: Departamento de Publicaciones y Centro de Estudios Dominicanos, Pontificia Universidad Católica Madre y Maestra, serial.

Esteban Deive, Carlos. *Diccionario de Dominicanismos.* 2nd ed. Santo Domingo, D.R.: Ediciones Librería La Trinitaria y Editora Manatí, 2002.

Moya Pons, Frank. *Después de Colón: Trabajo, sociedad y política en la economía del oro.* Madrid: Alianza Editorial, 1987.

Stanley, Avelino. *Tiempo Muerto.* Santo Domingo, D.R.: Cocolo Editorial, 1998. Fiction.

Wiarda, Howard J. *The Dominican Republic: Nation in Transition.* New York: Frederick A. Praeger, 1969.

ERA OF TRUJILLO

Alvarez, Julia. *In the Time of the Butterflies.* Chapel Hill, North Carolina: Algonquin Books of Chapel Hill, 1994. Fiction.

Bosch, Juan. *Trujillo: Causas de una tiranía sin ejemplo.* Caracas, Venezuela: Grabados Nacionales, 1959.

Crassweller, Robert D. *Trujillo: The Life and Times of a Caribbean Dictator.* New York: Macmillan, 1966.

Diederich, Bernard. *Trujillo: The Death of the Goat.* Boston: Little, Brown, 1978.

Turits, Richard Lee. *Foundations of Despotism: Peasants, the Trujillo Regime, and Modernity in Dominican History.* Stanford, California: Stanford University Press, 2003.

United States Senate Select Committee to Study Governmental Operations with Respect to Intelligence Activities. *Alleged Assassination Plots Involving Foreign Leaders.* New York: W.W. Norton, 1976.

Vargas Llosa, Mario. *The Feast of the Goat.* New York: Picador, 2000. Fiction.

1965 REVOLUTION

Archives of the Organization of American States. Columbus Memorial Library, Organization of American States. Washington, D.C.

Bennett, Jr., William Tapley. Papers 1930–1994, Richard B. Russell Collection. Richard B. Russell Library for Political Research and Studies, University of Georgia Libraries. Athens, Georgia.

Bosch, Juan. *Crisis de la democracia de América en la República Dominicana.* México, D.F.: Centro de Estudios y Documentación Sociales, 1964.

Dallek, Robert. *Flawed Giant: Lyndon Johnson and His Times, 1961–1973.* New York: Oxford University Press, 1998.

Gleijeses, Piero. *The Dominican Crisis: The 1965 Constitutionalist Revolt and American Intervention*. Baltimore, Maryland: The Johns Hopkins University Press, 1978.

Martin, John Bartlow. *Overtaken by Events: The Dominican Crisis—from the Fall of Trujillo to the Civil War*. New York: Doubleday, 1966.

Secretaría de Estado de las Fuerzas Armadas. *Guerra de Abril: Inevitabilidad de la historia (Textos del seminario sobre la revolución de abril de 1965)*. Santo Domingo, D.R.: Editora de las Fuerzas Armadas, 2002.

Szulc, Tad. *Dominican Diary*. New York: Dell, 1965.

RECENT HISTORY

[A]hora. Santo Domingo, D.R.: Revistas Nacionales, serial.

Betances, Emelio, and Hobart A. Spalding, Jr., eds. *The Dominican Republic Today: Realities and Perspectives*. New York: Bildner Center for Western Hemisphere Studies, 1996.

Fortunato, René. *La Violencia del Poder: Los Doce Años de Balaguer*. Santo Domingo, D.R.: Videocine Palau (distributor), 2004. Documentary film.

Metz, Helen Chapin, ed. *Dominican Republic and Haiti: Country Studies*. 3rd ed. Washington, D.C.: Federal Research Division, Library of Congress, 2001. Area handbook series.

Wiarda, Howard J., and Michael J. Kryzanek, *The Dominican Republic: A Caribbean Crucible*. Boulder, Colorado: Westview Press, 1982.

Young, Philip, et al. *The Dominican Republic: Stabilization, Reform, and Growth*. Washington, D.C.: International Monetary Fund, 2001.

FATHER ARTHUR MACKINNON, THE SCARBORO MISSIONS AND THE ROMAN CATHOLIC CHURCH IN THE DOMINICAN REPUBLIC

Báez, Ramón. *Sueños y Realidades de 20 Años*. Santo Domingo, D.R.: Impresora Dominicana, 1984.

Clark, Rev. James A. *The Church and the Crisis in the Dominican Republic*. Westminster, Maryland: Newman Press, 1967.

Moreno, José A. *Barrios in Arms: Revolution in Santo Domingo*. Pittsburgh: University of Pittsburgh Press, 1970.

Scarboro Missions. Scarborough, Ontario: Scarboro Foreign Mission Society, serial.

Steele, Harvey. *Why Kill a Priest!* Burlington, Ontario: Crown, 1982.

NOTES & ACKNOWLEDGMENTS

Dead Man in Paradise is a work of non-fiction—a true story. Records, interviews or personal observations support every detail presented as fact, and I have taken pains to ensure that speculation is identifiable as such. In reconstructed scenes, I have included no description or dialogue that is not based on documentation or recollections of the events described. There is, of course, a great deal that occurred during my time in the Dominican Republic that did not make it into the book.

A true story is also a living story. As this book was going to print, and more than a year after I left the Dominican Republic, I was contacted by two relatives of Second Lieutenant Evangelista Martínez Rodríguez. A dialogue has begun that can only be described as tentative. It is important to note, however, that these family members do not agree with my version of events. Like the sister and brother of Ramón Restituyo, they say that Father Art and the two policemen travelling with him on June 22, 1965, were killed in an ambush by Odulio de los Santos Castillo and possibly other soldiers. It is impossible to rule out this or several other more byzantine possibilities. That said, I remain convinced that the evidence strongly supports the conclusions presented in these pages.

All interviews with Dominicans in this book were carried out in Spanish. It is an unfortunate reality that I do not speak the language fluently; however, each interview was recorded and I consulted native Spanish speakers where there was any doubt as to what was said. Translation permits some latitude, but I have been careful to remain true to the meaning of my sources' words. In the translations, as with every other element of the book, any errors or oversights are entirely my own.

One often hears an author say that a book could not have been written without the support of many people. I have tried in these acknowledgements to show how literal a truth that is. What follows is not a list of thank-yous so much as a capsule history of the making of this book.

First, my thanks and love to Alisa Smith, who was with me even when she couldn't be. The same to the entire MacKinnon family, who offered support from afar, and especially to my father, Allan, and to my mother, Marian, who knew I would write this book years before I did. To my cousin Steve, who brought me back into the Cape Breton clan, *moran taing.*

The Scarboro Foreign Mission Society in Scarborough, Ontario, was a superlative resource at the outset of this project. John and Jean MacInnis graciously made possible my visit. Robert Cranley gave me the run of an excellent archive; Kathy VanLoon, editor of *Scarboro Missions*, dug into her morgue on my behalf. It was a pleasure and an honour to meet or correspond with the veteran missionaries Joe Curcio, Lionel Walsh, John Walsh, Vic Vachon, John Gomes, Ron MacFarlane and the late Joe Moriarty. I owe an enormous debt of gratitude to the late Paul Ouellette and Harvey Steele, Scarboro men who investigated the mystery of Arthur's death ahead of me and left behind the foundation for my own contribution to the story.

To Paula Ramos and Ludmila Marenco, and later Gabriela Moreno, many thanks for the gift of the Spanish language.

I will forever be grateful to the many Dominicans and Haitians who made me welcome and shared often difficult memories, and especially to the people of Monte Plata and San José de Ocoa. My good friend Yanira (whose surname shall remain private) helped me more than I could ever hope to repay. Rosa Hernández de Ayala and Juan María Ayala Regalo fed me body and spirit in Santo Domingo. My best regards as well to the family of Jesús and Dionisio de los Santos, to the Association for the Development of San José de Ocoa and to Roberto Santana, Frank Tejeda, José Luis Almonte and Fausto Moreno. Thanks, too, to "Charlie," who never gave up.

The Dominican Republic is a beautiful and remarkable nation that has given much to the world and will continue to do so. I would encourage anyone to visit it.

Two Scarboro priests continue their work in the Dominican Republic. Louis Quinn and Joe McGuckin live their faith profoundly and are an inspiration that transcends it; my thanks to both for suffering this fool gladly. Lenore Gibb, Susan Daly and Catherine O'Shea of the Grey Sisters of the Immaculate Conception in Ingenio Consuelo gave generously of their histories and dormitories. If I didn't believe in miracles when I arrived, I did by the time I had seen what it takes for Sister Mary Jo Mazzerolle and the Religious Hospitallers of St. Joseph (www.rhsj.org) to run the Padre Arturo MacKinnon Centre in San José de Ocoa. To support the important model of self-reliance and mutual aid being developed in Ocoa and elsewhere in the Dominican Republic, contact:

Scarboro Missions
2685 Kingston Road
Scarborough, ON
Canada M1M 1M4
Tel: 416-261-7135
Toll-free: 1-800-260-4815
www.scarboromissions.ca

Scott McIntyre at Douglas & McIntyre believed in this book from the first. Anne McDermid and her associates continue to take my words out to a wider world. My editor, Barbara Pulling, worked beyond the call of duty through a difficult time. I can only hope that I was among the lesser of her worries; the book would not be what it is without her efforts.

The FCC in Vancouver offered collegial guidance and friendship, in particular the following members: Deborah Campbell, Charles Montgomery, Brian Payton, Alisa Smith and Chris Tenove. Trish Baldwin and Aiden Enns were my first, best readers. Saeko Usukawa laid early groundwork for the edit. Mario and Eliana Canseco helped with translations. Former coroner Sherryl Yeager and forensic consultant Bob Stair (then manager of forensic services for the British Columbia Coroner Service) checked my forensics. John Graham and Jack Kepper helped me understand the state of the Canadian chancellery in Santo Domingo in 1965. My good friends Nils Riis and Tammy Rampone gave me rest and absinthe in Toronto. Louise Dennys and Pico Iyer showed me how gracious the Canadian literary crowd can be.

Ruben Anderson was a patient ear over pints. Jason Payne, a friend and a talented photojournalist, contributed author's photos.

I can't say enough about libraries. My compliments to Greta Reisel Browning and the staff of the Richard B. Russell Library at the University of Georgia for their assistance with the William Tapley Bennett collection. The information and services department of Columbus Memorial Library offered prompt assistance with the records of the Organization of American States. *Gracias también* to the staffs of the Pedro Henríques Ureña National Library and the General Archive of the Nation in Santo Domingo, as well as to the dedicated crews at the Vancouver Public Library and University of British Columbia Libraries.

Last but not least, I reserve special thanks to whomever I've forgotten—thank you for your forgiveness. I apologize in advance and owe you a beer, as always.